The Polish Nurse

A WW2 Historical Fiction Novel

LEAH MOYES

Producer & International Distributor
eBookPro Publishing
www.ebook-pro.com

THE POLISH NURSE
Leah Moyes
Copyright © 2023 Leah Moyes

Edited by: Dawne Anderson
Proofread by: MJ Jones

Contact: Leahmoyesauthor@gmail.com
www.leahmoyes.com

ISBN

The Polish Nurse is a work of fiction. Names,
characters, places, and incidents are either wholly
the product of the author's imagination or are used
fictitiously. Any resemblance to actual persons, living
or dead, events, or locales is entirely coincidental.

To Maria

Thank you for your endless support and love

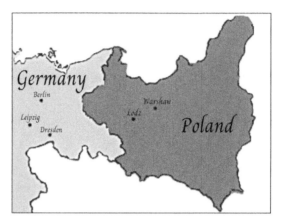

Map designed by Samantha Thatcher

AUTHOR'S NOTE

Both German and Polish languages are intertwined in conversation throughout the story, and although the author attempted to make it simple enough for the reader to understand the context, a language glossary can be found at the back of the book.

*"One day, one moment, one event...
can change your life completely."*

Anonymous

ReadMore Press

DISCOVERING THE NEXT BESTSELLER

Sign up for Readmore Press' monthly newsletter and get a
FREE audiobook!

For instant access, scan the QR code

Where you will be able to register and receive
your sign–up gift, a free audiobook of

Beneath the Winds of War
by **Pola Wawer,**

which you can listen to right away

Our newsletter will let you know about
new releases of our World War II historical
fiction books, as well as discount deals and
exclusive freebies for subscribed members.

CHAPTER ONE

19 August 1941

"Vorwärts! Kinn hoch! Arme nach oben!" The sharp demands in a thick German accent came swiftly. Step forward. Chin out. Arms up. I hardly had time to turn to my left to see Renia, my best friend of ten years, performing the same ridiculous movements with an equally sour-faced woman in front of her. The long horizontal line of students extended the length of our stone courtyard, chunks of concrete still littered the ground even now, nearly two years after the explosions rocked our school. Another dozen or so girls clustered near the outer gate, awaiting their turn.

"Open your mouth." The timeworn taskmistress inched closer to me, but even in youth, I towered over her by a head at the very least. She stretched her neck and leaned forward. The sulfurous scent of mustard reeked from her lips as they curved into an ardent scowl. When she spoke, her jowls wiggled loosely above her crisp, clean uniform collar, but it was the brown mole near her chin with the solitary hair protruding that captured my full attention.

"Do you have all of your teeth?" She inspected my mouth thoroughly.

I nodded.

She tugged on the end of my braid that hung freely down the right side of my chest, the lower locks nearly reaching my waist.

"Gute Länge."

I snuck a glance at Renia once more and wiggled my brows carefully, so this madam did not see my disrespect. What a relief the length of my hair had passed her inspection. I fought the giggle building in my throat. Such an odd thing for her to find so satisfactory.

A tall, reedy woman shadowed the ill-tempered one. She clutched a simple clipboard in one hand and a pencil in the other.

"Macht Notizen." The demanding one pointed for her to take notes, then turned back to me. "What is your name?"

I recognized my good fortune of having learned German years ago, even before they arrived in my city. While my fellow classmates struggled with the foreign demands, I understood her well enough.

"Aleksandra," I answered proudly, named after my *oma*, my mother's mama, who died before my birth.

"Family name?"

"Jaworski."

"Age?"

"Sixteen."

"Kennkarte?"

I pulled the small, beige paper book from my pocket. I rarely went anywhere without it since its issuance from the *Generalne Gubernatorstwo* at the beginning of the year. She reached for it and scanned its contents carefully, focusing her attention on the black and white photograph with my thumbprint and signature above the official seal. She turned the page for my family lineage.

"Schmidt?" she grunted. "Maternal?"

"Yes, Frau, my oma came from East Prussia."

"Hmmm." She handed it to the other woman and faced me again.

"Turn around."

I rotated my back towards her. *Why is she inspecting my person so closely?* My brother, Ivan, who had been enlisted through conscript eighteen months before had not been scrutinized so closely when the German soldiers came to our home.

My breath hitched at a wayward thought. A faint recollection emerged from an event I tried hard to forget…a collection of people—people with a unified belief—seized from their homes, lined up in the street, and marched away…*but I am not Jewish!* And as my papers just proved, I am not entirely Polish either, I justified, quite aware of the hostility directed towards Poles. When my grandmother, Aleksandra Schmidt, came to Łódź to attend art school, she met and married my grandfather, choosing never to return to Prussia.

The woman pinched my side. The movement made me jump. I was ticklish there.

"Stand still," she snapped. Though she had a solid grip on my waist there wasn't much to grasp and the tighter she held on the more it hurt.

She spoke to her scribe. "Tall, but skinny. Good posture and hips. Send her to Medical."

Offended at her command to see the doctor, I scrunched my nose. *I am quite healthy*, I wanted to argue. Other than a scare of scarlet fever at the age of four, I hardly got sick. And at this very moment, I could outrun anyone in this school, including the old bag.

The SS's sudden disruption of our school day had come unexpectedly. This had happened often at the beginning of the German occupation, but not recently, and none of the previous appearances required us to stand outside for hours in the sweltering heat.

Within a week of their arrival in Poland, the Germans had closed almost all the schools in the city…but not this one. New instructors, altered curriculum, and stifling rules were put in place. Rumors circulated amongst the girls as to why we were spared—whispered conjectures included suggestions as eccentric as our headmistress being involved in the Third Reich, to training a new generation of Hitler youth who could also offer child-bearing qualities, to the most realistic…we all had German familial ties. I ignored them all. Though we no longer had our beloved Polish teachers, Polish language, literature, culture, and arts, I excelled in math and sciences and, above all, being in school meant being away from the horrors and atrocities occurring outside of it.

"Dreh dich um."

When I turned forward again at the command of the clipboard woman, the female soldier had moved on to the next girl. The scribe scribbled something on a piece of paper and then shoved it into my hand.

"Siebzehn," I whispered as I read it. The number "17" appeared on the square sheet.

The Germans gave us little choice but to follow every direction given. The blatant slaughtering of Poles proved not only their power but their hatred for our countrymen. My family learned first-hand the consequences of having a father in the government. As a Parliamentarian, he should have been killed. Instead, the new commanders forced him to labor as the liaison between the Poles and our new German Mayor, Albert Leister… that, and a reminder bullet to each knee—they claimed he didn't need to walk to do his job. His brother, Borys, and a dozen other men who worked in his office were not so fortunate. Determined to be a threat by the Auskunftsabteilung, they were detained and sent to the Radogoszcz prison in November, then executed the following May 1940.

From the moment the soldiers entered our classrooms this morning until now, I hadn't been afraid. Though they were stern and forceful, nothing in their conversations led me to believe our lives were threatened.

This was far from the invasion in September 1939.

Though Łódź was smaller than Warsaw, its location became key to the Germans' continued pursuits against enemies of the state. Our lack of adequate equipment and poor defenses, especially against the Blitzkrieg, allowed for an effortless seizure when our Polish army collapsed in mere days under the pressure of the Third Reich.

Within that first month, not only did they sever our transportation, but they also carried out mass searches, committed crimes against the population, public executions, restructured the government with German officials, issued occupation decrees, renamed the city as Litzmannstadt, and annexed us into Nazi Germany.

My mind easily slipped back to those early days…the deafening sounds of gunfire, explosions, and above all, the horrifying screams that were forever etched in my memory. At fourteen, I lived through the worst nightmare imaginable, or so I thought with my limited life experience…until I witnessed the expulsion, the process in which the Germans managed the Jewish population.

They claimed that the people of the Jewish faith were diseased and brought filth and degradation upon us, but especially upon our new landlords. By February of 1940, the Judes had been removed to a *ghetto*—a controlled residential quarter in the northeastern section of town—surrounded by barbed wire and armed guards. My friend Erela, along with her parents and sister, who lived in the flat across from us, were subjected to swift removal and forced relocation. I didn't even get to say goodbye.

Occasionally, Mama and I would take the streetcar past the fences. Sometimes I would cover my eyes, afraid to see the downtrodden and defeated people. A people who just a year earlier were our baker, tailor, and seamstress. Then two months ago, train cars full of *Romas* arrived at the ghetto. Frau Weber, Mama's hairdresser, said the new detainees came from Austria. I overheard her conversation while she washed Mama's hair one afternoon. Her husband, Herr Weber, oversaw the *Judenräte*—the Jewish Council—in the ghetto and reported that the Romas were sent here temporarily prior to their transition to another camp.

"There are not enough resources for those filthy gypsies," Frau Weber exclaimed, callously unaware of my mother's cringe. "The Judes are already seven or eight to a room and nearly twenty in each flat," she continued. "While I don't care much for the Judes, I cannot tolerate the Romas.

The quicker they move them to an extermination camp, the better."

Mama never went back to have her hair done by Frau Weber, but she also never discussed with me the definition of an extermination camp. Something I eventually came to learn from Renia.

Over the past year, the number of residents in the ghetto increased and decreased with the constant arrival of trains. New faces replaced old though none seemed to last very long. I calculated the changes from the rotating children who lingered against the fence. The neighborhood had always had an eeriness to it but now a dark cloud hovered unceasingly. I now went entirely out of my way to avoid it.

The stories that circulated about town varied as to where the ghetto residents were evacuated to. Some claimed deportations were to other cities, countries, or work camps, but I never forgot what Frau Weber called them and when *Pan* Nowak, our butcher, said with undeniable certainty that they were sent to a nearby village called Chelmno, a hint of hope sparked within me…until he elaborated.

"Not the town mind you and not for better accommodations." He weighed the last of the veal.

Mama froze in place, but I watched him curiously.

Wrapping the meat in paper, he continued, "To a country estate specifically used as a killing center."

Mama gasped and looked at me, then before she could stop him, he added, "They use poisonous gas."

Mama's beautiful complexion drained of all color. Her red lips pulled into a tight line and, though I could not see her eyes, her lashes blinked repeatedly. When he finally handed over the meat, Mama slipped the money down on the counter and departed quickly with me tightly in tow and we began a very silent walk home.

That night, I prayed for Erela. I didn't want to believe the stories; I wanted to trust that she was somewhere safe and happy. She was by far one of the kindest girls I had ever met.

"Weitergehen!" The terse voice of the clipboard woman ordering me to *move on* brought me back to the present. I followed her long, thin finger in the direction of another door, but before I exited, I peeked back at Renia. She stood a few girls down from me and, though the tyrant had moved past her, she apparently hadn't gotten her square number yet to be dismissed. When she brushed her brown curls aside to reveal a smile, I winked at her before I turned away. We will have a good laugh about this at lunch.

CHAPTER TWO

WHEN I EXITED the courtyard and reentered the classroom, it looked nothing like the room I had left earlier that morning. The desks had been removed, and in their place were long tables separated by steel partitions with thin curtains both in front of the table and on each side. Because they hardly covered anything, I could see Gizela from my mathematics class sitting on one end of her table in a robe of sorts. Her shoulders were slumped, and her head lowered. *She must be sick*. I tried to recall the supper conversation with my parents the night before, but nothing was said about an illness spreading through the town.

I stopped in the center of the room, unsure of where to go next, until a man in a long white coat hustled toward me. His ungainly height forced his spectacles to slide down his shiny nose as he eyed me warily and grabbed the paper number from my fingers.

"Siebzehn," he hollered the number out and another woman approached with yet another clipboard. I bit the inside of my cheek and shifted nervously to my other foot. This could not be about sending young girls into battle—that's preposterous...*isn't it?*

Due to the uncertainty of our future, even before the war began, my father's keen foresight and sound finances gave me the best education a child could be privileged to have. My all-girls school was one of the finest in town. Along with my skills in numbers, I took easily to foreign languages. Outside of our native Polish tongue and German, I spoke a little Russian, and was currently learning English from my neighbor.

Though many of my elders mourned the hope of a free Poland, they were quite vocal about the value of other languages. "Knowing multiple languages, little Aleksandra," *Pani* Kalinowski said, "is quite equal to survival." Eight years after her comment, I have come to understand the wisdom of such a statement and valued our lessons immensely.

"Afleuchten." The woman waved for me to follow her. I passed three of the partitions before she rolled one of them away revealing an empty table.

"Sit."

Unsure whether she meant the table or the chair, I chose the sole chair in the space. I would do everything in my power to convey how healthy I am. Maybe Gizela was sick, but I most assuredly was not.

"Name?" The woman's eyes left the clipboard only briefly.

"Aleksandra Jaworski."

"Your age?"

"Sixteen." I sighed. They have already asked me this. Why didn't the clipboard woman from outside just forward the information? And where is my Kennkarte? It had not been returned to me.

"Have you been ill recently?"

"No."

"Broken any bones?"

"No."

"When was your last bleed?"

"Bleed?"

"Your monthly?"

My brows curved inward, and I stuttered for the first time. "L—last week."

"Have you had any imbecility in your family?"

I blinked twice then quickly answered so she didn't believe *I* was the simpleton. "Uh, no, no nothing like that."

"Do you have all of your teeth?"

I nodded, waiting for her to look in my mouth as the female soldier did, but she didn't.

"Zieh deine Sachen aus."

"What?" My heart thumped heavily in my chest. I could not have heard her correctly. Why would she need me to remove my clothing? *I am not sick!* She repeated the same sentence only with an urgency now pointing to the table. She held up a thin piece of fabric that unraveled into a robe as she lifted it up. "Put this on."

"Why?" My jaw tightened. "I am not ill," I responded in German so there was no chance of a misunderstanding.

"Do it now." Her stare pierced me threateningly. I waited but she made no move to leave my temporary quarters. I turned away from her and removed my collar and blouse slowly. While I unbuttoned my skirt, I desperately tried to devise a way to escape. *I am fast.* I could outrun her, the doctor, the female soldier, and any number of squaddies they had walking around here. What I could not outrun were bullets, and each of those soldiers carried a weapon.

"Quickly." She demanded.

I pointed to my camisole and underwear. "These too?"

"Ja."

I exhaled slowly and removed my undergarments with my back to her once again. I had never undressed in front of anyone besides my mother and that had not occurred for many years.

I put my arms in the lightweight robe and closed it tight with my arms across my torso. Only my tan leather shoes and knee-high woolen socks extended out the bottom. The woman didn't waste any time and grabbed my wrist, pulling me to the end of the table.

"Sit." She directed.

I did as I was told, but my cheeks heated with frustration.

"Dr. Kraus." She parted the curtain. "She is ready."

My eyes widened at her announcement. *Ready for what?* Looking down I could see my hands openly trembling just below the rapid rise and fall of my chest.

The same doctor from before stepped inside and closed the partition behind him.

I kept my head lowered and counted the black scuff marks on his brown shoes. *Four, five…no six.* They moved closer to me. His sweat, mixed with a pungent medicinal scent, preceded him. I wanted to pinch my nose, but he grabbed my arm and lifted it up, down, forward, and backward before he moved to my other arm and repeated the action. I eyed him warily. Maybe this is just a checkup, maybe somebody in the school really does have a contagious disease and we must all now be examined for it.

Couldn't they just tell us? I fumed. Though I had a health assessment when I registered to attend the school, nothing required me to completely disrobe.

He rotated my shoulders and tapped his fingers down my spine, calling off codes to the woman holding the clipboard. Codes I was unfamiliar with in any of my languages. I jumped again when he pinched my waist through the robe. He checked my ears, eyes, nose, and asked me to open my mouth. He untangled my braid and thoroughly searched my scalp, leaving my hair a ratted mess once he had finished.

There could be a lice infestation. *It has happened before.*

He put the listening tubes into his ears and pressed the rounded end against my chest and then my back, all the while telling the nurse with the clipboard to document his findings.

"Sie ist stark und gesund."

Of course, I was strong and healthy. I was not only the fastest runner at the school, but I could also jump higher than anyone as well.

The man placed his hands in the pockets of his white coat and rolled back on his heels. When he did this his jaw tightened.

"Name?"

"Aleksandra Jaworski."

I said my name at the same time the woman with the clipboard did. When she looked at me, she sent me a clear message…the doctor was speaking to her. I pursed my lips as he continued.

"Age?"

"Sixteen."

"Recent illnesses?"

"None."

"Hereditary diseases?"

"None."

"Menstruating?"

"Yes."

The doctor now scrutinized me from my head to my toes. A drop of sweat rolled from the edge of his hairline down his cheek, but he didn't pause to swipe it.

"Have you had relations with men?"

My eyes nearly popped out of my head and my mouth separated on its own accord.

The man peered at me over his thick glasses, his deep green eyes searing through me. He waited for my answer as if he was serious. I held my breath.

He is serious.

The heat in my cheeks made me want to sweat too. I shook my head almost imperceptibly, too shocked to manage any other response.

"Are you certain no boy has touched you down here?" He pointed between my legs.

I shook my head fiercely this time.

"Lie back."

I froze.

The woman placed her palm over my chest and pushed me backward.

"No, no, no!" I stiffened, and my hands wound around my waist again

15

holding tightly while fighting her pressure to restrain me. She set her clipboard down and used both hands to force me flat on the table, my legs dangled helplessly off the end. *What are they doing?* A thousand thoughts whirled inside my brain in that split second, and all the possibilities frightened me.

"Lift your shoes to the end of the table." The doctor spoke dryly as if the whole struggle meant nothing.

My heart thumped again. I glanced past them and toward the exposed opening in the partition. *Maybe someone out there will stop this.* I spied a soldier staring in my direction, a smirk spread across his face. I swallowed a lump, fighting the desire to cry.

"Bend your knees," said the doctor.

I shook my head, feeling my chest constrict. *This cannot be happening.*

The woman didn't wait and moved my legs upward to the hard surface. *Why?* My short breaths came rapidly.

When he lowered his torso at the end of the table, I gasped. The entire lower half of my body was now exposed to him and anyone else who walked by the curtain, including that awful soldier. A slight breeze blew through and caused goosebumps to cover my skin. In bold contrast, perspiration rolled down my forehead and mingled with emerging tears. Even though I closed my eyes tight, the moisture slipped through anyway.

I bit my lip to keep from crying out as the doctor's gloved fingers examined my private parts. I was too afraid to fight the woman who held my arms down, though I knew she did not care what was happening to me. I whimpered and sniffled through the horrifying seconds that followed.

"Very well." He stood straight again. "She passes."

I could barely catch my breath as the woman released her hold and the man pointed to the chair. "Get dressed and wait until you're retrieved."

My mind continued to whirl. Did the school believe I had been with a man? Did they suspect me of being with child? I was mortified over the idea of being touched in a place I had never been touched before and of all places…here at my school!

I dressed quickly, making sure every button was closed and every part of me covered, but no matter what I did to forget about what just happened, the incident haunted me.

Sniffling, I sat in the chair with both my hands covering my face, wishing to just go home. I wanted to see my parents, my dogs, and my rabbits. I wanted to feel the comfort of my bed and the loving embrace of my mother, and I never wanted to come back to this school ever again.

When the clipboard woman walked back in, I could have sliced her to ribbons with my glare. How would she like to be treated this way? How would she like it if I was holding her down?

She raised her chin in challenging defiance. "Hier."

She handed me a paper. I quickly perused it, finding that it had my name, age, details of my medical examination, and the word *pass* stamped in German on one corner.

"Do not lose this. It is your passport."

"Where is my Kennkarte?" I panicked, knowing no Polish person could be caught without it.

She handed me an apple and pointed to another door. "This is the only paper you will need. Do not speak to the soldiers, do not sleep with them, and do not leave their escort until you arrive at your destination."

"I—I just want to go home."

Her red-painted lips moved slowly enough for me to see every line she had brushed across them. "You have a new home, Fraulein. You are part of *Lebensborn* now."

Tears sprang from my eyes.

"I don't know what Lebensborn is," I whimpered. "Please, I just want to go home."

She grabbed my wrist and led me to a door opposite the one I had entered. Outside, a military truck rumbled to life as another young girl was physically forced inside the back. I stopped, but the woman shoved me forward and then called to one of the soldiers for help.

When he appeared at my side, he tapped his long gun with one hand. "Come, now," he commanded. Then he nudged me forward with the barrel end of his weapon.

"G—go wh—where?" I hardly recognized my stammering.

The soldier ignored me and directed me toward the back of the idling truck where additional soldiers faced me. Tears spilled freely down my cheeks. *Please, no, please no. I cannot be a soldier.*

Two hands pressed against my back and shoved me upward and I stumbled on the step, bruising my shin. With no tenderness in the responding touch, the same hands only lifted me to my feet to get me to move.

Once inside, my eyes adjusted to the dimness. I swiftly counted the frightened faces that peered back at me...*seven, eight, nine.* Nine girls already huddled together. I recognized two from my classes, but the others were strangers; they welcomed me to their embrace all the same.

CHAPTER THREE

B Y THE TIME the vehicle lurched forward into movement, there were eighteen of us assembled inside the back of the cramped military truck... and no Renia. Though slim wooden benches bordered the sides, we found comfort huddled together on the depressed center floor. Deep green, almost black-colored canvas surrounded us, allowing limited access to light or air.

"Where are we going?" A young girl curled to my side and whimpered. She could not have been more than twelve or thirteen.

I glanced down. If I had a sister, she could have very well looked a lot like her. Taking a deep breath, I brushed her flaxen bangs aside, exposing her watery blue eyes. "I don't know," I whispered, then contemplated the greater harm between telling her the insufficient truth I'd been told or a lie.

My tears had stopped the moment we departed. It did no good to continue to mourn the unknown, yet I couldn't prevent the fierce reaction that seared through my veins when I pictured my heartbroken parents. They would be awaiting my return from school, and I would not come. What might they think? *That I chose to leave?*

First, my brother was enlisted and today it was me.

I leaned my head down toward the girl once more. Her pale eyelashes bubbled with moisture and her cheeks flamed a splotchy pink. I wrapped one arm around her. "At least we're not alone. What is your name?"

"Karina."

"How old are you?"

"Thirteen." She paused. "But my *urodziny* is next week."

"Well, happy *almost* birthday, Karina." I smiled as best I could, trying to hide the rage I felt growing inside. Did they put her and the other young girls through the same violating inspection as us older girls? My eyes flitted over the group. There must be at least two girls here even younger than her. What could they possibly want or need from us? We were hardly fit for battle if that is what they expected. A bundle of harmless schoolgirls, some fresh out of primary school.

"I've never had a sister." I tightened my hold around her shoulders. "Would you be mine?"

She grinned back with a nod and nuzzled deeper into my chest until I heard her steady breaths ease into a sound sleep.

Still watching Karina, I rubbed her curls between my fingers. The softness reminded me of my pet rabbit, Oliver. I had rescued him from his mother at birth, afraid he wouldn't live a day, but that was over a year ago. He was quite the rascally bunny now. Tears lingered in the corners of my eyes as thoughts of home faded with the daylight and I wondered if I would ever see it again.

Elapsed time became difficult to follow as I struggled to stay awake. Early on, I fought hard to keep a grasp on the length of our journey. *Pani* Kucharski, my physics teacher, had once told us if we counted to two hundred it would be equal to a kilometer. I tried the theory out when my family visited a relative's house several towns away. I don't know if it was accurate or not, but I proudly announced we lived twenty-three kilometers from Auntie Duda. At any rate, father seemed pleased with my calculations; he always had a head for numbers himself.

Tonight, however, I gave up after I counted to twelve thousand.

Fatigue finally took over. We lumped together in our once-clean, blue blouses with white pleated collars and our gray, woolen skirts that flared slightly below our knees. Though I saw little of their faces in the growing darkness, their similarly braided hair stuck out in all directions. We appeared like a clumpy bowl of Żurek. Delirious thoughts, summoning my favorite celery root and sausage soup, only made my empty stomach grumble louder.

From the way the truck jostled and lurched seemingly over every rock, tree branch, or dip in the road, I didn't think sleep could be possible, yet as the light slowly disappeared from the gap above the door flaps, an eerie darkness descended and caused my eyelids to droop as well.

When the truck screeched to a stop and rocked, I jerked my head up in response. Listening closely, I tried to decipher if the halt was a temporary pause or longer.

Doors slammed and rattled the frame.

"Alle raus!" The command to *get out* came in German, but I wasn't certain if this direction was given to the fellow soldiers or to us until the men opened the flap and waved for us to move.

"Spricht jemand Deutsch?" One man glanced eagerly among us.

Silence.

The second time he asked if anyone spoke German, the whites of his eyes expanded with the volume of his voice.

I raised my hand. "Das tue ich." Although many of us understood the language well, especially since Polish had been banned, it seemed apparent I was the only one brave enough to answer.

"Inform the others to step outside and relieve themselves. This will be our only stop; we will reach our destination by morning."

I turned to the group and repeated the directions in our native tongue. Though I was certain the girls already understood, I wanted to see if the soldiers would stop us from communicating this way. They didn't. Once I realized none of our captors spoke Polish, I hoped this could be used to our advantage.

"Bewegt euch jetzt!" The demands to move grew louder.

The girls all stretched and rubbed their eyes, yet they didn't step out until I did. It was clear I had become the newly appointed leader of our group—much like my father—and, for a moment, I realized how difficult it must have been for him. Would he be proud of me, or would he think me foolish? Taking the lead had lost him the use of his legs…*what will I lose?*

Once outside, a light fog hovered below a thick black sky, forging an eerie scene. Several of the girls whimpered while the younger ones began to cry. They huddled together at the rear of the truck, angering the soldiers.

One hollered at me to get them to move. "Geht schnell!" He repeated the command three times while waving his fist angrily above his head.

I motioned them forward, but from the smell that surfaced from our rustling skirts, it was certain some of the girls had already relieved themselves in the truck either out of fear or lack of options. A second soldier, a large, burly man in a uniform much too small for him, aggressively pushed us toward a nearby line of trees shouting *Müll* and *Hündinnen* the whole time. We ignored the crude insults as we stumbled in the direction of a single lamplight.

As the girls followed me, I proceeded to tell the girls in Polish that we would be safe if we stayed together and did as we were told…at least until we knew more about where we were going or their reasons for keeping us.

Once the girls had moved past the light and toward the trees, the soldiers relaxed. Three of them entered a nearby building while the other two leaned lazily against the jeep that followed our truck. Immediately, they turned their attention to their cigarettes and drink. I peered between them and the girls, then strategically maneuvered myself within earshot of the men's conversation. If I could gather as much information as possible, it might help me know more of what awaited us or even in deciding our next move.

After a few drags of his short cigarette, one soldier blew smoke through his nose and mouth as he spoke. "Oh, to be an officer…" He shook one finger at the other. "Now that, that would be a desired occupation."

His comrade laughed and brought a thin silver flask to his mouth, gulping loudly. "Why? They only work harder and are only ordered around."

"*We* are ordered around." The first one laughed in response.

"Yes, but we don't work harder." He took another long sip. "And they never seem happy. They don't smile and they don't have any amusement."

The first one pointed in our direction. I glanced away and held my breath as he spoke. "These girls will bring plenty of amusement very soon."

"How so?"

"Don't you see, Dietrich—they are blond, fair-skinned, blue-eyed, long legs, the Aryan trademark…" He smirked.

My cheeks warmed when I peered back at the girls. *They spoke the truth.*

"But they are Polish, they don't come from pure German blood."

"Only part Pole, but that doesn't matter anymore." He scoffed. "My cousin in Munich had one himself—a Yugoslav. As long as they can birth fair children, they are what the Führer wants."

My muscles strained with irritation as my mind spun, trying to analyze their meaning. Instantly my heart faltered with the worst of possibilities.

"Are we not allowed to…uh…" The man called Dietrich nodded his chin in our direction. "You know…have a little fun?"

"Not this lot, comrade." The first soldier slapped his friend on the shoulder.

"But how will they even know?"

"They were inspected. They're clean…untouched and already marked for Berlin."

Dietrich scoffed in offense. "I am of a long line of pure Germans. I'm as good as any."

His companion laughed out loud. "But *not* an officer."

"Scheiße." Dietrich clicked his tongue and nodded. "I want to be an officer now. Glückliche Männer."

Lucky men? My heart thumped in double time. I knew very little of the intimate ways of men and women and only knew some because Renia caught her older sister with her boyfriend behind their house and told me what she saw. Though something about the soldiers' tone caused my mind to wander dangerously. Could we really be the "amusement" he implied?

I watched the girls once more as they tried desperately to make a wall with their skirts, scrambling for any minuscule amount of dignity while they peed on the side of the road. I gasped as the soldier's words became clearer. *We are all blond…fair…and blue-eyed.* Could we really be going to Berlin? For the officers' pleasure?

The disparaging remarks from the men whirled inside my head, but I repeated nothing to the girls when I rejoined them. It would have only caused fright. The words of the clipboard woman back at my school entered my mind with surprising relief, reminding me that these men were only transporting us to Lebensborn, wherever that was, and nothing more. At least we should be safe on the journey…or so I wanted to believe.

CHAPTER FOUR

"**K**OMMT HER!" The soldiers shouted for us to come and ushered us all back onto the truck. Before I stepped inside, the sound of approaching vehicles forced me to pause. Three additional trucks and two jeeps had come from the opposite direction and pulled up beside ours. A handful of soldiers riding in one jeep jumped out to speak with our escorts. I scanned the trucks, wondering if they were also filled with schoolgirls.

"Die beschissenen Briten haben die Hauptstraße gesprengt!" One soldier shouted angrily then spit on the ground.

I gasped at his announcement that the British planes had blown up the road. From their frustrated expressions, I assumed it was the road we were traveling on.

Back in Poland, the German papers printed much on the wanton destruction from Britain and France. The Nazis claimed their enemies increased their bombing attacks on transportation and supply lines in an effort to destroy all, including women and children. Though my father only spoke of this in the privacy of our home, he occasionally expressed his doubt that the Allies sought to kill the innocent.

One of the newly arrived soldiers pointed to me and scowled, alerting the soldiers to my delay.

"Geh hinein!" He pushed me forward roughly and hollered for me to get inside. The other men's belittling remarks supported the man's anger. I held my chin high and pushed the flap aside as I entered, but once it closed behind me, I kept my cheek pressed against the canvas to hear their continued conversation.

"What is it?" Katia, one of the older girls, asked.

I placed my finger to my lips and held my breath.

Once the hum of voices ceased, I turned toward the girls where I was met with wide eyes and a volley of questions.

"What happened?" Katia pressed.

"More soldiers," I said, once again in Polish, but quickly restructured my answer when the girls began to whimper and cry. "I mean, they were only talking. There is nothing to fear, we are safe inside the truck." I glanced back to Katia, but she appeared unconvinced.

Leaning in, she whispered, "What is *really* happening?" This was the most she had spoken to me in all the years we had been at school together. Our friends were vastly different. Katia lived up to the ladylike ideals our school promoted…I, on the other hand, lived more for the thrill of life.

Making sure none of the other girls could hear, I whispered back. "The soldiers who just arrived said that the road we are traveling on was bombed by the British. We must backtrack and detour to another road. From the men's displeasure, I imagine this change will only lengthen our journey…and our time in the truck."

She frowned. "Do you know where we are going?"

I nodded subtly. "After the uh, examination…" Katia's eyes shifted downward and her cheeks turned ruddy, confirming that she, too, was subjected to the horrifying inspection. "…the woman, the one who gave me my new papers told me we were going to Lebensborn."

Her brows raised and her eyes met mine once again. "Is that a village in Germany?"

"I thought so." I paused. "But then, just earlier, the soldiers said we are going to Berlin."

She chewed on her bottom lip. Through her dishevelment, she still appeared as lovely as I always believed her to be, but also as shy as I remembered. At eighteen, Katia was one of the oldest in the group, and her beauty had been admired by her classmates for years. Even after a day of less than humane conditions, her pale blond hair naturally curled around her shoulders and, though her cheeks appeared a bit hollow, her striking cheekbones and angled jaw still emanated beauty in the moonlight.

The back flap was thrown open vigorously. The girls jumped and squealed at the sudden exertion. The soldiers who had entered the house appeared at the opening with two loaves of bread and only one canteen of water. Tossing it inside to whoever was nearest, the men closed the flaps once again with a callous chuckle. It took only a moment to register the offering, then an urgency to get a hand on the limited liquid brought the girls to nearly clawing each other over it.

"Zatrzymać." Stop, I cried. Skimming the dim space, wide eyes met my gaze. "We must all work together." I rose upward on my knees. My shock at seeing these once proper pupils from a high-born private school fighting over crumbs frightened me. I imagined they, much like me, were not used to experiencing hunger, however. It reminded me quite clearly how in a matter of just a day, life and circumstances can change quite quickly. *We must keep our wits about us.*

"We are better than this." I waved for the food and water to be passed in my direction. The girls remained frozen at the anger in my voice. Though I was not the oldest or the smartest at my school, I had gained a reputation for being the bravest, having stood up to Madame Juska, our language instructor, on more than one occasion for her harshness toward some of the younger girls.

"One at a time." I grabbed the canteen. "And only one swallow." I handed it to Karina and nodded for her to be first. "We must use it sparingly."

"We're going to diiiieee…" A whine came from the far side of the huddle.

My head snapped to the girl's direction, but I couldn't make out the voice, though to my defense, I could only reasonably identify five or six of the occupants.

"No!" I retorted swiftly. "We are not going to die."

As the whimpers increased, I looked to Katia for help. Now would be a good time for her to move past her characteristic reserve and speak up.

"We really arrreee." The whine continued. "We are n—nnnever going home and n—nnnever going to see our families againnn…"

"Who is saying that?" I attempted to stand in the cramped space. My fists curled at my sides. Though I had promised to stop my occasional fist fights years ago, I was not about to let this girl send everyone into hysteria.

"That's enough, Hanna." Katia's gentle voice rose above mine with more exertion than I had ever believed possible. My mouth fell open as she continued. "We will *not* forget who we are, where we come from, or who we represent." Her finger flew forward pointing at each girl individually. "We come from honorable families and a noble country. Though we do not know where we are going…We. Will. Not. Die!" She stole a breath before she continued. "Think, girls! If they wanted us dead, they would not have given us even this parcel of bread or smidgeon of water. You are stronger than you think. Be brave…you are Polish." Once finished, she crossed her arms over her chest and settled back into her original seat.

Not a sound came forth.

I quickly reached for the loaves of bread that had been placed on the bench and broke them into eighteen equal parts. Handing them out slowly, I added, "I know there isn't much, but you might want to save half for later, we don't know when the next food might come."

Quiet nibbling and swallowing commenced once all the pieces had been distributed. Katia peered cautiously in my direction; her wariness returned. I smiled my thanks.

Within minutes the girls were quiet once more. When the canteen reached me, I took my allotted sip and replaced the cap. "I will pass it around again in the morning. Try to rest."

As we rumbled down the road in complete darkness, I struggled to fall back asleep. My mind spun with anxiousness, attempting to formulate a strategy. I had no military experience. I was no planner or policymaker, though I had seen my father organize and direct for years, the unforgiving reality emerged...I was not *him*.

Eventually, the clanks and clatters of the truck replaced my contemplations and I resigned myself to the dark reality of an unknown future as the distance from our home expanded. There were too many of us with very little strength to defend ourselves, especially against weapons. Defeated in thought, I allowed my eyes to close. Only a miracle could stop our nameless fate now.

CHAPTER FIVE

As the sun peeked through the back flap, the truck came to a stop for another pee, another loaf of bread, and another canteen of water. Eventually, I had to tell the girls the truth about why our travels had lengthened. In response, Hanna's increasing grumbles and moans brought others to her side and, though Katia and I did our best to offer encouragement, a clear line had been drawn between those who believed our positive reassurance and those who didn't.

With the detour, I took mental accounts of our altered environment whenever possible. We rumbled along smaller dirt roads lined with thick leafy trees and since our last stop, the convoy had now increased to almost a dozen trucks and jeeps. The same stop-and-go routine occurred two more times, but food and water were tendered only once, most likely due to our isolation from civilization.

The increased numbers of soldiers offered us less and less privacy as we stepped outside for our short breaks and brought more leering and unpleasant comments in our direction. In contrast, however, the discomfort gave sight to at least one other truck filled with girls in similar circumstances. Though I didn't recognize any of them and we were kept separated on purpose, shared glances brought a glimmer of collective hope. We still knew little of our captors' intent, but now we knew we were not alone.

By the third day, we had gone a full twenty-four hours without food and only one sip from the last of our water. The continued malnourishment spurned illness and vomiting. Though we had eaten nothing, it didn't stop the bile from surfacing and left the stronger half barely able to care for the weak above the rancid smells in the confined space. Eventually, as time passed, we grew used to the odors…overpowered mostly by our own limitations and fatigue.

Overwhelmed at first, I wrestled with my own nausea to the greatest degree—mostly because the others needed me, or at least the few of us older girls still resilient enough to help the younger ones, though I took no thrill in leading. Recognizing the fine line between yielding and enduring, I fought the desire to give up.

I cannot give up, I vowed secretly.

As the daylight faded and the glow of sunset once again fell upon us, we labored to make the ill as comfortable as possible—for the nighttime, somehow, brought a whole different level of fear.

"Here, Karina, rest your head on my lap." I guided her matted hair gently downward to my dirty skirt.

"Aleksandra?"

"Yes?"

The young girl, who had practically been glued to me since the day we left, looked up at me. The light that shone at one time from her baby blues had dimmed and a gray tint had started to form across her hollow cheeks.

"If I die, will you keep this?"

She opened her tight fist and a little wooden doll lay flat on her palm. It was the size of my thumb. The hair was fashioned from a couple of threads of yellow string, two black dots indicated the eyes, and a swatch of red fabric formed a skirt. The imprints on her skin from the grip told me of its importance to her.

I picked it up and examined it as best I could in the limited light. "What's her name?"

"Adela."

"She's beautiful and has a lovely name," I whispered and placed the doll back in her hand then closed her fingers over her figurine. "You will not die, Karina. I promise to keep you safe."

It was a promise I had no business making.

She whimpered quietly into my shoulder.

I rubbed her cheek tenderly. "Tell me about your home, *motyl*."

She glanced back up at me and bit her lip as if she might cry from my endearment.

"My papa calls me that. I'm his little butterfly."

"Well, then that will be your nickname. You remind me of a blue one I saw just a week ago."

"I saw one too," she sighed, "but it was green."

I smiled. "Do you have a pet?"

"Oh, yes." She nodded with a bit more energy. "I have a dog named Vuk. He is big and hairy and likes to chase the chickens." She wiped her nose on my sleeve. "Do you have any dogs?"

I nodded. "Three."

"Three?"

I chuckled at her surprise. It was true; most people in the city did not have more than one dog, but our property size allowed for it.

"What are their names?"

BOOM!

The vibration against the truck rattled my body. My head jerked upward, and my heart thumped nearly clean out of my chest. Along the journey, we had grown used to hearing various explosions from afar, but nothing seemed to come this close. I held my breath and peered around at the girls. Some remained still, lying atop one another, but others jerked awake, and when my eyes settled on Karina, I knew from her expression that she had heard what I had.

"What is that?" she cried.

A succession of explosions burst through the darkness and as the truck veered wildly to the side, my body tossed easily with it. I reached for the metal bar between the canvas walls with one hand and clung to Karina with the other as another blast sent the truck erratically on two wheels, then a second later, it slammed back down on all four. Screams erupted as the girls were thrown about from the violent movements.

Another turn and jerk forced my hand to slip.

"Karina!" I shouted, trying to keep her close, but instead, something hit me roughly in the back and a knee to the jaw sent me back against one of the truck's canvas sides. "Karina!" I tried reaching for her again, but I could not get my bearings long enough to locate her. After having listened to the tone of her voice for three days now, I recognized her cries getting farther away.

Momentary bursts of glowing whites and yellows penetrated the blackness. A loud crash sounded behind us as if vehicles had violently collided. The screams continued as wild shifts in the driving vaulted us aggressively upward, downward, and side to side... then all of us smashed forward as our truck thundered down a decline. With each roll of the truck wheels, the sounds of large tree branches scraping and tearing the exterior cover filled our ears. Violently rocked back and forth, the girls' voices surged with fright. The leadership capabilities I had shown throughout the journey thus far vanished in the split seconds we were thrown helplessly about. I could do nothing to stop the screams or help the others. I had never felt so weak.

Continuous explosions shook the truck, slamming my head against the same metal pole I had clung to earlier for stability. Searing pain shot through the side of my skull as I grappled for composure—reaching behind, I felt the distinct sharpness of a protruding screw from the truck frame. It now tore viciously at the palm of my hand where I gripped the post. Before I could assess my head injury, the truck hit another large bump or rock, propelling us upward, and I felt the warm trickle of blood splash across my forehead and nose.

Three more thundering blasts rocked the truck, finally sending it careening onto its side. The sickening sound of metal screeching along the rough ground pierced the air as we felt the truck, once again, sliding down a slope, only steeper this time. Deafening cracking sounds competed fiercely against bloodcurdling screams…

Then the truck slammed to a stop.

CHAPTER SIX

Smoke blinded me as the scent of blood and vomit reeked from every direction.

With the truck on its side, our bodies remained tangled and paralyzed for several minutes. I prayed the unnatural silence originated from shock and nothing more permanent. Wiping the moisture from my eyes with the back of my hand, I looked down upon the dark smear. *Blood.* When I attempted to move, new screams erupted around me.

"It hurts!"

"Help me!"

"Please!"

I froze. My own movement could very well be hurting someone else. A massive pile of bodies lay between me and the back opening of the truck where one flap hung in shreds and the other one had vanished. I couldn't risk hurting another person just to get to it. Scanning the side that had now become my ceiling, I analyzed my options. *I can maneuver upward.* A murky night peeked through the severed canvas above me where faint light—possibly a full moon or very bright stars—kept the space free from complete darkness. The colorful lights that had illuminated the sky during the deadly attack had now vanished and only the echoes of booms reverberated in the distance.

I secured one foot against the bench and pushed my body upward. The action brought a memory to the forefront…three years ago, Renia and I had climbed the gate of my school to reach the ladder leading to the roof. She had stolen a pack of cigarettes from her sister, and this was to be our first attempt at smoking. We chose that particular perch on the gymnasium not only because the school was closed that day but once the sun reached high noon, its rays warmed us better than any coal stove ever could. Plus it overlooked the city. Of course, I gagged and choked so much after three short puffs on my first ciggy that I vowed never to partake in the sinful feat again, but at least the view was spectacular.

Shaking the memory from my mind, I forced my focus back to the task at hand. Stretching for that same metal pole, which was now above me, my fingers gripped it firmly, though a raw sting pulsated from my palm where the screw had torn my flesh just moments before. With renewed energy, I heaved my body upward until my waist hit the bar. Swinging one leg up and over a different bar, I noticed my right shoe was missing. "I never liked those shoes much anyway," I muttered as I wiggled upward, managing to get the rest of my body securely on top of the sideward vehicle. Though the cries below had not ceased, the hazy blackness that hung about me carried the most contradictory feeling of peace I had felt since this ordeal began. Tempted, a part of me wanted to remain up there away from the dreadful reality that most certainly awaited me once I descended.

Ignoring the burning pain in my right leg, I slid toward the ground outside the truck, but the hem of my skirt snagged and tore partway. At this point, it hardly mattered what condition my clothes were in... aside from the soiled blouse and skirt, the fabric absorbed the odors from the drive quite thoroughly; thankfully, my stomach tolerated them more than most.

Despite the momentary entanglement, I managed to land on solid ground where thick vegetation canopied us in all directions and made a lush carpet underfoot. From brisk glances, nothing nearby resembled a road, but my theory was entirely at the mercy of the night.

The faint glow that I first assumed to be the moon, actually came from the truck headlamps...or at least one of them. The twisted beam cast upward forming a haunting silhouette against a very large tree trunk. It did not take much to speculate its presence as the very reason we must've been brought to a sudden stop. The other lamp, closest to the ground, was buried in shrubbery.

My observation ended with a quick reminder of the cries from within the truck. As I stumbled backward, feeling my way to the vehicle's rear opening, I issued a silent prayer of gratitude that the sounds meant that air still pumped through their lungs...*somebody was still alive.*

Several girls had already started crawling out when I arrived. Reaching in, I grabbed the first arm or leg I could find and tugged. *More cries.* When my hands finally reached a torso, I gripped it tightly with two hands and pulled the person out. With no time to spare, I laid them down, one by one, in the most unencumbered area I could find—which happened to be where the tires had trampled the foliage flat.

Katia and a girl named Ruta exited on their own, each carrying one of the youngest girls. The ashen, lifeless form in Katia's arms surely was the reason for her flowing tears. Once she laid the girl down, she assisted me in helping the rest out of the truck.

Once the truck was emptied, the weight of the depressing scene was crushing. My clouded eyes struggled to identify life from death. The bodies lay in all directions, intermingling moans with heartrending cries. I wrapped both arms tightly around my torso, attempting to keep my legs from buckling underneath. A sob snaked its way upward from my chest past my throat and forced its way out of my clenched teeth.

Peering upward, I pleaded for help. Having been raised Roman Catholic, I trusted God watched over us from heaven above, but the more misery I witnessed, the less I believed. *Life is bitterly cruel!*

"Aleksandra."

A voice muttered my name, but I could not place the speaker.

"Aleksandra."

Thin fingers gripped my arm and squeezed. Katia stood next to me; her brows furrowed severely. "Are you alright?"

I tried to grasp that question…*Of course I'm not alright, none of us are.* I blinked.

She stared at me, her cheeks streaked with a combination of tears and dirt. "We need your help to check the girls." Her lips trembled. "Some, I fear, are already dead."

I watched her mouth move, yet I could not register her words clearly.

She shook my arm with more force. "Aleksandra, I *need* your help."

The exertion freed my limbs, and I shook myself from my stupor. "Yes." I took a deep breath and rubbed my eyes. Though the trees around us were thick, a nearly full moon provided random streams of light. I began counting heads.

Ruta stood up from one girl and wiped her cheeks. "Irena didn't make it."

Katia choked back a cry. When I looked over, her lips were pinched tight and her eyes glistened. They both must've known Irena.

Zuzana, the first young girl Katia brought out from the truck had been carefully laid aside while help was rendered to the others, but now Irena's death brought the number of deceased to two.

Trying to assess injuries in the dark proved difficult. We separated and spread out, making initial evaluations as best we could. I carried one girl toward the still glowing headlamp at the front of the truck. Once the light shown on her, I could make out extensive bruising along her arms and legs, but she was alive.

Several times in my young life I had found a way to detach all emotion from what I was witnessing or experiencing. This method of survival started shortly after the German occupation—seeing families torn apart, men brutalized or shot, and women beaten or violated became a daily occurrence. The figurative severance of my heart from my body continued while the ghetto was being populated…then depopulated.

At times, the process appeared more like a curse than a gift, but tonight it came in handy as bodies became numbers. It was simply a list, I told myself…a list of who is living and who is not. It wasn't until I caught sight of Karina that a tangible sensation returned with overwhelming sensitivity. I dropped to her side and reached for her hand.

"Karina," I cried and squeezed her cold fingers. "Please, please open your eyes."

As if on command, they fluttered open. I could taste her salty tears on my lips as I leaned in and kissed her cheeks out of relief.

"Aleksandra," she whimpered. "What happened?"

"We've been in an accident, but you are all right, you will be fine."

When she attempted to sit up, a blood-curling scream burst forth. I shook at the exertion from such a petite form. Through her cries, she drew attention to the cause. Her right arm dangled helplessly to her side. When I tried to lift it, she screamed again. My fingers gently traced over the flesh for any open wounds, but it was the peculiar angle in which it was bent that confirmed to me her pain. It *must* be broken.

I laid her back down and carefully placed the injured arm over her stomach. Her breaths discharged so rapidly that she sounded like a rabid animal. Brushing her hair off her face, I modeled slow, even breaths myself to get her to calm down.

"It hurts," she wailed.

"I know, and I'm so sorry." My eyes blurred as I kissed her cheeks once more. "Do you have pain in other places?"

She nodded. "I hurt everywhere."

"Any part as bad as your arm?"

"No," she cried again. "My arm is th—the w—worst."

"Rest," I whispered. "I need to help the others, but I promise to return as soon as I can."

She clutched my hand tightly with her good hand. "D—don't leave m—me."

I had to gently untangle her fingers. "Karina, I promise to hurry back but there are other girls…girls who might be worse than you."

She bit her lip and nodded, but a deluge of tears continued.

Though my spirit wanted to collapse, curl up, and disappear, a spark of fortitude drove me forward. *If not me…who? Who will fix this?* It was at this moment that I recalled the day the Germans arrested my father. He alone carried the combination to an administration safe. They forced us, his family, to watch his submission to their will and subsequent "sentencing" for his role in the former government. Right there on the street in front of our home, I feared I would witness my father's execution. My mother's cries begged for mercy, but I remained silent. Silent and confounded at what I saw in his eyes when they met mine. Strength as I'd never seen before emerged—an inward battle of finding a balance between obedience, integrity, and one less obvious element…challenge. It wasn't until the soldiers held pistols to *our* heads—his wife and children—that he relinquished. In return for his cooperation, they only took his legs.

I must be strong.

I stepped over to another girl who lay silent. Placing a palm on her chest, I rested my cheek against her mouth, yearning for any sign of life…a wisp of breath, a moan, an eyelash fluttering upward…nothing.

Three.

Katia held up a finger. *No, four.*

I turned away from the girl I had come to know as Marzanna and fought the quiver in my chest as I looked to Ruta for her update as well. She, too, held a finger up and my heart sank deeper.

Five.

CHAPTER SEVEN

Several minutes passed in near silence before we had a final count. Out of the eighteen girls, five were confirmed dead and one was missing. Two may have even died before the bombing took place—their cold skin and rigid muscles evidenced that suspicion.

Facing the girls once more as a whole, I surveyed the scene. Had it been broad daylight and not the shadow of night, I might've fallen to the ground in absolute despair, but what little I could see at this hour would surely be ten times worse in the morning.

"You lied." The hiss came from a person sitting only a few steps away. She huddled next to the body of a dead girl. "You said we wouldn't die."

Hanna.

Her eyes met mine and, even in the darkness, they sparked with a revulsion only hate delivers. Unable to speak, I turned away. I neither had the strength nor desire to argue tonight, despite how inexcusable her selfishness was. I returned to Karina who had since passed out. I held the hand of her good arm as I wrestled with the urge to just give up and walk away, allowing whatever fate God intended to transpire.

Then I watched my "little sister's" suffering etched in every line on her face and I knew I could never do that. *She needs me.*

Katia came and sat across from me. Though she didn't speak, our eyes had a full conversation.

We stood on tenuous ground. We were lost, with no help, no medical supplies, no food, no water, and from our initial inspection, the survivors bore varying injuries, some quite severe.

"We need to remove the dead," I spoke so only Katia could hear.

Her eyes widened momentarily, then choking back a sob herself, she nodded.

Though we were clearly exhausted, the deed must be undertaken tonight. Not only for the sake of the living, psychologically, but if there were any sort of predators lurking about this forest tonight, the scent of death would surely lead them in our direction. It was dangerous—the reeking odor of blood lingered everywhere, and a dead body brought a whole new level of peril.

Katia enlisted Ruta and a girl named Olga to help. Between the four of us, we removed the bodies to the opposite side of the truck and placed them securely beneath the thick underbrush…all but the one Hanna held on to. She clawed and fought to keep the body near, for what reasons I didn't know, but with the little patience I possessed, I didn't trust myself and I let Katia and Ruta handle it. Eventually, they returned to the brush carrying the fifth girl's body.

Though I had seen dead people after the Blitzkrieg attack, there was something so much more personal about the deceased this time. The sobering reality reminded me with each trip we made…I could very well have been any one of them.

Though the girls' clothes might have provided needed resources such as bandages, I could only bring myself to remove their socks and shoes and even then, it felt like a spiritual violation of sorts. Despite my current doubt in God, I feared going to hell.

Placing additional leaves over them, I vowed to give them a proper good-bye as soon as possible, but for now, our focus must be on the injured.

Ruta's father was a doctor and she, herself, had some training and made the initial assessments—cuts and bruises, a broken nose, broken fingers, a black eye, one head wound that might under normal circumstances need stitches, lost teeth, sore muscles, sprained or broken ankles, Karina's broken arm, and one gaping stomach wound with significant blood loss. These were the ones we could see. It was entirely possible some of the girls sustained internal injuries, but those were wounds we could not heal.

While Ruta saw to Julia, the girl whose gash was severe, Katia and I walked to the front of the truck, hoping to find some supplies of any kind. I had tried on all the extra pairs of shoes to replace my lost one, but they were all too small and tight. I blamed my father for my wide feet.

While the light of day would have made the task of gathering supplies easier, we needed to find what we could now, for a harsh truth lingered… some girls might not make it to morning.

Scanning the truck's outline in the dark, a shiver ran up my spine. Its damaged carriage seemed to emit its own morbid demise. Smoke continued to swirl from the mangled hood and the pungent smell of petrol assaulted us on our approach. No other vehicle from our convoy seemed to be nearby, though this was based solely on sound and not sight.

"Do you think the soldiers are…um, that they are…" Katia stumbled over her sentence.

"Yes, I think so."

She referred to the men who drove and rode in the front. We weren't sure how many, we only knew there were five of them between both vehicles the day we left Łódź.

Approaching the truck from the side, the entire bottom exposed twisted metal and torn rubber. Glass crunched under my one shoe as I walked to the front. This forced me to step more carefully with only a sock on my other foot. Once we reached the front, I realized the only way we could access the cab would be to climb up to the only free door. What was left of the windshield was shattered up against the tree.

Despite the sharp throbs that pricked my hand and leg with each movement, I mounted the hood and inched my way toward the passenger door, though it was missing, having been ripped off at some point. With the headlamps' limited light, I peered inside—the three soldiers were dead.

Without a second thought, I maneuvered within, trying to avoid any sharp edges or twisted metal still protruding. It took only a minute for me to conclude that the search for resources would be much easier if the bodies were out of the cab.

I wrenched one soldier free from the pile while stepping on the body of the second. Thankfully, his thin form made the task possible. Fueled by a rush of hatred, I clutched the sides of his jacket, somehow summoning an inordinate amount of strength as I had never felt before and was able to heave his lifeless body to the top. Katia's face appeared through the gap. Reaching for his arms, she tightly gripped his limbs and pulled him the rest of the way until his weight shifted and slid down the side, hitting the ground with a sickening thud.

With awkward footing, I repeated the motions with the second soldier, whose bloody head rolled lifelessly against my chest before I could push him up and out. I tried to wipe the stain, but it had already seeped into my blouse. He was heavier than the first, but once again the powerful emotions that surfaced led my muscles until Katia could duplicate her part.

Leaning against the mangled seat, I took a moment to breathe.

"Are you alright in there?" Katia called from outside.

I wiped a layer of sweat from my forehead and whispered so she could not hear. "I don't think we'll ever be alright."

"Aleksandra?" Concern surfaced in her tone.

"I'm okay," I answered. "Although, I don't think I can get the third soldier out."

I recognized the driver as the overly large man. There was no choice, he would have to remain. In the darkness, I studied his contorted body and had the greatest temptation to spit on him. My family was not as religious as my friend Erela's was, but we attended church enough for me to know God would not want me to hate my enemies. *But where was God now?* Where was He when we were taken from Łódź and were brought here, now burying innocent young girls?

My jaw tightened. The man was dead, and I wanted to believe he would face some sort of judgement in the afterlife, yet when I maneuvered to climb out of the truck once more, I used his head for leverage and didn't feel an ounce of regret as I did. If any of these men had been alive and only injured, I might have been tempted to finish them off myself if it weren't for fear of my own salvation.

Once I pulled myself up and out, I joined Katia on the ground where the other two men lay limply atop one another.

"Did you get hurt in there?" Katia pointed to the dark stain on my chest. It matched the other stains all over, but this one was new.

"No, it's not mine." My eyes dropped to the soldiers.

She nodded.

Emptying their pockets, we found a pack of cigarettes, a lighter, a stick of gum, and a ten *Reichsmarks*.

"We can use their clothing for bandages," Katia suggested.

I nodded in agreement. These men did not deserve the same respect our friends did.

We stripped them of their boots, shirts, pants, and jackets, piling to the side the belts, watches, chains, and any other metal we found, including a small pack of ammunition—no good without a pistol of course.

Once finished, she narrowed her eyes in my direction and examined me more carefully. "Actually, we can use *your* clothing for bandages. You should put these on." She held up a pair of the soldier's pants.

I glanced down. My skirt, torn in multiple places, could hardly be called practical any longer and though I had not noticed before, my underclothes were entirely exposed.

"And put these on, too." Katia set aside one pair of boots. From the looks of them, she had chosen the smaller size. "You're missing a shoe and will be no help if you injure your foot."

Again, she spoke with a clear mind.

I nodded, removing the rags resembling clothing and slipped my legs into the baggy pants, cinching one of the belts tightly around my waist. Having never worn pants before, I tugged at the initial awkwardness the fabric caused between my legs, but the coverage somehow also brought an element of relief. The man was taller than me, but once the boots were on, I tucked the ends inside the thick sides.

Tying up the shoelaces, I peered at the nearly naked bodies of the men. A maddening bitterness rose once more as I remembered their vulgar remarks and callous treatment.

"They got what they deserved," said Katia at my side. "Now what should we do with them?"

I looked around. There was no way I was going to place their bodies next to the dead girls...*our* dead girls. They did not deserve to even be in their vicinity. "Just a minute." I walked past the front of the truck and around one side of the tree when my new boot, a size too big, slipped forward. "Oopf." I quickly grabbed the hanging branches of the nearby tree to keep from falling forward.

"Aleksandra?" Katia called out as she approached me.

"Wait!" I cried. "Don't come any closer."

Her footsteps stopped. "Are you okay? What happened?"

I inched my way back to solid ground. The fading headlamp provided just enough light to show a drop I had not noticed. I swallowed hard. Had the truck not hit this tree, we could very well have plunged down this ravine to our deaths—*all our deaths.*

The consuming thought humbled me.

Facing Katia again, I bent over to catch my breath before I spoke. "There's a big drop-off." I pointed behind me. "It's a cliff of some sort. I would need to see it in the daylight."

I could hear the quiver in Katia's voice. "Are you saying that if this tree wasn't here, we would have..." her voice trailed off.

I raised myself upright and reached for her hands. "Possibly." I squeezed her cold fingers then let go. "Let's leave the men where they are for now and take the clothing back to the others."

We gathered all the supplies in our arms and returned to where we had left Ruta in charge.

As we approached, Ruta lowered her eyes to where her bloody hand pressed against Julia's body, the socks we had used from the dead girls now soaked through. Katia clumped one of the men's shirts in her hand and moved to Ruta's side ready to relieve her, but she refused. "Save them for someone else," she said dismally.

From Julia's coloring, it was almost certainly too late.

Katia and I made the rounds, taking a few minutes with each of the others. Aside from Julia, there were two additional girls who were not faring well, Felka and Henrieta. The specific causes of their weakness and pain were more difficult to identify, likely internal injuries that we could not remedy.

Using the soldiers' jackets, we covered the two of them for the night, then proceeded to tear a larger part of the canvas siding off the truck to shelter the rest. My eyes skimmed over the restless forms…twelve of us remained…a little over half from what we departed Łódź with. The very idea subdued me into silence.

"Let me look at your injuries, Aleksandra." Katia motioned for me to sit down on a nearby log, pointing to the dry blood caked on my nose, cheeks, and chin. It was then that the stinging sensation on my leg returned— or more likely, never actually went away at all, but only resurfaced once I became idle and the adrenaline wore off.

"Wrap this around your hand." She handed me one of the strips she had torn into bandages. I looked at the cut on my palm caused by the exposed screw in the truck. It wasn't too deep, but I did as she said and wound it around, tucking the end inside the wrap.

As she did her best to wipe the blood off with a piece of the soldier's shirt, I unbuckled my belt. When she was finished, I stood to lower my pants to the ground so I could inspect my leg. Intense pain flared as my finger traced a jagged cut from my knee to my ankle, ending right above my new boots. I winced from the touch.

"That looks bad." She followed my line of sight.

"I'll be fine." I pulled my pants back up and secured the belt once more. "What about you?" I tried to see how she fared. A large bruise swelled on one cheek and several cuts on her neck had dripped blood on her collar.

"I'm okay." She looked down. "Bruises and cuts mostly."

I reached for her hand and squeezed. "Thanks for your help, Katia." I smiled faintly, then turned to Ruta who stood a few steps away. "And you, too." She hadn't moved from Julia's side. "I could not have done this alone."

"You could have." Katia smiled back. "You're strong. I've always admired that about you."

I was struck by her words. *Always admired?* We truly only met for the first time three days ago.

"Sometimes," I whispered, "I don't want to be the strong one."

She nodded. "I know, but I, for one, am grateful *you* are the one who is here." She patted our hands with her other one before she released them both and stood up. "Let's get some sleep and tomorrow in the daylight, see what else we can find."

I nodded, exhausted. Climbing underneath the one large cover, I settled in next to Karina, carefully avoiding her arm. We had wrapped it with fabric, more for comfort than anything, then clasped the other belt around her shoulders securing it to her chest. It was a rudimentary sling at best and the process had Karina screaming in pain—something that would likely last quite some time. As I listened to her uneven breaths, I could only hope that she would be one of the lucky ones who made it through the night.

CHAPTER EIGHT

Though I believe I slept well for a few hours, the moment the dawn cracked through the trees, I was up, anxious to better assess our situation.

Ruta awoke shortly after me. Julia lay lifeless at her side.

I frowned in their direction. "I'm sorry."

I wasn't sure if they were friends, but Ruta's cheeks appeared swollen from crying. The quietness of the morning augmented our reality and, more specifically, my determination not to lose anyone else.

"Can you come with me?" I whispered. "I want to check for any supplies."

She nodded and fell into step behind me as I walked toward the cab of the truck once more.

I climbed up the same way I had the night before and disappeared inside. Ruta followed me and peered through the opening as I searched the space. The dead soldier, too big to remove, remained crumpled in a lump on the bottom. I could not move without stepping on him, though I did not feel remorse over the action. Pulling his jacket off took a great deal of effort. His limp body was heavy and awkward to move around, but we needed anything we could scrape off him, and one more jacket to use at night became priceless. Once freed, I handed it up to Ruta.

"Toss it to the ground. I will keep handing you whatever I find."

She nodded, then cried with a lift in her voice. "Is that, is that bread?"

I followed the direction of her finger and reached into a tight corner crevice, withdrawing a half loaf of bread.

"Yes!" I smiled broadly and brushed some of the dirt off the dry crust before I handed it up to her.

Turning back to the soldier, I reached into one of the pockets of his pants. I found another lighter and a pipe. The other pocket contained a thin silver flask. I shook it. A sloshing sound answered back. Twisting off the cap, I sniffed. "Hmmm. Plum." *Schnapps, certainly.* My mother loved the plum and cherry flavors the most, though I expected something more like vodka from such a beastly man. I replaced the cap and handed it up.

Examining the soldier, I tore off his shirt, despite a small blood stain on the front of it. A putrid scent wafted up from his exposed skin. Pinching my nose, I wanted to retch. His body may be decomposing, but it was clear he likely hadn't bathed in weeks. As much as the shirt material could surely be used for more bandages, I doubted anyone could stand the smell, but I handed it up to Ruta nonetheless.

With nothing more this man could offer us, I took one more glance about, then noticed a green strap protruding from beneath his twisted legs. They were as heavy and as large as the rest of him, and it took all of my effort just to lift one up a few inches. When I peered underneath, a pack of some sort appeared stuffed beneath him. Wrangling my way around in the tight space, I pushed and pulled his limbs in various positions, then finally with one last tug, I wrenched it free. The pack wasn't heavy, but not empty either. I peeked inside. *A canteen!* I slung it over my shoulder as I clambered back out of the truck and to the ground.

Kneeling, Ruta and I inspected the contents. It was more than we hoped for—a half-filled canteen, a pocketknife, two chocolate candy bars, a can of sardines, a girlie magazine, more cigarettes, an unknown salve, and a couple more Reichsmarks. It was as if we found a chest of gold…although the money would hardly do us any good in the woods.

The two soldiers that Katia and I had left the night before remained in their same curled positions…only bugs had begun appearing. I walked over to see the drop-off I had nearly fallen down the night before and saw a deep ravine. I returned to where Ruta waited for me and handed her the pack. "Hold on a minute. These soldiers need their obligatory burial."

Her nose wrinkled in confusion and, before she could argue, I held my hand up for her to wait.

Dragging one of the soldiers by his legs around the wide tree trunk, I let his head hit every rock and tree branch along the way. When I reached the edge, I let go and pushed the man forward until he rolled down on his own, hitting more branches and shrubbery until he disappeared. "Decent burials are reserved for decent people," I whispered. I repeated the process with the other one as Ruta's bewilderment turned into a satisfied smile.

Gathering the supplies, we moved back around to the rear of the truck. An odor similar to that of the dead soldiers immediately hit us. My stomach rolled with a clear view of what we survived. In the light of day, the mangled mess was worse than I imagined.

The night before, we had settled our group of injured girls a good ten meters away, but the rotten stench still lingered around what was left of the frame of the truck. Despite both the removal of the canvas last night and a breeze, the floor and seats still reeked from everything from vomit to urine, feces, and blood. It was the main reason we couldn't use it for shelter—one step inside would have all of us puking once more.

"What are you looking for here?" Ruta stared at me blankly.

My jaw tightened in an effort to keep my throat from releasing the contents of my churning stomach. I took one step forward. "I was hoping the canteen we were given was still in here."

She nodded but it was apparent from her expression she doubted it... *so did I.* It most likely had been thrown out when the truck fell to its side and the canvas ripped open. Truthfully, I was surprised that more girls hadn't fallen out during the upheaval. The missing girl, identified as sixteen-year-old Ramona, had not been located last night, though our weak attempt was superficial. It would have been unwise to search in the dark. We would do our best to try and locate her today.

I peered around the space briefly. The days and nights we had spent holed up here now seemed like a lifetime ago. I fought the emotion that wanted to surface in response. "It's not here," I mumbled, frustrated. We needed water more than anything—the canteen from the soldiers was only half filled with water and a flask of liquor was hardly an adequate substitute.

When we made our way back to our camp, most of the girls had awoken. I offered a sip of water to each. Enough to only wet their tongues, not knowing when and where we might find more. It would be a blessed day when I could tell the girls they could drink more than a sip. I hoped that day really might come to pass.

When I reached Katia, her hands covered her face, and the gentle shudder of her shoulders told me she was crying. I placed a hand on her arm. She sat crossed-legged between Felka and Henrieta who, just as we suspected, lay as lifeless as Julia. Our numbers were dwindling at a rapid speed. The reality of their deaths and our precarious survival weighed heavily on everyone's minds.

After moving the most recent dead to join the others, I sat down on the log, disheartened. A sluggishness seeped through my limbs and overwhelmed me. *How could we even believe we had a chance?* Glancing over the broken and bruised bodies of the survivors, I pulled the bread from the pack and held it tightly between my fingers. Nine of us remained. Would there be any purpose in delaying the inevitable? Am I only postponing our fate with this pittance of nourishment? The weight of the bread paralleled the weight on my heart. It grew heavier with each passing second.

As if she could read my mind, Katia approached and sat next to me. Though no words were initially spoken, she brought an element of calm that soothed me as none other, not even my mother. When she put her arm around my shoulders, I wanted to cry.

When several minutes had passed in silence she reached for the bread. "Let me help you," she said. Breaking it in half, she handed one part back to me. "Save this for us for tomorrow." Then using her skirt for a table, she broke her half into nine equal pieces.

I tucked the other half back into the pack as she stepped around each of the girls and handed them their small allotment. "This is all we have for today," she said. "I'm sorry."

Pitiful cries multiplied. Hanna grumbled unintelligibly through a sob when Katia handed her the food and another girl, who I didn't know, snatched it roughly out of Katia's hands without the slightest note of gratitude.

I peered around. Heat trickled up my neck and flamed my cheeks. Rising to my feet, I fisted my hands at my sides. "What will crying accomplish?" I shouted. "Crying doesn't get us more food or water or shelter or transportation."

Once again, the girls stared at me as if I had grown a second head. Some placed their hands over their mouths to muffle their cries and others buried their heads in their shirts.

"I realize we don't have the comforts you are accustomed to, but you are alive!" I tried to soften my tone, but it was useless. "If any of those girls over there on the other side of the truck could trade places with you right now, I bet they would."

Nobody spoke…and now, they didn't even move.

Katia walked over and placed her hand on my forearm.

"I'm sorry." I shook my head. "I should not have lost my temper."

Her face emitted compassion. "You are right to be angry. It angers me too, but let's let them have their cry this morning," she whispered. "And this afternoon, we will make a plan."

My lips pulled into a thin line. She was right, but their selfishness provoked my frustration. We were all facing the same dire circumstances.

"Alright." I turned away, recognizing the need to keep myself busy, to do something…anything. "I will be back. I'm going to search for Ramona." I pointed to the path the truck had taken coming downhill, easily identified from the weighty depressions on the shrubs and a line of broken branches from the trees. Maybe there was some chance that I would find her near the roadway, that perhaps she only suffered minor injuries…it was all I could hope for.

Katia nodded and took a seat next to the youngest girl, Inga, who was just eleven years old. With a number of missing teeth and a broken nose, her cries through the night were louder than the others.

Threading my hair into a braid and then tying it into a knot at the crown of my head, I felt instantly lighter when I stepped onto the smashed part of the grass where the tires had rolled down the hill. Though walking uphill with an injured leg wasn't easy, I was determined to see just how far off the road we had ended up and hoped to find answers to where the other vehicles went…and possibly a solution to our disastrous predicament.

CHAPTER NINE

AFTER WHAT SEEMED like an hour of walking and rifling through the shrubs and undergrowth for any sign of Ramona, I reached a dirt road above. Unsuccessful in my hunt for the girl, I encountered the remains of several soldiers instead. It was their boots I recognized—the same black standard-issue boots I wore on my own feet. Though the footwear was ripped and even melted in parts, they fared much better than the soldiers' bodies—too burned to salvage anything.

Though I was certain the bombing occurred from above, I glanced warily about, wondering if the enemy who attacked last night somehow lurked nearby. I stepped cautiously onto the road. Based on the tire marks, it was surely the same road we had been traveling along before we veered off. The lingering scent of petrol and fire preceded my every step and offered a spine-chilling prelude to what lay before me.

I maneuvered through pieces of burnt and twisted metal scattered all over the road, some embedded deep into explosion cavities and some even hung from nearby branches. Smoke churned in loops over what may have been a large metal frame…one that looked vaguely like our truck but burnt to a crisp. I refused to step closer, fearing the sight of more charred bodies, but more specifically…more charred *girls'* bodies.

I glanced up at the clear blue sky above me…*can someone see me now?* Were we being watched somehow by another airplane with more bombs? I shuddered and walked backward. Stepping farther away from the destruction, I nearly fell over my own feet in panicked flight.

Dashing swiftly into the refuge of the forest, I leaned against a thick tree trunk to catch my breath and brush the growing sweat off my cheeks.

Though everything around me represented horror and death, I took comfort in the thought that there were still nine of us breathing and alive. If we could find a way to survive this, I imagined we could survive anything.

Taking a minute to calm my shaking hands, I retied my boots and justified my quick departure. "There are likely no survivors here," I mumbled to myself. Knowing that my energy would be best used in searching for Ramona, I began the hour journey back down the hill.

The sun was high overhead by the time I reached our "camp". Though I shared the basics of what I had seen on the road with Katia and Ruta, I didn't elaborate on the details, and they didn't pursue it. A search of the wreckage might have yielded some sort of supplies, but I couldn't dwell on my shortsightedness and how I let fear overtake me—it was done.

"I suppose you didn't find her," Katia whispered. "Ramona."

"No." I lowered my head. "I tried, but this forest…" I waved my hand about. "It just seems endless. It goes on and on."

She nodded and patted my hand. "It's okay. We can try again tomorrow."

"So, we are on our own?" asked Ruta. "No other survivors?"

"It is what I expected." I sighed. "There was no sign of life up there and no working vehicles."

"Should we try to make our way up to the road? All of us?" Ruta asked. "Surely the road is still used by *someone*."

Katia and I exchanged looks. She didn't know what we did. Being found by soldiers once more may not be a rescue after all.

"No," I said. "The hike is too strenuous. The girls wouldn't make it."

Though I didn't have an alternate plan, I couldn't bring myself to allow these girls to face what was initially intended. I glanced over them as they rested. Each moment that had passed since the crash felt like an additional weight being added to my shoulders. *How long before it crushes me?*

Before the sun began its descent, we offered each of the girls another sip of water. Though most of the girls understood the need to conserve, it didn't stop them from complaining. Hanna, by far grumbled the most, but she had managed to get others to join her occasional outbursts. Both Yetta and the impressionable Inga followed suit.

Once again, I embarked on ways to be useful and deliberately labored to avoid the crossness of Hanna and her friends. I knew she was young, spoiled, and hurting, but we all faced these same awful circumstances, and my patience ran thin. I hoped that if I kept myself busy and functional, I could avoid saying or doing something I might regret.

Retrieving the knife from the backpack, I moved back to the truck and cut away the rest of the loose canvas attached to the bars. With three decent-sized strips, we could use them for more bedding or bandages. Next, I maneuvered back down into the cab. I plugged my nose as best I could to avoid the soldier's stench, which, in the heat of the day, had grown even worse.

Glancing around, I inspected the space for anything else we might use. Most military trucks I had come into contact with were basic, with no embellishments, and this one seemed to be no different. There wouldn't be much to utilize…except maybe the seats. I plunged the knife into the cushion and crudely carved the thin padding out of the seats. If anything, they will make decent support—one for Karina's arm and the other for Aneta's ankle.

With a great deal of hankering and subsequent bruising, I also freed several metal wires that coiled within the seat casing and underneath the steering wheel. They may come in handy for something, though for what, I wasn't yet sure.

When I returned to where the group rested, I threw my recent acquisitions to the ground and sat on the same log I had the night before and watched the others. Resting my fists under my chin, I tried to strategize. If only I had a pencil and paper to collect my random thoughts…at the moment, my head felt too muddled to hold onto anything sane.

Ruta moved over toward me. As she stood nearby, her words came out strained. "They are hungry and weak. What should we do?"

Pressing my bandaged palm to my forehead, I exhaled slowly. "I don't know." We had very little supplies and even less hope. When Katia joined us, I glanced between the two and whispered. "I only know we won't survive on one or two sips of water a day."

"True," Ruta mumbled.

"Do either of you have any ideas?" I asked.

Katia shook her head. "I'm not very good at this," she mumbled. "I understand we're the oldest and healthiest, but I don't know much about this." She waved her hand around. "Being outside…in a forest."

Neither had I really, but I'd spent some time on a farm before we moved to the city.

"The girls are looking to us for guidance." Ruta grabbed Katia's hand. "We need to use our heads and work together."

Katia's eyes lowered to the ground and her voice squeaked. "I just don't know what to do."

I placed my hand over their linked fingers and squeezed. "None of us were meant to be out here. We should have never been taken from home, but now that it's happened, we can't just give up."

"What options do we have?" Katia looked as though she might cry. This was the first time that I had seen her start to crack. She had been so strong up until now.

"There are only two choices." My eyes flickered between the two. "We fight to survive, or we lie down and die."

The silence between us expanded.

Inhaling deeply, I prodded them, knowing this burden could not be carried alone. "Which do you choose?"

They looked at each other, then together they said, "We fight."

My responding smile was weak at best. "Good, because I'm not ready to die."

Another quiet scan of the area and another sigh escaped Katia before she spoke. "But leaving here might be more dangerous than staying." Pointing to the thick trees, she lifted her shoulders. "We don't know what's out there…or who is out there."

She was right. We were in the middle of what I believed to be part of Germany…an unknown area with unknown threats. If we managed to get back up to the road and follow it again, would we risk being picked up by more German soldiers? Or worse, the Soviets? I wasn't even aware of what part they played in the war…I only knew of their rumored brutalities.

Our official papers had been taken from us before we left the school and only a few of us still had the temporary passport tucked into our clothing. Mine was missing, and as young women, we risked worse outcomes than starvation if the wrong type of rescuers crossed our paths.

I chewed on my bottom lip in thought. "We can do short searches around here to get a grasp on our surroundings. Maybe there is a town nearby, or a home or farm."

"Yes," Ruta agreed.

I tried not to be the constant bearer of bad news, but we needed the facts to be clear. "Because honestly, if we don't try to find help, nothing will matter without water."

Danger loomed whether we decided to stay *or* leave. *Such a daunting choice.* I just hoped we could pick the lesser of two evils.

Katia pointed to the far side of the truck. "We might need to move the dead girls." Her lips pulled into a frown. "I can hear things over there… animals and such."

My head tilted in her direction. "Animals?"

Her forehead creased, but my mind wandered a different way…an animal meant the possibility of food.

"Have you seen what type of animals they are?"

She looked at me blankly. "No, I've only heard them."

51

My mind continued to whirl with possibilities. "If we can somehow catch one of these animals, we might be able to cook it…and eat it."

Both pairs of eyes widened.

"We need food," I reasoned.

I was as far from a hunter as humanly possible, and I was willing to bet none of the other girls had any experience either. I could not even bear the thought of seeing a dead rabbit at home, but losing more girls was not an option. We had to try.

"We have two priorities. Catching food and finding water." I faced them again. "Which one do you think you could do better?" I looked between both girls; their pale faces and slack jaws assured me of their shock. When neither spoke, I urged an answer. "Do you have any other suggestions?"

"No." Ruta shook her head. "You're right. I will look for water."

"Me too," Katia spoke up.

I pursed my lips. Of course, I would be the one to kill the animal. "Fine. We need to figure out a way for you to not get lost while you search and only search in the daylight." I glanced upward to see the sun beginning its descent behind the trees. "For today, look down the ravine in front of the truck. Maybe you can see a path or a creek from that height, then tomorrow, you can look somewhere else."

They both nodded and stood to leave.

"Open the can of sardines; it's small and will likely only offer one or two bites per girl, but the oil might quench some thirst," I said before they left. Then quietly added, "And thank you."

"For what?" One of Ruta's eyebrows raised.

"For doing all this, for helping."

Katia smiled and placed a hand on my shoulder. "Thank *you*, Aleksandra. I'm certain we could not do this without you."

After they departed, I sat still for several more minutes. Nobody will care one whit about anything if we can't find food or water.

I glanced over to where we had covered the dead bodies. I needed to figure out how to trap an animal and then, the even greater dilemma of preparing it for consumption. I walked back over to the truck and studied it to see if there was anything that could be manipulated into a crude trap of some sort. I would use anything available to us. However, my shortcomings in the area of survivalism were evident— I really had no idea what to do.

I returned to where we had left the bodies.

The smell of death had intensified in the heat of the day and smacked me with the foul odor a good three meters away. When I pulled back one of the shrubs to inspect out of curiosity, a wide variety of insects had begun to appear on the bodies. I jumped backward. If only we had a shovel, we could have buried the girls this morning. I turned my head upward to allow the slight breeze to clear my nostrils and fill my lungs. Looking around, I felt discouraged. *What can I possibly do?*

Eyeing several large rocks piled nearby, ideas flowed. My father grew up on a farm in a rural part of Poland. It was the same farm, we lived on until I was six. I recalled him telling the story of when our chickens were being picked off by a fox. The wiry little predator was too fast for him to catch with his hands, so he fastened a trap out of stones. The stones were large and flat, similar to the shape of a tire and were heavy enough to cause harm if dropped on something—something like a small animal.

I examined the rocks before me until I found several that might meet my needs. *Now, how do I get them to fall on the animal as they approach?*

I scolded myself. From the care of my bunnies, I knew they sensed when danger was near. I had to figure out a way for the rock to fall without me being right there. I studied the area again, hoping to find a stick big enough to prop underneath for balance and wait for the animals to come, then somehow have the rock fall upon them.

Working out the details in my head, I realized this was the first convincing plan I'd come up with. Now I needed something to move the stick...*the wire!* I snatched the coiled wire from the camp and tied the random pieces together into a long crude rope.

Studying the contraption, I tried to mentally work out the process. I would have to sit somewhere out of sight but close enough to monitor the trap and pull the wire at the very moment the animal crossed underneath. That would mean, of course, that I would be out here with the bodies, animals, and any other unearthly thing in the dark. My only light would come from the stars. The full moon from our first night had long disappeared into the sliver of a new moon...entirely useless. I shook my head at such a foolish notion, then sighed; I truly had no other choice.

Motivated if not by anything more than my innate stubbornness, I looked around for several thick sticks, strong enough to hold the stone in place, but not too strong to remain in place. Once I located the best sizes, I placed a half dozen of these large rocks in front of the shrubs that shrouded the bodies. One at a time I heaved them up on one side and propped the stick underneath holding it precariously a foot above the ground. If I timed things just right, this might be our first meal in days, but I wouldn't let that pressure weigh me down. Thoughts of Karina, Katia, Ruta, Aneta, and even Olga, who was helping in any way she could, kept me focused. *I will do this for them.*

Tying the wire to two different traps, I marveled at the contraption. Even if it didn't work, though I truly hoped it did, I found strength in the belief that I wasn't going to go down without a fight. My father would be proud.

CHAPTER TEN

Later that evening, after Katia and Ruta told me they hadn't discovered anything new in their earlier inspection from the top of the ravine, I explained my plan. Both were quick to share their concerns, though they, like me, knew it was the best idea so far. Everything about our situation troubled me and my drive to *fix it* had become an obsession.

"Do you want me to come with you?" Katia asked. She did so with a great deal of courage; I knew that was the last place she'd want to be. She continued, "There might be, well, there might be bigger or more hostile animals than you expect."

I wanted to smile at her words but refrained. If there were, neither one of us could really fight them off. There was no sense in both of us getting injured. "No, get a good night's rest," I suggested. "Water is much more important than food. You'll need your energy for your search tomorrow."

They handed me one of the soldier's jackets. Now, all I needed was a helmet and I might be mistaken as one, despite the baggy appearance… *and* my blond braid. I made my way cautiously toward the traps and the dead girls.

Before I had left earlier this afternoon, I had rolled out the wire that was attached to the sticks across the ground toward a separate hedge. This was where I would sit and wait for some unsuspecting meal to come along.

As the night grew darker and the sounds of the girls' chatter in the distance lessened, I grew more uneasy. Every sound of every insect amplified around me. I tried to keep my shaking body to a minimum, despite my overwhelming fear.

Even though life became challenging when the Germans arrived, I always had family to rely upon. Here, I had no one but the other girls. And despite the cruelty I witnessed in the occupation, in the end, I had been spared the worst of it. Yes, I observed the harsh cruelty against the Jewish population, even the public executions of the teachers and priests… but it wasn't *me*.

My father's position allowed our family to remain in relative comfort after the invasion and, between his usefulness to the Third Reich and our ties to German ancestry, this allowed us privileges many lacked. Even when food and other luxuries were hard to come by for the average Pole, we suffered little compared to others. Yet, now as I reflect on it—the arrangement pilfered a silent cost. My father was never the same. A once proud and confident politician who drew crowds in the thousands had been reduced to a morsel of a man…not only physically, but he became withdrawn, angry, and hateful. Any light that once existed had been effectively dimmed within a few short months.

"I have sold my soul to the devil," he would say.

And though I didn't quite understand the significance of his declaration at the time, I understood it now.

Father planned twice to stand up to the SS, yet it was Mama's unrelenting persistence that stopped him. "We will do whatever they ask," she vowed. "I refuse to lose you." She even stomped her heel for added emphasis. "For I will not become a war widow, Szymon Jaworski!"

Rustling nearby shook my core. I held my breath, fighting to stay hidden, then allowed minuscule inhales and exhales to escape. Though distinct movement rustled around me, I couldn't see much. As time wore on, the sounds increased. Creatures continued to creep, but what they were or precisely where they were, I didn't know.

Eventually, my eyes adjusted to the darkness in a way that I could recognize the shape of the bushes and what wasn't a bush. With the escalating sounds of scurrying feet in what sounded like the direction of the shrubs, I sat up slowly and gripped each line of wire in my hands. When low growls emerged, my heart raced half a second faster and perspiration layered my skin. When I finally caught the outline of several furry animals, larger than a rabbit but smaller than something like a fox, I refused to let my mind wander with guilt…*they were food, that was all that mattered.*

Once they grew closer to the rocks, I timed the fall, hoping the stick would be yanked in time to allow the full force of the stone to do its damage. When the animals seemed to be in place, I quickly pulled the line, and a peculiar bark erupted at the same time the rumble from the rocks occurred. The noise rattled me through the stillness.

I had no idea what was over there, but my legs suddenly refused to move any closer. I shivered from the breeze that had picked up with the setting sun and pulled the uniform jacket tighter against my chest as I waited for more sounds to come forth. I heard nothing. *Could whatever it was be dead?* I crawled forward on my hands and knees then stood to my normal height upon approach. I tilted my head to listen better, but no moans or whimpers materialized. Examining the pile as best I could in the limited light, twinges of disappointment sparked as I lifted the rocks one by one. Nothing protruded from the edges. No tail, paw, or piece of fur. I wanted to cry. Nothing had been caught.

Discouraged, I clung to little hope. For several minutes I debated returning to camp empty-handed. Katia and Ruta would understand, they knew how hard this would be, but the others? Would they also relinquish their splinter of hope because I failed them?

I reluctantly lifted each rock and set the trap once more, positioning the stick and disentangling the wire. Over the next couple of hours, I pulled the wire several more times to disappointment. Once, I must've been close because a chunk of fur was left behind.

While I waited on my fifth attempt, I picked up a sharp rock near my feet on the ground. My fingers rubbed over the pointed edge. Feeling around, I found another rock similar to the ones I used for the trap though not as large. I pressed the pointed end against the smooth surface and began to scrape. The sound was nothing compared to the night screeches, and at times was swallowed by the brutally violent clashes that erupted as if the prowlers were fighting over something...*or someone.*

Another pull on the wire...another miss...another scrape against the rock.

One straight line materialized on the stone—deep and rhythmic, then another one intersected it. When a light gray sky began to drive the darkness away, the etched image came to light.

A cross.

I could do very little for those girls lying a stone's throw away but hoped in this limited way, they would be memorialized—to never be forgotten in this dark corner of the world.

When a splinter of orange cast a light behind me indicating a sunrise, I feared my window of opportunity might be closing. I settled flat on my stomach as before and fought the fatigue that spread through my limbs, then waited once more for the scurrying sounds that I had grown accustomed to. I closed my eyes and controlled my breathing. An unearthly screech emerged, followed by several more. I jumped to my feet and tugged the wire so hard I felt flesh searing in my palm—then watched as it bled freely through my makeshift bandage. I squeezed my fist shut, my injury being the least of my worries.

When the thunderous sound of toppling rocks gave way to more strained barks and squeals, I stood frozen in place, waiting for all the shrieking cries and scurrying to cease again. It could have been my exhaustion and possibly delirium, but I wondered if the animal was lying in wait for *me*...whatever the predator was, was it watching me?

Eventually, I crept forward. All the large rocks were piled unevenly. I shuddered as I stood over them. Could something be underneath? Could I finally have caught an animal? I removed them one by one. *Nothing!* I tossed the final stone angrily aside and dropped to my knees. My breathing sounded unsteady and guttural...I pulled my mouth tight...wait! *That isn't me!*

The labored sounds came with a peculiar wheeze, but from where? I stood up and searched the bushes around me. Near the foot of one of the girls an animal laid prone, its black paws extended outward and an irregular rise and fall of its blackish-gray fur indicated severe distress. Red streaks lined its head where the only white patch of fur could be found. They were claw marks...fatal claw marks, but the animal was not yet dead.

Once, when I had arrived too late for the birth of a litter of bunnies, I found several already dead, but one was left to suffer. Its own mother had bitten off its limbs. As a seven-year-old, the image had never left me. My father placed the injured animal in one of his socks and smashed a brick over its head. He explained that the bunny could not survive but that we gave it mercy...a swift death.

I glanced only briefly at this tormented animal before me and knew what to do. While I didn't have a sock to place it in, at least not one it would fit, I reached for its back paws and slid it out into the open. If I waited, it might be dead over time, but I could not stomach its suffering. Reaching for one of the flat rocks, I lifted it high overhead and smashed it down. The long, ragged breaths ceased.

Shoving my shaking hands into the pockets of the jacket, I finally took a deep breath and allowed myself a bit of relief with this strange circumstance. The only logical explanation for my good fortune had to be the hand of God. Nothing else made sense, and for the first time in several days, something other than hopelessness filled my heart. Maybe He hadn't completely turned his back on us.

As the morning sun rose higher and released the darkness that had a stranglehold on me, I scanned the area in the new light. There were paw prints and evidence of skirmishes everywhere. The unknown predator before me surely became victim to one and I could not be more thankful. With no success at the traps, had a fight not ensued, we would've spent another day wondering how long before we'd perish ourselves.

I leaned over and removed the rock and, in a spontaneous response, made the sign of the cross by pointing to my head, chest, and each shoulder. Though the deceased before me was not human, its death could very well prolong our lives, and for that, it deserved some respect.

Though our situation had only slightly improved with the possibility of this meat, I still had no idea how we would cook it or eat it. I secured its tail in the palm of my hand and walked toward camp with a lighter step than I had the day before.

CHAPTER ELEVEN

"Eww! What is that?" Inga cried the moment she spied me.

"Eek!" Yetta shrieked, taking several steps backward.

"This," I held it up proudly, "is our breakfast…and supper."

Varying cries erupted until Katia hushed them to silence. "Do you ladies have some bread in your pocket or a bowl of soup I am unaware of?" She looked at each of the girls. "Maybe you, Hanna? Yetta? Some potatoes or even a cucumber?"

The girls lowered their heads.

"I didn't think so." She glanced in my direction. "You should all be thanking Aleksandra for staying up last night and working hard to get you something to eat. She is the reason you might live another day."

I fought back a smile. If Katia and I survive this ordeal, we will be great friends.

I set the animal down on the log and began to pile sticks for a fire.

"Maybe we should skin it first." Ruta walked up and inspected it.

"Skin it?"

"Yes. My brother caught squirrels and rabbits for a poor family in our neighborhood. He always removed the fur before he gave it to them."

"That makes sense." I winced. I didn't recall eating hair in any of my meals before. "Do you know how to do it?" I looked at her with hope.

"I've never done it myself, but I watched him." She wrinkled her nose. "I suppose I could try." I didn't hesitate to retrieve the knife. If she was willing, I was more than eager to let her.

Getting a fire started was not as easy as I had hoped. I'd seen my cook start one on the stove but had never done it myself. The lighter I found on the first soldier had been misplaced somehow…or taken, and the lighter we found in the large man's pocket didn't seem to work. I hadn't had much experience with such a gadget, but I had seen enough smokers to know what to do, yet after many attempts, I could not get a flame to appear.

I retrieved the small cigarette pack next. *Camel Cigarettes.* The box had a picture of a camel on it, of course, and it was in English. *How odd*. I knew that the Nazi party restricted the German soldiers from smoking but most soldiers I encountered always stole a drag here and there. Somehow, this soldier must've gotten some cigarettes from the enemy. Opening the small pack that only contained three cigarettes, I knew the same number of matches would be found on the inside flap. Renia showed me this when we snuck up to the roof that first time.

Taking an armful of sticks, I piled them on top of each other and lit the first match. Nothing caught on and the match quickly extinguished. I only had two matches left. Olga appeared at my side holding the girlie magazine.

"Here, let me help." She tore out one page at a time and crinkled it in her fist. Once she had about eight or nine balls of paper, she restructured my sticks to form a hole underneath, then stuffed the paper in there.

"Have you done this before?"

"Once." She smiled. "My family went on a picnic a month before the occupation. I watched my father build a fire like this one, then we cooked our sausages over the open flame."

It was apparent this was a very good memory for her.

"Sausages sound delicious right now." I sighed as I watched her light the match.

She nodded. "I would give anything to go back to that day."

As Olga got the fire going quite effortlessly, I watched her with fascination. I suddenly realized I didn't know very much about these girls and their families.

"Is your family still in Łódź?"

Olga's jaw tightened. As the flames grew higher, they reflected a bright orange orb in her eyes. "My father was killed. It's just me and Mama…only now, she's alone."

I touched her arm. "I'm so sorry, Olga."

She shrugged and pointed to the fire. "Just keep adding more sticks and paper to keep it going. You don't want it too low; it will go out…or too high so it burns the meat."

"Will you help me cook it?"

"Sure. I don't really know much about it. The only reason I even know that is because I scorched my first sausage."

I smiled. "Anything will help, I've never done this before."

By the time we had a decent fire going, Ruta brought the odd-looking animal over to me with a stick through its mouth and out its bum. She had been able to scrape most of the fur off, missing a few places. But it didn't matter, I was so hungry, I would have probably eaten it even with the fur on.

Ruta handed me the meat. "If you want to start cooking it, Katia and I are going to hike a bit farther down the ravine looking for water." She grabbed the canteen. The contents swished lightly; we only had enough water for one more night.

I handed the meat to Olga and then grabbed Ruta's arm before she left. "But how will you know how to get back here, how can you mark your way?"

She held up some of the shredded pieces of fabric that had been torn for bandages, but not yet needed. "We are going to tie these along the way, especially where we exit to the ground below. It's the best we could think of."

"Okay." I found myself getting teary-eyed. "Be careful." I could not imagine continuing without them. It was a lot to ask for Katia and Ruta's safe return and even more for their successful retrieval of water, but we now realized our very survival depended on the risks we all took.

I held one end of the long stick over the fire while Olga held the other. We slowly turned the animal over, allowing the flame to reach all sides. When our arms grew tired, we asked Hanna and Yetta to take a turn. They did, albeit begrudgingly.

Once the animal's hide looked darker on all sides, I retrieved the knife from where Ruta left it and cut a portion away to check the inside. I had seen this done before when our cook roasted chickens. I knew the look and texture of a well-cooked fowl, mostly from my dinner table, and whatever this was, I hoped it shared similarities…especially in taste. The meat appeared ready.

With a couple of the lesser offensive pages of the magazine laid flat on the ground, I carved the meat from the animal's bones. I picked at every nook and cranny and as the meat piled higher, I was pleased with the results. This could possibly last us two days. Several times, the girls wandered over to inspect my work and a couple of them even commented on the enticing smell. It could have been a sewer rat for as hungry as we were; regardless, we believed it would taste like *Duck à l'Orange*.

When Katia and Ruta returned three hours later, I sent a silent prayer upward. Though their expedition yielded no water, they excitedly claimed to have found railroad tracks below. According to their inspection, the steel lines and wood planks appeared in working order. This small revelation boosted our spirits. If we followed the tracks, we might find our way to a town.

As my mind whirled at the possibilities, it simultaneously cringed at the reality. Several girls were still weak and injured, and even with rest, they would not recover well without adequate water. As excited as we were about the possibility of the tracks leading us to nourishment, they could just as easily lead us back into the hands of the German soldiers.

I shook the negative thoughts from my head—tonight we would eat and though our bellies might not be full, they would be much better than the last four days.

"How did the meat turn out?" Ruta asked.

"Good, I think." I grinned. "At least it smells good."

"Are we going to eat now or are you going to make us just look at the food," Hanna grumbled.

Katia's eyes rolled. "Ignore her," she whispered as we gathered by the fire. When I returned to my neatly heaped pile of meat, I noticed a small depression. It appeared as if someone had either knocked it over or taken some. It was hard to tell if any was missing, but why else would someone touch the food?

I glanced around. My first thought was Hanna or Yetta, both of whom had been thorns in our sides from day one, but taking in each forlorn girl's face, it truly could have been anyone. We were all starving to death.

I separated the meat into two stacks. Katia and Ruta divided the first half into nine small lots and handed them out while I gathered the second half and wrapped it tightly in paper from the magazine. I would need to somehow keep it away from animals, bugs, and now possibly a thief for the night.

The girls eagerly accepted the small offering and ate with no complaints. This made my sleepless night worth it in the end. If we could each contribute in different ways, we might not succumb after all. The greasy meat tasted a little like pork, and at times I struggled to chew the fat fully before swallowing, but not one piece went uneaten.

As we readied for sleep, I took the wrapped meat and dug a hole between Karina and myself. The dirt should keep it cool. Then I placed a flat rock on top. If anyone tried to take it overnight, I would know.

That night, the sounds of the scavenging animals near the dead bodies grew louder and more aggressive. The smell, too, had increased and the pungent odors reeked. It was becoming more and more apparent that our need to move on had to be soon.

The next morning, I dispersed another small portion of the meat, keeping only a handful for later—enough for each person to get one bite. It was apparent the protein the girls consumed had strengthened and helped them, but we were in desperate need of water, so Katia and Ruta departed up toward the road in search of anything they could find. They left before I could warn them about what they might see.

While we awaited their return, I checked the area around the bodies once more to see if any other skirmishes resulted in more animal victims. It was a longshot…the fact that it even happened the first time was a miracle in itself. After pushing the brush aside, I quickly retreated. The decay and smell had worsened…almost to the point I wasn't sure I could tolerate another night out here. Of course, I would do anything to keep us alive, but it would take a great deal of effort to keep my stomach from reacting.

Finding myself on the opposite side of the truck, I took advantage of the privacy and pulled my pants down to reveal the cut on my leg. Though I had ignored it as best I could, it had grown more tender the last couple of days.

Examining the injury, I noticed there were parts of the cut that appeared inflamed and a particularly ugly section near my knee that oozed with puss. I retrieved several of the unused strips of fabric from my pocket and wrapped them tightly around the worst of it. Tying the ends, I hoped this would keep it from rubbing against the rough uniform pants. Thankfully, both my head and hand wounds had since scabbed over. The salve we had found in the dead soldier's pack was used on some of the more serious lacerations in the group, and though mine was bad, others were worse.

As time wore on, everyone seemed to be healing at different rates, but the best news was that each girl appeared to be past any critical stage of injury. Our biggest concerns now were Aneta's swollen ankle, which prevented her from walking, and Karina's broken arm, which caused her terrible pain.

"Hey, look what we found!" Ruta hollered down to us as she and Katia made their descent.

I had taken a seat on the log again while the other girls sat in varying positions around the firepit, but we all stood to her shouting.

"We found some supplies." She and Katia ran down the rest of the way.

As they emptied the dirty, torn sack, the girls moved into a half circle around them and watched as two cans of tinned tomatoes, a can labeled *Wurst*, a couple of hard biscuits, a whistle tied to a rope, and an additional canteen rolled to a stop before us.

"Oh," I gasped and reached for the canteen first. The weight brought a smile to my face. *It must be nearly full.* I opened the cap and sniffed. "Good," I mumbled. "This is very good." No sweet or bitter scent of liquor transpired.

Katia peered over at me. "We saw the wreckage up there…and the bodies." Her voice faltered momentarily then picked up speed. "But we found these as if they'd fallen out of a vehicle before the fire burned everything. When we first saw the tomatoes, we just searched all over and found the other stuff."

I grinned, but inside I felt terrible. I could have found these two days ago had I had the courage to check around the burned-out vehicle myself. I had let my fears overpower me.

"Thank you for going up there," I said. "This water is a miraculous find."

Katia patted my hand. "I prayed while I was up there, then within minutes Ruta found it."

Another testament that we were being looked after.

I passed the canteen around with the usual warning…one sip only. Once everyone received their allotment, Katia and Ruta sat down with me to share the details of their discovery, then we moved on to a much more serious discussion—the need to leave. The canteen water would be gone by tomorrow and without a water source, staying here only led to one thing… certain demise. *We must leave.*

"How is Aneta going to walk out? She can't even put pressure on her ankle?" I questioned.

"I have an idea." Ruta picked up a nearby stick. "My father made splints for his patients' limbs. Some, he even fashioned out of items around our house when people would show up unannounced."

"But can she get down a mountain or even walk along the railroad tracks?" I asked with skepticism.

Ruta looked at me. "What is the alternative, Aleksandra?"

I looked down. Now, *I* was being the skeptic.

She continued, "We got very lucky finding that canteen, but we've found nothing here to help us survive much longer."

Katia joined in. "We've looked all around here. We can't stay."

"I know." I fidgeted with the hem of my shirt. "I just worry about what's out there." I pointed toward the ravine.

Katia patted my shoulder. "Whatever is out there…we'll face it together."

Ruta stood up. "I'm going to search for anything I can use for splints for Aneta and Karina. Do you think I can cut some strips of canvas?"

Katia stood to join her. "Yes, they're over here. I will help you."

Once Ruta had found what she considered to be the right sticks, she positioned them on each side of Aneta's ankle and wrapped the thick canvas strips tightly around, then tied the ends. At the very least it appeared to give Aneta support and keep her ankle from bearing too much pressure.

She then did the same for Karina but continued to use the belt as a means of keeping her arm snug against her torso to reduce its movement.

I filled the soldier's backpack with the few items we would need for our journey including both canteens, one now completely empty, the cans of food, the small portion of meat, one uneaten candy bar, and the flask, which was also now empty. I had used it several times for the girls who suffered the most, including Karina. The liquor took the edge off and helped them relax. Additionally, we rolled up several pieces of cut canvas and tied them with the wire to be used for bed rolls as we traveled. Though we despised our current circumstances, a part of me feared leaving the comfort of our little camp only to venture out into the unknown.

When the time came to share our plans, we gathered the girls together. Up until now, Katia, Ruta, and I had kept our conversations private, mostly to reduce any disagreements, but now they needed to understand the whole of it.

Once explained, most understood the need for us to go. There was the typical whining and complaining from the same girls who had done so since the beginning, but we also told them if they wanted to stay and not go with us that was their decision, we wouldn't force them. That quickly quieted them.

It seemed many had realized on their own that survival required us to leave.

Though I didn't know it at the time, the young girl that Hanna clung to who died that first night had been her younger sister. It justified some of her anger and resentment toward me; I might feel the same if Karina hadn't made it, despite the short length of our relationship.

When Hanna stood up and gathered some of the random wildflowers off to the side, we realized what she was doing and joined her. Each of us, with fistfuls of green stalks and colorful buds, made our way to the shrubs.

It was time to say goodbye to our friends. I retrieved the stone I etched the cross into from my hiding place and placed it near the flowers.

Katia encouraged everyone to clasp hands while she offered a prayer. Oh, how I wished we could have given these girls a proper burial. It seemed so awful, so incomplete to leave them as they were. Though hidden from the elements, their bodies were still exposed to the wilds of the forest.

Katia wrapped her arms around Hanna's shoulders that shook with sobs, then silently we walked back to the camp, gathered our limited supplies, and followed Ruta to the edge of the ravine.

CHAPTER TWELVE

Hiking down the mountain proved to be easier than I had anticipated. Katia and Ruta had already mapped out the easiest descent and carefully led the way to the bottom edge of the valley and in the direction of the railroad tracks. Though we hadn't heard any train whistles or engine sounds in the five days since the accident, we had high hopes that these tracks would lead us toward a town or any type of civilization…we weren't picky, we just needed resources.

We didn't make much progress that first day with Aneta's injury slowing us down, but by nightfall, our prayers had been answered in an odd way. One might not think walking in a rainstorm would be a particularly pleasant experience, but the rain brought the moisture our bodies needed more than anything.

After trying to catch as much as we could with our open mouths, we sought shelter underneath a canopy of trees. Soaked to the bone, we were not strong enough to fight off exposure or colds, so we wrapped the three soldiers' jackets around Karina, Aneta, and Inga. Then the rest of us used the canvas pieces we had brought for warmth.

While the rain continued to fall around us, we placed both canteens out in direct contact to catch the water, as well as several large leaves that allowed the moisture to pool within like a bowl. Each time one of the leaves filled to capacity, we carefully lifted it up and brought it to a different girl, encouraging them to drink the entire amount.

Once all nine of us had a chance to drink, we settled down for the night beneath the thick trees. Somehow, despite our wet clothing, we seemed to fall asleep easier than we had in over a week. The gentle pitter-patter of moisture dripping through the night may have been the reason or possibly that our dehydrated bodies had been satisfied to some degree. Regardless, it was welcome.

By morning, only the ground showed remnants of the rainstorm; the sun shone brightly, and the sky was as dry as the week before. Thankfully, both canteens were filled to their rims with water and our leafy bowls had not yet dried up, providing us with another bountiful morning drink. It was astonishing how something as simple as freshly showered trees rekindled our faith and gave us the courage we needed to forge forward.

Now it was the lack of food that lingered on my mind. Especially since we only had two cans of tomatoes and the sausage remaining. Despite all the reasons we could be discouraged, there was a lighter step amongst the girls as we walked that day. Even Aneta and Karina pushed forward despite their pain.

I tried to ignore the growing inflammation along my leg. I had changed the bandages last night in the dark, and though I could not see the injury well…I could feel it. By late afternoon, the swelling had increased, and my temperature had started to alternate between sweats and chills. I wanted to believe it was from the exertion and not the possibility of something worse.

In the twenty-four hours since we left the truck and moved along the tracks, no trains had appeared, yet somehow, we knew each step brought us closer to *something*. We could sense it.

That night, after an excessively warm day, we took shelter once more under the trees. The heat mixed with a dense humidity that lingered from the summer rainstorm had brought an unfortunate influx of insects— mosquitos and flies—that drove us nearly out of our minds.

Though we should have awoken better rested than the night before, I could feel every crack and bump in the muscles of my neck, back, and shoulders. Fatigue spread through my limbs, and it took me twice as long to stand and stretch. Then on top of that, aggravated bites seemed to reach every part of my exposed skin and even some that hadn't been quite so visible. I hid my discomfort from the others. My needs were not a priority.

Reaching for the canteen that morning, I noticed the cap was not as tightly screwed on as I had left it. Removing it, I peered inside. The darkness prevented me from seeing the entire contents, but I could tell just from shaking it that someone had helped themselves to the water.

"Who touched this last night?" I shouted at the girls as they all struggled to their feet. Every pair of eyes was settled on mine except one. Yetta fidgeted with the hem of her skirt with a fascination that seemed to encompass all her attention.

"What's wrong?" Ruta asked in her approach.

"Someone helped themselves to the water," I spoke loud enough for all to hear.

"Are you sure?"

"I'm positive." I didn't shift my gaze from Yetta, though she didn't seem to notice since she never looked up.

"What about the canteen Katia has?"

"We used most of that yesterday and now it appears as though we will run out of water quicker than planned."

Frightened gasps and cries emerged.

I took several steps closer to Yetta, who straightened upon my approach. Though she said nothing, I could see the defiance in her eyes.

"You don't get any water today," I declared angrily.

"What?" she huffed. "You can't do that!" Her fists curled at her sides. She and I had only met in the truck, but none of our interactions since had been pleasant. She and Hanna were two peas in a pod when it came to complaining the most.

"I can and I will."

Yetta reached forward to grab the canteen from my hand, but my other hand blocked her attempt and shoved her to the ground.

I glared hard, then turned around to face the others.

Karina's eyes went wide. "Watch out!" she shrieked.

I turned the very moment a stick whacked me in the shoulder. Part of the broken twig caught my blouse and tore the material, scraping my skin at the same time.

I tossed the canteen to Ruta and leaped towards Yetta. She was not as tall as me but carried a bit more weight in the chest and hips than I did. She used her weight to her advantage and we both hit the ground with a thud. Her fingers clutched my hair and yanked as I punched her arm free from its clasp. Once I found solid ground, I straddled her and held her body down. Both of my knees restrained her wrists at the side while my hands gripped her throat.

When her arms stopped flailing and her legs stopped kicking, I released my hold just enough for her to catch her breath. Breathing erratically myself, I shoved my finger in her chest and threatened, "Don't you ever, ever do that again, or I will make sure you regret it."

Katia appeared at my side and lifted me to my feet. The pain in my leg resumed and I hobbled a few feet away.

"Are you hurt?" Katia asked.

I shook my head, though I knew the struggle aggravated my injury. "Just shaken." I coughed. "I didn't expect that."

Brushing the dirt off my pants, I motioned for Ruta to let the girls have their one morning sip while I caught my breath. Anger still charged through me, but I tamped it down nearly as quickly as it surfaced.

Yetta stayed on the ground.

I truly didn't care if she remained there. In fact, I nearly told her to.

Once our few belongings were packed, we set out along the tracks again, albeit much slower than yesterday and the day before, and with very little conversation. Most of the girls seemed stunned over the turn of events and trudged along wearily. Between the tension and a return to a shortage of supplies, the end of our misery seemed out of reach…we were losing hope.

"How much farther, Aleksandra?" Karina whimpered at my side as the sun reached high overhead with the encumbrance of another blistering day.

I wrapped my arm through hers and helped her trudge along. "Hopefully not much longer. There has to be a town along here somewh—"

"Buildings!" Olga cried. "I see buildings ahead!"

Sure enough, several structures appeared no more than maybe a kilometer away. Though we were tired from lack of sleep and hunger, our adrenaline surged, and we began to run. Our movements were clunky and awkward but filled with anticipation. When Aneta fell we all stopped and helped her to her feet before we continued. That was when I realized the majority of us had become more than friends.

As we closed the remaining distance to the first brick building, our steps slowed. All the windows had been shattered, some missing entirely. The smoky black streaks that spread like skeletal fingers across the brick confirmed a fire had destroyed most of the timber parts of what would have been a home, and it was abandoned.

Olga and Ruta disappeared around the side while I looked through the holes that were once windows. The inside wasn't entirely burned out, but debris littered the space. One of the front doors hung loosely on a hinge, crashing to the ground the moment I tried to push it open for entry. I shuddered at the sound but stepped inside anyway. Dirt and rubbish seemed to cover the floor and if there had been any furniture at one time, it was now missing. After a quick glance about, I exited back to the porch where a few of the girls dropped in anguish. Their cries intensified.

"Don't give up now," Katia soothed in her motherly voice. "We have come so far."

Inga stumbled away from Hanna and fell to her knees, laying her head down on a pile of large stones before her. "We are going to perish here," she sobbed.

"No," Katia insisted. "No, we will not."

Karina looked at me to confirm what Katia said. I shook my head. "No, Karina, we won't die, we are the ones who fought to survive, remember?"

Tears pooled in her eyes, though she didn't respond.

"There are about another dozen buildings here just like this one," Olga said upon return. "It may have been a small village. It's hard to tell with all the damage."

"Do you think there are any supplies? Water or food maybe?" I asked while moving to look behind the first house.

"I doubt it." Ruta joined us. "They appear picked over, but it won't hurt checking." She pointed to the far side. "Looks like there are a few barns in that direction and what may have been some farms, but everything is so overgrown, it seems like it's been deserted for quite some time."

I glanced over the girls' worn and weary faces, now dotted with insect bites on top of everything else we had endured.

"Let's stay here for the night," I suggested and pointed through the door of the house I had just inspected. "Even though it's still daylight, I think everyone is in need of some rest."

Hanna peered inside. "It's filthy," she cried.

"Everything this entire journey has been filthy!" Olga snapped back. She had said very little since the accident, but she might have reached her limit now with Hanna.

I fought my smile. It was good to see I wasn't the only one fed up with the ongoing objections.

"It will, at the very least, keep us away from the bugs for tonight." Katia scratched her arm where a line of bites bulged. "But you are welcome to sleep under the trees again if you want to. We won't force you to stay here."

Hanna and Yetta exchanged disgruntled looks as they entered the house. Once inside, they cleared a space farther away from the rest of us, then huddled in quiet confidence. Normally, Inga would have joined them, but this time she lingered near Ruta.

I used my boots to remove the clutter from a section of the floor in one corner and rolled out the pieces of canvas. It would not be an overly comfortable night, but the way the girls were scratching their skin, we all needed a break from the insects.

Once all were seated either on the canvas or the floor, I pulled out the canteen. Irritation over the earlier incident with Yetta quickly resurfaced when I unscrewed the cap. "Only one sip." I passed it around, though I didn't make the effort to walk it over to the two girls who had isolated themselves in the connecting room. "If we are careful," I spoke to those nearby, "this might last us through tomorrow." Turning to Katia and Ruta, I whispered, "Once they are settled, I will go out and check the other buildings before dark. Maybe there is water somewhere here."

"You shouldn't go alone," Katia responded first. I figured that's what she would say.

"Yeah." I glanced out the window as the sun began to lower. "Maybe one of you can come with me, but let's try to get them to sleep first."

Curious about our surroundings, I scavenged the two small rooms for any source of comfort, although they yielded very little. Several empty cabinets with missing doors lined one wall, the remnants of a metal bed frame with no mattress lay upside down, ceramic glass shards and brittle leaves layered the hard wooden floors, and ash blackened our fingers from nearly everything we touched.

Despite the presence of a jamb stove in the center of the room we took refuge in, its plates were seriously cracked with a missing throat. *Worthless.* Thankfully, with as warm as the nights had been, its presence hardly mattered.

Katia, in her typical tenderness, helped the girls to settle in while Ruta pulled us aside. Her eyebrows pinched severely, making her mouth curve into a deep frown. "I think Inga might be allergic to the bug bites," she said.

We glanced over to the youngest of the group as she tried to lie down but moved restlessly about, scratching her arms and legs. Even from our distance and the descending sun, we could see that her skin was swollen and red. We stepped over for a closer look.

Ruta knelt down and placed her hand over Inga's. "Try not to scratch the bites, that could make them worse."

"It itches so much," she whimpered.

Katia and I joined them on the floor. With all that Inga had faced thus far, she had survived with a strength I didn't expect from such a young person, but now as I looked upon her, she might have reached her threshold—even her cheeks and lips were puffy.

"What would your father say to do?" I turned to Ruta. We had relied on her medical insight day in and day out.

"Without proper medication, it would be honey."

"Honey?" I choked, glancing around. If honey was anywhere nearby, I would have tried to harvest some just to eat. "What else?"

Ruta pinched the bridge of her nose. She did this often when she tried to remember. "Um…basil, yes, I believe basil might work."

I sighed. "Alright. I'm going out to look beyond the buildings. Maybe the residents at one time had a garden and some wild plants survived." I knew what the glossy green basil leaves looked like from my mama's garden— along with the garlic and rosemary she grew for her headaches.

Ruta glanced nervously between us.

"I doubt I will find honey." Peering back to Inga, who moaned and cried at the touch of another, I stood to my feet. "Keep her comfortable. I will try to make it back before dark."

"You shouldn't go alone," Katia repeated her concerns from earlier, only now circumstances had changed.

"I have to. Ruta needs to take care of Inga and there are five others who need you both."

Katia frowned. She knew I spoke the truth.

"I won't go far, and I promise to return before dark. There's still enough light for me to explore the area around the outer buildings."

Katia and Ruta both looked over to the window as the yellow glow of a sunset shone through.

"This doesn't seem to be a large village, so it won't take long," I assured.

Katia sighed. "Should we open the tomatoes? The girls haven't eaten today."

Ruta and I nodded at the same time. The girls needed strength.

I retrieved the backpack. Handing what was left of the food and the canteens to Katia's care, I used the knife to open the tinned tomatoes, then slipped the blade into the side of my boot. Without the cans, the pack was much lighter and would help me carry anything I might find.

I waved goodbye as I headed toward the next row of houses. With little variation, they too had been picked over and burned. Nothing seemed to be of use…certainly no food or water, and from what I had seen of the air attack on our convoy, I suspected something like that may have happened here…*but why?*

Maybe the rumors of the Allied forces were true after all—the ones where they were trying to destroy everyone…even women and children. Nothing in this war made sense.

Standing in the center of what appeared to be a main road, I could see most of this small village. Approximately ten houses lined each side and a handful scattered beyond with what was left of a few barns. *What would be the purpose of bombing such a place?* It didn't appear to have harbored anti-aircraft weapons or stored mortar or tanks, but I had stopped trying to find reason in this illogical combat some time ago.

As darkness fell quicker than I anticipated, having lingered too long in the structures with no luck, a grayish-purple sky settled around me as I headed toward the farms. I hoped to find wild herbs or anything edible along the path. Maybe by some chance, I would even find a plant that could stop the burning sensation on my leg. Now I knew the chills I fought earlier came from a fever and not the weather.

The first barn I approached was in worse shape than the brick buildings, most assuredly because of its wooden exterior. Three sides had collapsed inward, but the fourth remained standing. The waist-high overgrown weeds between me and the structure could very well be hiding some fertile soil based on the successful overgrowth. I tiptoed closer then bent down and checked the ground for any kind of edible root, possibly abandoned potatoes.

I clawed through the dirt and sifted past the tangled weeds. *Nothing.* I crawled forward making the same motions with my hands for a good five meters when my fingers fumbled over a pile of random nuts. I lifted one up toward the vanishing light, its hard brown shell was unmistakable… hazelnut! Inspecting the nut closer, a shadow moved next to the farm wall.

I froze.

A silhouette rose slowly from its crouched position and faced me.

CHAPTER THIRTEEN

THE DARK OUTLINE grew taller with each passing second. My shaky exhale was all I could hear before the rustle of moving clothes overtook it. The movement came toward me. *Katia was right.* I should not have come alone.

I stood and turned on my heels to run when a rush of air caught up with me and fingers yanked my shirt and body backward. "Eek," I squealed as I hit the ground easily from the force and rolled underneath the stems of thick vegetation. *I am dead*, I repeated over and over in my mind. I had little strength to fight whatever it was.

"Stille!" A man's rough hand covered my mouth and held tight. The way he silenced me should have been frightening but once his eyes were parallel to mine as we lay prone in the weeds, a piercing element of fear surfaced. *He* was afraid...*but of what?*

"Sprich nicht." His voice softened when he pled for me to keep quiet. My eyes remained wide and curious, only inches from this stranger's green eyes, but oddly enough, despite his broad shoulders and obvious strength, I no longer felt frightened.

I scanned his clothing. The typical gray tunic with its dark green collar and matching shoulder straps, large buttons, and four pleated pockets clearly identified his position as a German soldier, but his uniform was dirty and disheveled and he wore no hat or helmet, which allowed his dark blond bangs to hang low near his eyes, much longer than a typical squaddie's cut might be...and as he watched me with his deep, intense eyes, a solitary dimple emerged on the right side of his mouth as he pursed his lips tightly together. He was handsome in a mysterious, dangerous sort of way.

I opened my mouth to speak when he pressed harder. "Bitte," he whispered— *please*— the same moment other voices emerged from possibly another side of the barn. My breathing increased. *There are more soldiers?*

His eyes begged. I nodded and he released his hand as we listened quietly for their approach.

"Wo ist er hin?" A gruff voice rose barely above a whisper, but in the quiet of the night, it was clear as day. The soldier was looking for someone.

"Er wird bezahlen." A different voice…only accompanied with a threat.

I watched this stranger carefully. His smooth skin exposed a fine layer of sweat. The men were talking about him. *They were looking for him.*

I resisted the temptation to stretch up to see how many were present; to do so would give away our location. I hoped it was only the two. Then my heart shuddered…what if they make their way toward the other buildings? What if they find the girls?

The soldier must've seen my expression because his hand went to mine, and he squeezed it gently…a strange consolation from a man I knew nothing about, and a soldier no less. I took a silent inhale and allowed air to fill my lungs. Panicking wouldn't do either of us any good.

I listened for the men's footsteps as they tramped away from us, then rolled to my back. Sighing a momentary relief, I waited several minutes until I could no longer hear their voices and their movements grew faint.

Glancing back over to the soldier, I met his eyes once more. "You are a deserter," I whispered in German.

The soldier's square jaw grew rigid as he moved to his knees, but he said nothing.

I peered upward. My father would have never tolerated the presence of a coward but knowing what the German armies did in my hometown, I didn't feel like desertion under a cruel dictator was entirely wrong.

"It's okay." I struggled to stand to my feet and brushed the dirt off my trousers. The soldier's gaze went to my attire and ended at my borrowed boots. I waited until his eyes reached mine again. "I don't like what you are forced to do."

The sharp green eyes from before softened in the moonlight. He adjusted his tunic. "What do you know of that?"

I wondered how much I should say. But in the end, he did not seem to be the one I should fear. "Your soldiers invaded my city," I mumbled. "I know plenty."

He stood impassively in front of me. His demeanor tried to initiate a hardness but something more akin to compassion broke through. "Did you kill someone to get those?" He pointed to my boots.

"No!" I snapped. Then whispered, "but I would have if necessary."

His forehead wrinkled in surprise, and he folded his arms across his chest defensively. "I do not run from my country," he said. "I love my country."

"Then why did you leave?"

His tall form turned rigid. "I refused to continue to do what my commandant requires of me."

My mind wandered with vivid imagination, but in the end, I really *didn't* want to know. I had witnessed torture, threats, shootings, and assaults…I didn't ask him to elaborate. What I had seen in my own country spoke volumes of the atrocities with which the German soldiers were tasked.

"I must go." I stepped around him.

He grabbed my arm. "Why are you out here alone?"

"We—" I hesitated. Though I strangely felt as if I could trust him, I feared telling him the whole truth. After all, it was German soldiers who had taken us from our school in the first place.

One of his eyebrows raised as he waited for me to finish.

I didn't.

"My name is Günter." He released his hold and held out his hand for me to shake it.

I peered down at it in awe. None of the previous soldiers I had encountered cared to know who I was or anything about me.

"I'm Aleksandra." I met his hand. Then eyed him carefully. "Where are *you* going?" I was curious where a German soldier could possibly go as a deserter and feel safe.

He shrugged his shoulders. "I'm not sure. France maybe, or Spain." Then his eyes narrowed. "You're not well."

I gasped. How could he know this with just a glance? I had successfully kept it from the girls thus far.

He pointed to my cheeks. "You are feverish. Are you injured?"

I swallowed hard. "I wish you good luck, Günter, and…thank you for alerting me to the other soldiers." I took a breath. "But I must go."

I squeezed his hand, then turned to leave, though he held on a bit longer. "You are not safe out here."

My eyes went to our clasp. He quickly released his hold and continued, "There are soldiers everywhere."

My heart thumped, remembering that the two soldiers could still come upon my friends and my urgency to rush back to them arose again. "I must get back to my friends," I confessed.

"There are more of you?"

I nodded.

"Girls?"

I nodded again. His complexion paled and his jaw tightened once more.

"I do not mean to frighten you, but I have seen how these men treat women they come across."

My chest burned. It was too late; I was already frightened. He wasn't telling me anything I hadn't already seen happen in my own city, but now my friends could be at risk.

I turned and walked briskly toward the buildings when a faint scream materialized. I stiffened, then sprang forward when Günter grabbed my arm and whisked me swiftly to the side of the nearest house. Once again, he held his hand to my mouth for me to shush. I pushed it off and tried to run when he leaped in my direction, grabbing my injured leg, and causing me to tumble and roll.

"Aleksandra! Halt!" He tightened his grip—the length of his fingers went nearly around my leg's circumference. All I could think of was the girls. I pinched and slapped in an effort to get him to release his hold on me. I needed to get to them…fast. They needed my help.

"Please," I pleaded desperately. "I must go."

His whisper came out firm and strained. "You cannot go now. If you are seen, you will face the same fate as your friends."

"Then so be it!" I shot back. "And they're not my friends…they're my family!" I hissed angrily through gritted teeth. Wrestling free, I scrambled forward only to have my shirt snagged by him once more. Then his arms went fully around my waist as he pulled me backward.

"Just wait!" he mumbled through my hair. "You cannot stop these men." His grip around my waist tightened until my back reached his chest. "They are soldiers, and they will kill you."

I broke down in sobs. My entire body went limp and helpless. I knew he was trying to help, but the physical torment my wandering mind put me through made me cry out. "I can't just stay here and do nothing!"

Günter turned me around to face him. Though he had lessened his grip slightly, he still held me tight enough to prevent me from leaving.

"I can't just let bad things happen," I whimpered.

"Sometimes you can't stop the bad things from happening." He leaned in. "Trust me, Aleksandra. I am a soldier, and the one thing I know quite well is that you don't rush into a situation you know nothing about."

When he drew back, my eyes stared hard at his, but I found nothing cruel within them. His intent to help was sincere.

Several seconds passed by in total silence. "You can let go now," I whispered.

His hands still clutched my waist. "Are you going to run?"

I shook my head. He must've believed me because his hands immediately dropped to his sides, and he took a step backward. I fell to my knees and both of my hands pressed against my chest. Searing pain tore within me at this sudden turn of events. Devastated, I wept.

When I finally raised my head, I saw Günter moving carefully around me. For a brief moment, he was near, then he disappeared, reappeared, and disappeared again. Finally, he reached his hand down for me to take. "Come now, let's go."

We maneuvered carefully from house to house down the main road until we were one house away from where I left the girls. We had not seen or heard anything since the scream.

"Where did you leave your friends?"

A feeling of trust settled upon me, and I pointed to the last house. The building stood so quiet, it was as if they slept soundly within. "Maybe it was only a nightmare, and all is well," I reasoned.

Günter paused at my side. "I hope you're right."

Suddenly, he grabbed my arm again and pulled me back toward him. Urgently, he tugged me downward to take cover beneath the overgrown vegetation against the building. Putting his finger to his lips, he whispered, "Shhhh, I hear something."

I winced in pain. My leg throbbed tremendously, but my eyes followed his pointing finger to the dark line of trees about twenty meters from where we were. Short rapid breaths expelled from my lips. This whole day has been nothing but a terrible nightmare. *When will it end?*

"Is it your leg?" He looked to where I rubbed it. "Your injury?"

I nodded.

He turned back to where the noise came from, and the next few minutes passed so slowly and painfully that my mind conjured the worst. Why was I so naïve to believe there wouldn't be dangers here? Why did I risk the girls' safety over a few insect bites?

Günter's keen eyesight scanned the surroundings judiciously as I silently and repeatedly admonished myself for my foolishness.

"There are nine of us," I mumbled.

His eyes widened in horror.

"I left them when I went searching for a certain plant. A girl in our group is sick from the bug bites."

He pressed his fist against his forehead. He seemed clearly angered by this bit of information, but he didn't know…he didn't know the horrors that we had come from. We had no choice. He squeezed my hand. "Stay here, let me go check the house first."

"No," I cried. "If they are there, they will be frightened to see you and not me."

"I know how to approach unseen." He unholstered a pistol from his waist. It had been concealed so well I hadn't even realized he carried one. "I will check to see if they are in there." Then he frowned and looked away from me. "The soldiers would have likely checked every building here looking for me."

I knew he was right, but I could not sit still.

"I will follow behind you," I insisted.

"No."

"Yes," I demanded.

When he pursed his lips, the dimple reappeared. Like Katia, he seemed to have learned quickly how stubborn I can be. Reaching for my hand, he lifted me up and pressed his back against the outer wall. When we inched through the tall grass, we kept low and quiet all while keeping an eye on the trees to our left where we heard the earlier sounds.

When we reached the corner of the structure, he held up one hand for me to wait as he crept forward. I crouched down again against the brick siding and waited. He didn't look my way when he moved to the doorway. He was only gone for several seconds, but when he returned, I could see from his face the news was not good.

"There is no one in there," he said when he reached me.

I gasped. Tears immediately filled my eyes.

"There is debris everywhere, but no people," he continued.

I covered my face with my hands. I should never have left them…and with nothing to defend themselves with, for I had the knife.

Günter moved closer. He didn't touch me, but I could feel him near. When I removed my hands, he handed me a handkerchief. It was thin, frayed, and dirty but I readily accepted his meaningful gesture.

When I attempted to return it, he motioned for me to keep it. Most likely because I could not stop the tears from falling. *Katia, Ruta, Olga…Karina!* These girls who had become my family in the last ten days were *gone.*

"What do you think happened to them?"

Günter failed in his attempt to keep his frown hidden. "I'm not sure." Though I hadn't known him for long, his words were not convincing.

I think he knew.

"I must find them." I brushed the wetness off my cheeks. I would not sit here and do nothing.

"We need to move away from this position. The soldiers could still be near." He grabbed my hand and led me back to the thick shrubs near the second building. I sat down where he pointed and fought my urge to cry again. My heart felt the heaviest it had in days.

"You are courageous, Aleksandra."

I listened but said nothing. *Is it truly courageous if you are fighting for survival? Wouldn't anybody fight to live?*

"How did you and your friends get here?" he asked when he sat down next to me. "You are not German."

My breath hitched. I had hoped my accent wasn't that obvious. Taking a deeper breath, I relaxed. This man had been kind. "No. There were eighteen of us taken from our school in Poland."

After I relayed parts of our accident and attempt at survival, he unbuttoned the front of his tunic and pulled out a covertly hidden knapsack. When he untied the opening, he retrieved an envelope and handed it to me. "Put this on your wound."

I read the label. *Sulfanilamide.* "What is this?" I opened one end and stuck a finger inside. A bright yellow powder stuck to my skin.

"It's sulfur powder. It will help with your infection."

"How did you know?"

"I've seen it hundreds of times." Then he turned his back while I lowered my pants and sprinkled half of the contents of the envelope onto the red and puffy parts of my leg, then replaced the bandages.

"Did you say Lebensborn?" Günter returned to our conversation.

I nodded. "Where is that?" I asked as I sat back down next to him.

He lowered his head. "It's not a place. It's a program," he said quietly.

Just then movement sounded nearby. Somebody was approaching the first building. He held his finger to his lips, and we crouched lower to listen as the steps grew closer. Someone entered the structure.

"Stay here," he whispered but did not wait for my answer as he inched forward again.

I watched as he crept up to the window. Within seconds, he quickly spun around and bolted back to me.

"It's a girl!" he declared.

CHAPTER FOURTEEN

"What?" My eyes lit up and I jumped up, but his hands held me back.

"Don't frighten her, she might scream."

I nodded and moved quickly toward the same window that he watched her from. Sure enough, the tall, slim form was picking up something from the floor. When she turned around, I gasped.

"Katia," I whispered, loud enough for her to hear but not too loud.

She squealed.

"It's me, Aleksandra."

Her eyes found mine and she rushed through the door and around to where I stood but stopped short when she saw Günter behind me. A small cry escaped her lips.

"It's okay," I assured and closed the distance. "He is good." I went to her and hugged her tightly.

"Oh, Aleksandra." Her arms went wide around me in return. "We thought something happened to you."

"Where are the others?"

Her eyes lowered and tears freely dripped down her cheeks. "We couldn't get everyone out in time."

"Who?" I panicked. "Who *did* you get out?"

"Ruta helped Inga. Olga and I got Aneta and Karina out."

I allowed myself to breathe when Karina's name surfaced. "So, Hanna and Yetta?"

Her shoulders fell as she sobbed.

Günter stepped forward. "We are too exposed here." In a stern voice, he continued, "We need to leave."

Katia pointed to the trees. "We've been hiding over there."

"That explains the noise I heard." Günter shot me an anxious look. "We should go."

As I wrapped an arm around Katia's shoulder and let her guide us toward the trees, I leaned in and asked, "What happened?"

She continued to sniffle as she spoke. She told me how she awoke to sounds outside the building. When she saw the outline of men walking around the building across from theirs, she awoke the girls, but only Ruta and Olga listened to her. "Once the six of us had exited the door closest to the forest, I watched as the men entered our building shortly after." She could barely get out her next words. "I heard a scream, some cries…then nothing." She wept. "I came back to see if they were here."

Günter had kept quiet this entire time.

"How many girls are gone?" he asked.

"Two."

I shook my head. Though I had little feeling for those two, I would never have wished for this.

I looked to Günter. "Where would they have taken them?"

His lips pulled tight. "I don't think they would have taken them back to camp. Too many men to share them with."

His honesty and implications were clear. My heart sank at the thought of the harm that could be occurring to these girls at this very moment. Katia nearly fell to the ground. "Please," I pleaded as I tried to keep her upright. "Please, Katia, let's get back to the others."

"It's possible the men didn't take them far." Günter scanned the outline of the structures and back toward the barn where we had met, tightening his grip on the pistol.

"Wait." My hand covered his. "You could get killed."

His eyes met mine. "I have two sisters, Aleksandra. I wouldn't want anyone hurting them. I can't walk away and not try to help."

I glanced back to Katia, securing her in her stance. "Please go back to the others. Stay quiet and stay hidden in the trees." She wobbled as if she might fall again. "I will come to you. I promise. Here, take this." I handed her my pack.

"No." Katia's fingers gripped my arm. "Come with me, Aleksandra."

We stood halfway between the house and the trees. "I can't let Günter try to save them alone. Think of Hanna and Yetta. I must try." I pulled the knife from my boot.

Once I convinced Katia to return alone, I watched where she entered the trees so I could return to them…if I returned at all.

Günter faced me with a sober expression. "You should go with her."

"I can't." Guilt overpowered me. I felt responsible for leaving the girls in the first place and then not rushing back to warn them when the soldiers first appeared. Though the whole idea was ridiculous since I would have only exposed myself and Günter in the process, I couldn't help but feel responsible.

Günter stood in front of me. His proximity forced me to look up as he spoke. "Stay behind me and do as I say."

I nodded. I feared any word out of my mouth would reveal how truly frightened I was.

"I will lead us slowly back toward the military camp. It is only a couple of kilometers from here. We can check the area along the way."

When only the crunch of leaves beneath my feet and an occasional bat flapping its wings in the trees could be heard, I finally spoke up, though kept it low and hushed. "Why didn't the—the soldiers just, um, uh," I swallowed against a dry throat. "You know, uh…

"Why didn't the soldiers just take the girls right there in the house?"

My question came out awkwardly but at least he knew what I was trying to ask. In a terrifying memory, shortly before I stopped walking past the ghetto, I watched two soldiers force a young girl my age on the other side of the fence into a nearby alley. It was broad daylight and despite her cries for help, nobody came to her aid. I can still hear her horrifying screams in my sleep. "Why didn't they?"

"I'm not sure, but…" He stopped himself.

"You won't offend me," I whispered. "I've already seen many horrible things happen."

I heard his deep inhale. "I stopped them once before, in a village north of here. Maybe they believed I would come upon them in the house."

I cringed, both terrified for the girls and relieved, knowing the man I stood next to attempted to stop such evil.

Günter watched me closely. "As we walk, keep watch in all directions…if you hear anything, drop to the ground."

"Okay." I gripped my knife tighter. My hand trembled at the different scenarios that could develop, then my mind marveled at how far I had come in less than two weeks. Though I never considered myself to be weak or frail, I would have never imagined myself capable of killing another… until now.

The night had grown significantly darker since I left the girls the first time and, though I tried to walk as silently as possible, I was not as skilled in this as Günter was, though he said nothing.

By the time we had scoured the barns and fields, we reached a place to stop and rest. Discouragement easily crept in. We hadn't come across anyone.

Günter stopped behind a tree and pulled out a flask. Taking a swig, he handed it to me. I hesitated, certain it was not water, but thirsty all the same.

"Go ahead." He nudged. "The vodka is watered down."

I reached for it and took a small sip—just enough to wet my dry throat. Though the taste was bitter, it was not bad.

"Thank you."

He replaced the cap and returned it to his tunic pocket. "I'm sorry this happened to your friends…your uh, family."

I glanced up to Günter who towered over me. His strong physique and handsome face should have him at a university studying, playing sports, or courting…not creeping through a forest. "I am sorry, too."

He pointed around the tree. "The camp is just down through here, but they have people on watch outside of camp. I need you to stay here."

"I should help."

"Please stay." His pleading tone silenced me, and I marveled at his honest desire to help. He had just risked his life to get away from these men, for whatever reasons he had, and now he risked his life to help strangers. There is at least one good German in this world. I promised to heed his advice and crouched near the thick trunk of the tree before he moved away.

Sending a silent prayer upward for Hanna and Yetta, I followed up with one of gratitude for Karina's safety. I had promised to keep her safe and if it weren't for Katia and Ruta, she might not have been.

After what seemed like a lifetime, Günter returned. When he drew closer, a deep frown filled his face.

"What?" I whispered.

He shook his head and led me farther away from the camp and back toward the village. When we had reached the safety of an outer wall and appeared to be alone, I asked again.

He looked at me with troubled eyes. "Detlef and Jörg have returned."

"Are those the men who were looking for you?"

He nodded.

"Were the girls with them?"

He shook his head. "No. I watched them for nearly an hour. I'm positive they returned alone."

I wasn't sure if this answer was good or bad. If Hanna and Yetta had been taken to camp, they may have still been alive, yet now that we believed they were not with the men, they could be dead—or left for dead— anywhere in this vast forest. My heart sank again. Günter knelt to my side and let me bury my face in his jacket. Images of the unknown plundered my mind.

Günter's warm breath blew against my cheek when he spoke. "You and the others need to get out of here."

"To where?" I snapped unfairly. "We don't even know where to go."

He glanced around, then back to me. "I can lead you to Dresden. It's about eight kilometers west of here."

I sniffled and wiped my nose on the handkerchief again. "Why would you do that?" I spoke in a softer tone as we stood up at the same time. "Why would you risk getting caught for us?"

His head lowered once more. "It's because of me that your friends were discovered." Though no tears fell from his eyes, I could hear the anguish in his voice. "They were looking for me."

Though his words held some truth, it wasn't entirely accurate. "Had I not run into you, we would not have even known there was a military camp nearby." I lifted his chin upward until he faced me again. "All of us could have been hurt if not for you."

This brought a bit of relief to his countenance, but we had little time to waste. On the walk back to join Katia, we remained silent—I contemplated how to break the bad news to the others, and Günter surely contemplated his future.

CHAPTER FIFTEEN

When I rejoined the girls, Günter lingered behind out of sight. The hope Katia carried with our departure faded when she saw my return came without Hanna and Yetta.

"I'm sorry." I faced Inga who had attached herself to them in the last few days. "I'm so sorry we didn't find them." My voice broke. "We tried, we really tried."

Inga wailed out loud until she caught sight of Günter, who had stepped forward at the sudden eruption of cries.

"You need to be quiet," he said in a severe tone which only forced the girls to cry louder at the sight of a soldier until I spoke up.

"Stop! Stop, it's okay. He's okay."

"No, he's one of them!" Inga hollered.

"No," I rushed forward and placed my hand over her mouth. "He saved me from the other soldiers, but if you don't be quiet, they will be back."

The girls quieted down and I introduced Günter properly. "He has offered to show us the way out of here and to the closest town."

"He's going to help us?" Katia asked me without taking her eyes off him. "Do you trust him?"

I nodded. "Yes, yes I do." I exchanged glances with him.

"Okay." Katia stood up. "We will listen and do what you ask."

"We can't leave Hanna and Yetta!" Inga shrieked.

Katia rushed to her side this time and pulled her close, attempting to silence her again.

"If we stay here, we could all be in danger," I said. Peering over to Günter, I pointed. "He is going to help us, but we need to leave now."

Katia caressed Inga's hair as she cried into her shirt. I didn't want to leave Hanna and Yetta either but couldn't risk the rest of us by continuing to look while this close to the military camp.

Once again, our numbers had fallen in an unbearably tragic way.

"Collect your belongings," Günter said not knowing we really had nothing.

Katia handed the pack back to me and gripped the one canteen she retrieved when she went back to the house, but everything else was left inside.

"Let's go." Günter led the way.

I stepped over and pulled Karina to my side. "I am happy to see you, motyl." I didn't hide my gratitude as she met my embrace.

"Me too," she whimpered.

I leaned down and whispered in her ear. "I'm so glad you listened to Katia."

She looked up at me with tired eyes. "She told me you would want me to."

I winked and held her tighter.

Since the night of the accident, we didn't do much in the dark of night other than sleep, or attempt to sleep, with the exception of the one night I tried to trap the animal. Tonight, we walked in near blackness along the line of trees rather than the even ground next to the railroad tracks. This made our progress much harder, yet nobody complained. The sobering reality of Hanna and Yetta's disappearance occupied all our minds. Out of fear of the other soldiers, it was apparent we were willing to do whatever Günter asked us to—to stay alive and stay safe.

He guided us with caution, giving the girls the same instructions he had given me—be aware of your surroundings, be quiet, and drop to the ground the moment you hear something.

We walked in twos in case somebody slipped or stumbled, then the other person could help, though occasionally both fell down. I held Karina to my side, Katia was with Aneta, Ruta with Inga, whose skin was now covered in the yellow sulfur powder from the envelope Günter gave me, and Olga walked alone at the rear.

We stopped twice to briefly rest. Günter shared the contents of his flask with the others despite my protestations, which actually had nothing to do with the alcohol.

"You'll need your provisions for when we separate," I said after I left Karina in Olga's care and walked beside him.

"I know where to find more." He glanced over at me. I had seen how the sight of us had affected him. "Besides, it's apparent you all have suffered more than I."

"Things would have been so much worse if you hadn't been there." I kept my voice low so as not to alert the others. "I can't thank you enough."

He nodded and kept a vigil lookout ahead. There was no doubt in my mind…this man had a good heart.

He was also a perfect gentleman. He kept a proper distance, never berated us for our snail's pace, or sneered at our foolish questions. The more time I spent with him, the more I found myself wishing I could help him get to where he wanted to go safely.

"Günter, may I ask you a question?" I had asked Olga to walk with Karina while I moved a tad closer to him.

He nodded warily.

"You mentioned Lebensborn was a program, not a place. What does that mean?"

His sigh was heavy and prolonged. "You are familiar with the Master Race, aren't you?"

"Uh, some." I swallowed hard. "In school, our German instructors taught us more about those who did not meet certain criteria…you know, those who were unworthy to live…like the Jews, Roma, and mentally retarded."

He nodded again, "Yes, all whom you've mentioned are considered quite inferior. Adolf Hitler and Heinrich Himmler thought it would be wise to protect the Aryan *Herrenrasse* for future generations. In order for that to happen, pure German breeding must occur."

"Breeding?"

Günter kept his eyes forward. It seemed he wasn't entirely at ease speaking on the subject, but I persisted. I wanted to know exactly why we were taken from our homes and brought to Germany. I just didn't want to believe it was for iniquitous purposes.

"Yes." He tugged on his collar. "Women being with men to reproduce."

My cheeks warmed though I was certain he couldn't see me blush in the dark. "But we are not of pure German blood," I whispered.

"True. Personally, I'm surprised they abducted Polish women." He wiped his brow. "But I am aware of their desperation as the war proceeds and the number of Germans has been reduced. I have heard of their desire to speed up the process through occupied territories." He pointed back to the girls all clustered together. "The appearance that you and your *family* possess…well they fit the Führer's needs."

I clenched my teeth. *We were tokens.* "I heard the soldiers speak of our fair features. All eighteen of us had blond hair and blue eyes…is that what they seek?"

"Yes. My younger sister, Ana. She looks like you. She was approached to participate in the Lebensborn project two years ago. She was seventeen at the time."

"She was not kidnapped?"

"No. She was selected and encouraged, but not forced."

I struggled to wrap my head around women who would participate in something like this willingly. "Did she do it?"

"No, though she considered it. They made the prospect quite appealing, but ultimately, she declined. However, two of her friends joined. Ana didn't speak of it after that."

I took a minute to absorb all that Günter shared. Of course, it all made sense—the inspections, the special passport, the strict rules on consorting with the soldiers, the talk of Berlin…we were to be used to birth German babies.

"You will be safe in Dresden," Günter added, most likely deducing my thoughts. "It's not like other German cities."

I fumbled to retie my braid. My hands shook as they wound through my dirty hair which practically stuck together without the twisting plaits. Günter's eyes found mine. I wanted to forget our conversation. I wanted to believe we would be okay once we made it to a town. I wanted to believe the worst was over. I returned his stare. "Where is *your* family home?"

He hesitated, likely assessing my discretion as I had his earlier in the night, but then he answered. "My home is in the Moselle Valley."

"How far is that from here?"

"It's in the west, well over five hundred kilometers away."

"Will you ever go home again? See your parents or sisters?"

I couldn't see his face clearly enough to see if there was emotion, but his breath quickened as he spoke. "I fear I might never see them again or, at least not until the war is over."

I reached for his hand and tenderly squeezed it. "I'm sorry, Günter, I truly am."

He stopped momentarily and, in that brief moment, his eyes revealed regret. It then passed as quickly as it arose. "Do not worry for me, Aleksandra, I will be free."

He turned to the others. "Keep going, we are almost there."

When the sun finally peaked through the blackness and we were nearly dragging from complete exhaustion, a shriek came from Olga who had climbed to the top of a pile of debris. The additional height gave her a view of things we couldn't see. "It's a town!" she shouted, pointing to the ground before us. Had we been paying better attention, we would have seen our one small railroad track end, and several others appear from other directions. This explained the lack of trains on our route.

The rest of us scrambled up to join her. Sure enough, structures of every size appeared on the horizon. If I had to guess, it was less than a fifteen-minute walk.

Fifteen minutes...the idea shocked me. After all, we had been through since the day we were taken from our school, this very sight nearly brought me to my knees, but I stood strong and clasped my hands together in joy. Though I had cried in private often and wanted to dissolve into tears a thousand times, I often held my emotion captive—never wanting the girls to see how weak I truly was. Yet, nothing, nothing at all could stop my tears at this moment.

I searched for Günter from above, but he was gone. Glancing around the area, I could no longer see his face as I had for the last twelve hours. Part of me felt disappointed, I had grown used to being near him. Though he was a German soldier, he brought an element of security to me unlike anything, or anyone, had in over a week. I understood his reasoning, however. With his decision to abandon his unit, he became a target and, if discovered, he would most likely be killed. He risked a great deal to help seven destitute girls conquer the forest and reach civilization. We owed him our lives.

Suddenly, hands, fingers, and arms were flung around me from all directions. I peered around to see the girls had converged on me. All clutching and embracing one another, but all enveloping me with a love that couldn't even be put to words.

"Thank you," I cried.

"No." A response came from one I couldn't immediately place. "It is you we should thank."

After several moments we released, stood up straight, and marched in a pack down the tracks toward what we hoped was our new beginning.

CHAPTER SIXTEEN

W<small>E HUSTLED FASTER</small> the closer we got. The first building we came to appeared to be a small train station, a solitary brick building with a vacant wooden deck. A broken board hung from the one remaining chain. The name "Bohemian Station" etched upon it was nearly faded.

Concern leaked through. *Please, not another abandoned town*, I muttered under my breath. I wasn't sure any of us could handle such news.

Each of us fell upon it with an unparalleled mixture of eagerness and exhaustion. Both doors were missing and the rooms inside the building were eerily vacant, though not as dirty as the houses from before.

"It's not a working station." Ruta said what we all had been thinking. Cracked walls, spider webs, and layers of dust and dirt indicated a neglect had started quite some time before.

"Noooo," Inga cried.

"Over here," Katia hollered from the far end of the building. "There's another one over here." We stepped back down to the tracks and walked quickly to where Katia stood. She pointed to an additional structure, that even from our distance, was certainly bigger and in better condition. Its unmarred stonework and carved eaves brought forth a collective relief. "And it's surrounded by other buildings!"

"Ohhh, good," Karina sighed.

"Yes, it is." I took in the grandeur of the building from its wide windows and carved doorways. A brick column extended upward with a round clock at its peak. The clock chimed—its bold, black hands pointed right on the eight o'clock hour. The whole structure was picturesque. Of course, it could have been anything, as long as it appeared occupied. A larger sign above our heads read *Hauptbahnof*. Central Station.

We entered the deck from the side and, once again, found it to be completely empty, however as we moved around the expansive walkway to the front…a bustling city appeared.

"Oh," Aneta burst with delight. "It's a *real* city."

I peered over to Katia who met my smile with one of her own. "We made it." Tears ran freely down our cheeks.

I squeezed Karina at my side. "We're going to be okay!"

We stood all together and stepped slowly toward a busy road. Several automobiles and a trolley passed by, people were walking, children were playing—it was like a scene from a painting. *Where were we? Did they not know a war was going on?*

Beep, beep. An automobile horn honked as a hand gripped my shirt and pulled me back off the road. I had been so mesmerized by the sights, I hadn't watched where I was going. I glanced toward Ruta with gratitude as she released my shirt, but the blaring sound had suddenly alerted others to our presence.

Some people stopped walking. Others whispered and pointed in our direction.

We stood still in the growing silence.

I could only imagine how we appeared. Most of the girls wore the same clothes they wore the day we were taken from the school, much of which were torn, smelly, and covered in dirt. In addition to our soiled skin and matted hair, we were certainly a sight to behold.

People continued staring.

One man and a woman, walking arm in arm, rushed toward us from across the street.

The man wore a handsome gray suit and black hat. Several girls instinctively stepped backward at his sudden approach.

"It's okay." He spoke in fluent German, raising his hands cautiously. "I'm a doctor, I can help you."

A doctor? Why would he think we needed a doctor? I muttered to myself. I knew we appeared haggard, but our wounds were no longer life-threatening—and we had walked all the way here. I glanced at the girls, nothing I hadn't seen for days... we needed a bath, that was certain. *Oh, yes, Inga's allergy.* Her face had nearly doubled in size and was still covered in yellow powder.

A fashionably dressed woman appeared behind the man. Then another couple followed shortly.

All four stood before us with varying expressions...mostly wide eyes and grim looks, shifting uneasily from one girl to the next. I examined the girls on each side of me once more. I wanted to see what the strangers found so shocking. Yes, we were dirty, but we were alive...*and we had made it!* This was something to celebrate.

When the two men stepped forward to assist, Inga screamed. Though there was nothing in the men's actions to fear, the very sight of a man approaching so swiftly caused her to cower, especially after what happened to Hanna and Yetta.

"Here." The first woman seemed to recognize the problem and threw her reticule toward the doctor then beckoned her friend. "Helene, help me get them to the bench."

The men stood helplessly by and watched as the two women tenderly assisted all seven of us to a set of wooden benches nearby.

"I will alert the hospital," the doctor said. "Josef, can you retrieve your coupe? Not all of them will fit inside the ambulance."

He nodded and both departed quickly.

Ambulance? Could it really be that bad? I rubbed my knee through my pant leg, the powder had eased the pain, but it was still tender to my touch.

"My name is Frida, this is my sister, Helene. Do you speak German?" the first woman asked.

"Ja." This time, Katia and Ruta nodded their heads with me.

"Good." She clasped her gloved hands in front of her pristine attire. "Can you tell me what has happened to you?" Her black eyelashes fell in perfect synchronicity against her flawless skin. She was lovely. "Was your home bombed?" She went about assessing each girl one by one. "Can you tell me of your injuries?"

My eyes widened at the word *bombed.* So, they weren't entirely shielded from the ravages of war.

"We, um, yes…" Katia spoke first. "We were in a military truck that was fired upon and then crashed."

"Oh, my." The second woman's hand flew to her mouth as she gasped.

Frida winced but did not react as emotionally. "Why were you in a military truck?"

I bit my lip. The kindness I felt from these women allowed for some truth to come forth. "We were taken from our school, uh," I counted the days as best I could on my fingers, "ten days ago, I believe."

"Taken?" Frida gasped this time. I caught Helene exchanging an odd look toward her sister. She had been silently hushed.

"We have been wandering in the woods for a while. Do you have any water?"

Both women shook their heads though I could see tears forming in Helene's eyes. "I'm sorry, I don't."

"One moment," Frida said, then ran to a nearby market.

Helene removed the gloves from her hands and let the warmth of her touch reach my skin as she rubbed my arm. "We will help you. You will be alright now."

When Frida returned, she had two mugs of liquid. She hustled so quickly in her heels that the liquid sloshed up and over the rim several times. She handed one cup to Helene and between the two of them, they lifted it to our lips. The water soothed our burning throats.

"Where is your home?" Helene asked.

I lowered my head. Could we risk telling the truth again?

"Far away," I mumbled.

This time Frida couldn't school her fine features. Her pink lips pursed together, and I was certain I saw tears pooling on her lower lashes before she turned toward the wailing sound of a siren coming down the street.

"Let's get you to the hospital." She reached for Aneta's hand, easily recognizing her youth and subsequent fear. "You will be well taken care of, sweetheart, I promise you." She looked to me again. "Please convince her of that."

Though Aneta's German was coming along, I repeated the woman's words in whispered Polish. Though I felt these women were here to help, I knew how Germans, in general, looked upon Poles. If they know where we truly came from would they refuse to help?

When the ambulance arrived, the doctor stepped out. He didn't wait for the attendants to open the back doors and approached with caution this time.

"Frida, love. Please assure the girls I mean no harm, but I need to evaluate their injuries. Some appear more serious than the others."

Frida looked at me "Liam is my husband," she declared. "And a very good doctor."

I nodded and looked at the girls. "He needs to check us. It will be fine." I nudged Inga forward. "We are safe now."

Though they still clung to one another's hands, the younger girls were lightly examined.

"This one." He pointed to Inga, and Frida walked over to her, then led her to the back of the ambulance. "And these two." Karina and Aneta were next. "Since no one requires the use of the stretcher, we can accommodate these three, but Josef will be here shortly with his automobile."

Helene moved to the back. "I will go with them, too."

This allowed me to fully exhale. I knew the younger girls were frightened.

Within minutes of the ambulance's departure, a car pulled up next to us.

"Please," the man said. His voice was soft and kind. "Please allow me to help. I can transport three."

I pointed to the others. "I am not so bad. I can wait for you to deliver them, then return for me."

Frida stood next to me. "I will wait with you."

The man was introduced as Josef, Helene's husband. He assisted Katia, Olga, and Ruta into his vehicle.

Glancing over to Katia, I winced. This would be the first time we would be separated since the awful ordeal had started. We were friends now, possibly as close as Renia and I had been.

"They will be okay, won't they?"

"Yes," Frida answered. "I'm certain of it."

As I waved goodbye, she put an arm around my shoulders. "You have looked out for them, haven't you?"

I nodded. "That's what family does."

"You are all related?"

I bit the inside of my cheek. "Not necessarily by blood…but they are my sisters."

Her pretty lips curled into a warm smile. "I understand. What is your name?"

"Aleksandra."

She led me back to the bench to sit. Peace enveloped me. I could hardly believe our luck. We made it! We made it to a city and now the girls would get all the water, food, and medical care they needed.

Glancing around the bustling intersection, I turned to Frida. "Where is Dresden?"

She looked over at me with furrowed brows. "East Germany." She placed her hand over mine. "Where exactly is your home, Aleksandra?"

I pursed my lips together.

"I have a suspicion," she whispered, "but I would like you to tell me."

Instantly nervous, any comfort I felt, vanished.

"You can trust me," she added. "I promise."

I exhaled. "Łódź."

"Poland?"

I nodded. Tears filled her eyes. "Are you…" she glanced around warily. "You aren't a Jew, are you?"

My thoughts briefly returned to my Jewish friend Erela and the ghetto. "No, I'm not and neither are the others."

Her relief was quite evident though her eyes continued to tear. "I have heard the stories from Poland." She paused. The silence between us had us both reflecting. "I am sorry you have suffered so terribly." She pulled a small handkerchief from the inside of her hand glove and wiped her nose. It was significantly more delicate and refined than the one I still carried in my pocket from Günter.

"You and your friends will be well taken care of. My husband is a good doctor and a good man…but there are others who…"

The sudden caution in her voice caused me to stir with an uneasiness I hadn't felt before.

Her fingers now fidgeted with the embroidered hem of the linen.

"Others who, what?" I asked warily. Though I instantly felt indebted to her for everything she had already done, her sudden anxiousness concerned me.

"Please do not mention Poland while you are in the hospital."

I was only mildly surprised at this request. "Are we in danger?" My eyes shot to the street where both the ambulance and the man's car had disappeared. Could I possibly have put my friends in greater harm?

Her mouth pulled tight.

I lowered my head. "Do you hate us that much?"

She stuttered, "No, no not me, love."

I looked up. Her cheeks took on a rosy hue as she pulled me closer. The fresh scent of oranges infiltrated my senses. "Just please, Aleksandra, please do as I ask."

When she released me, dirt from my shirt had transferred to her impeccable dress, yet she didn't seem to notice or mind. She reached for my hand as I whispered, "What about my friends, how do I give them the same warning? What if they tell someone before I arrive?"

"We will get word to your friends in time." She stood up. "Josef is coming back now."

Sure enough, the same black coupe came flying down the road as if he were the ambulance driver himself. Once inside the automobile, we didn't speak again. I could only pray and hope that nothing of our journey had already been discovered and my friends had not been put in harm's way… once more.

CHAPTER SEVENTEEN

O NCE INSIDE THE hospital, the rush to get medical help had the nurses bustling about. Brought to a large ward, I saw the other girls had already been assigned beds. Olga was nearly asleep. Her hair was still wet from a bath with her blanket tucked up to her chin and she looked as though she smiled. I instantly realized that I had never seen that expression on her before.

"Where's Karina?" I inquired at the sight of Katia, who was being directed into a different room. I panicked a bit when I didn't see my little sister immediately.

"She and Inga are being examined, but their beds are over here."

Aneta, several beds down, smiled wide in my direction. She held a cup of water in her hands. She also was no longer covered in dirt from head to toe and wore a clean white nightgown.

I looked down at her foot, resting above the blankets. The temporary splint had been removed and she was heavily bandaged. "What did they say about your ankle?"

She frowned this time. "The doctor said it's too swollen to properly diagnose. The swelling must go down first. I will be in bed for at least a week."

"This way, please." A nurse rushed over to me. "Let's get you cleaned up in here." She led me to a separate room where there was a large basin, a stack of towels, and a robe-like cover. I shuddered at the door, remembering the last time I had to wear something similar.

"Come along." The nurse urged me forward.

"It's okay. I'm fine, I only need a wet towel to wipe off the dirt."

The nurse put both hands on her plump hips and sighed. "You cannot wear those rags presuming to be clothing any longer, my dear. Wash fully and I'll get you into something clean and warm."

I nodded slightly. A wash did sound wonderful. Peering down at my clothing it was hard to discern where the fabric ended and the flesh began. Dirt caked my entire body.

"Do you want me to stay?" She woke me from my rumination.

"N—no."

"Very well. When you are finished, put the robe on and I will take you to the examination room."

"I—uh, I don't need to be examined," I quickly responded. I was not about to let another person check my body.

The woman stared at me. Though her expression revealed very little, her words were soft. "You are safe here. We just need to make sure you don't have any severe injuries."

"I don't." I took a step back. "I only had cuts and bruises and they've mostly healed." I knew my leg was worse than I let on but felt it could be managed with rest and clean linens.

"Well then, you're far luckier than your friends."

My head shot up with worry. "What, what is wrong with them?"

"They have not all been fully examined but I believe some bones might need to be reset."

Karina. I cringed at the pain she must've endured on our lengthy journey and now only to face more.

"But they will all be okay, right?"

"Yes. They will recover."

She pursed her lips then nodded. "I will be back in fifteen minutes."

She closed the door behind her. The sound of that small piece of privacy overwhelmed me and I broke down in tears. Leaning over the basin, I gripped the sides with my fingers and let all the torment of the last eleven days flow outward. *The worst must surely be over.* Eighteen of us left Łódź on the 19th of August, today, seven of us were here in a hospital and alive.

I was most grateful for the strangers' kindness, but Frida's warning still lingered. I needed to make sure the girls didn't reveal too much about our means of arrival or where we came from, although Frida did say she would take care of it. Maybe she would let the girls know while I'm in here.

Before I removed my rags that were part of my once proper school uniform, and the trousers belonging to a dead man, I located the handkerchief Günter had given me. Pulling the dirty linen out, I set it aside as my thoughts went to him. I hoped he'd made make it somewhere safe for the night. If only we had given him our canteen before he disappeared, then maybe I wouldn't feel so guilty.

I glanced down at the boots and marveled at the only part of my clothing that survived the trek intact. Everything else had rips and tears in them.

When I slipped them off my feet, the knife hit the hard tile floor with a clink. I retrieved it and held it in my hand. The blade appeared so different here under the bright lights of the room…patches of blood and hair from the skinned animal still stuck to the silver finish. Quietly, I expressed my gratitude that the only beast to require use of the weapon was an animal and not a human being, although there was no doubt—I would have utilized it to save Hanna and Yetta, if necessary.

Standing naked before the basin, I slowly stepped inside. Though the water was only lukewarm, it was clean and allowed me to feel like a real person again. I submerged my body up to my chin and winced as the water soaked the damaged parts of my skin. Most of the bruises from the accident were faded now, only scars from the cuts remained, like the one on my forehead and palm, but the long slash down my leg never really healed, and upon first glance without the dirt, the gap between the edges was deep.

My hair took the longest time to clean. Because of its length, it was filled with all manner of earthly grime from end to end. By the time I stepped out of the tub, the water was nearly black.

As promised, the nurse returned promptly. I wore the robe because it was clean but clasped both arms tightly around my torso with Günter's handkerchief balled tightly in my fist. She led me to another private room off the main ward.

"Are you cold?" She pointed to my trembling arms.

"A little."

"This won't take long. Please sit down." She pointed to the examination table.

Please, no. Please, not again!

She reached out and placed both of her hands over my arms to calm my shaking. "I promise this will be quick and you will be in a warm bed shortly."

I said and did nothing. I didn't even move toward the table. When the doctor entered, it was the man from before, Frida's husband Liam, though he no longer wore his nice suit, but a doctor's white coat.

Tears involuntarily leaked out of my eyes and trailed my cheeks.

He remained by the door and watched me carefully. "I am told you are the reason these girls are alive."

I blinked.

"They credit you for helping them survive in the forest after a bombing."

It was his own wife who warned me to not say where we came from and, since our arrival, I had no opportunity to caution the girls. Was it possible he already knew everything?

He continued to speak softly though stayed a good distance away. The nurse moved to my side. My eyes flinched at the clipboard in her hands and my breath hitched.

"Hmmm." The man rubbed his clean-shaven chin, then turned to the nurse. "It appears our patient only has minor injuries, Nurse Huber." He pointed to my head. "Is that your assessment as well?"

She looked between the two of us. Her eyebrows gathered together in confusion. "Y—yes, I believe she has only suffered cuts and bruises. No broken bones that I am aware of."

He nodded in my direction. "Does it hurt anywhere else in your body other than that cut on your head?"

Finally at ease, I lifted the hem of my robe to my knee and pointed at my leg. "And here."

He tilted his head slightly to the left for a better look then nodded. "Very well." He smiled warmly. "Would it be okay if Nurse Huber, put some stitches in that? It won't look pretty, now that the skin is trying to repair itself, but could prevent further infection."

I nodded. Once clean, I realized how wide the wound was.

"And Nurse," the doctor pointed to her clipboard. "Make sure sulfanilamide is applied topically, and penicillin is administered twice daily." He then looked back at me. "And you must rest, Aleksandra. Lots of rest."

When he left the room, I exhaled with relief.

"Come," said the nurse. "Let me suture the wound then I will show you to your bed."

Once I joined the others, Karina and Inga had also returned and were safely tucked in their beds. Karina's arm was bandaged and, in a sling, though you could still see the bow in the bone. Helene stood next to her bed but spoke to me. "The doctor said he must rebreak her arm."

Karina looked as though she had been crying and, at Helene's words, began again. I knelt down at her side. "Be strong, sweet motyl." I kissed her cheek. "We are safe now." Though I wanted to believe those very words, I didn't let on that there was a fair amount of doubt. Nothing seemed safe in wartime.

"When?" I looked at Helene.

"A few days. They want her to regain her strength first. The procedure is quite painful, and you are all suffering from starvation."

I sighed quietly and held my sadness back when Karina buried her face in my shoulder. I patted her hair. "Get some rest, little sister."

She nodded and snuggled down as best she could.

A nurse came running from the opposite direction holding something up in her hand—a little stick doll with barely any life left in it. The stringy hair had vanished as well as the red fabric, but it was her little Adela doll, no doubt. "This was found in her pocket." The nurse smiled. "I didn't want it to become part of the rubbish."

I smiled at the nurse and then down to Karina as she handed her the toy. "Oh, Karina, see, Adela is a survivor too."

Karina grinned as she gripped the tiny doll then closed her eyes.

"Your bed is over here." Nurse Huber, who had patiently waited for me during the tender exchange, pointed to the bed next to Karina. Pulling the blanket back she said, "Several girls insisted that this one be yours."

I smiled. It was exactly where I wanted to be. When my bare feet slid beneath the clean sheet and my body nestled down onto the mattress, I closed my eyes. It was hard to believe I was in a bed…*an actual bed*. When my head hit the pillow with a soft thud, I smiled, truly smiled at our fortunate turn of events.

Two hours later, I was awakened for a warm bowl of chicken broth. Though my body insisted I stay asleep, the scent had me salivating the moment it was placed before me.

"Your stomachs are not capable of more at this time." A different nurse propped up my pillows for me to eat in bed. "We must nurture you back to good health slowly. You were all severely dehydrated and malnourished." Turning away from me, she did the same for Katia. "With proper care and rest, I imagine some of you will be released within the week. Others," she glanced at Karina as she struggled to wake, "others might take longer."

Even though I wanted to finish the broth, I felt full after a few sips, then slept for half the day, waking only again for more broth. This routine went on for several days.

Memory of those days came only in snippets. Occasional visits from the nurses, medication tablets, and more broth. Conversations with the girls rarely happened since I suspected they too were spending the same amount of time asleep. It wasn't until I heard Karina's horrific screams that I fully awakened to her empty bed four days later. I jumped to my feet and struggled to gain composure.

"Aleksandra, you must go back to your bed." A nurse met me before I attempted to enter the room the screams sounded from.

"What's happening? What is happening to Karina?" I cried and tried to fight my way past her until a man, possibly another doctor, joined in my restraint.

"She is having her arm reset."

"I should be with her!" I shouted.

"There are two nurses with the doctor. She will be fine. They will give her something for the pain."

Once the screams slowed, I stopped fighting, but I was physically sick to my stomach. Though I allowed the nurse to return me to my bed, I didn't lay down. I sat on the edge and fidgeted nervously every minute Karina wasn't there. When she did come out of the room, the doctor was carrying her. I gasped at the sight of her in this frail and weakened state. I jumped up and waited for him to lay her down before I fell upon her with my own hands, checking her arm and kissing her cheeks. She was asleep. *They must have put her to sleep.*

"She will be fine, Aleksandra," Dr. Meier assured me as he stood next to the bed. "It healed so poorly; that if she was ever to regain use of it, rebreaking it was inevitable."

I nodded. Ruta had told me it was a possibility when we first bandaged it with the crude fabric and belt.

"How long will it take to recover?"

"Months. And even then, it may not fully mend."

I bit the inside of my cheek fighting the cries that wanted to come. "Thank you."

He nodded and left the room. I crawled in next to her and slept the rest of the day by her side.

The next morning, Frida and Helene arrived during breakfast. This time we each had some porridge and a piece of bread…and no dirt. I wondered if I had ever tasted anything so delicious before.

"Good morning, ladies."

Frida entered the room with the same elegant grace we had seen the day we met her. Her golden-colored hair curled impeccably above her shoulders topped by a light pink hat with netting. She sported a floral, fitted jacket and matching skirt. Everything about her was perfect.

She stopped in place as she scanned the beds. Some girls were still too weak to sit up, but most were eating.

"My goodness." Her gloved hand went over her mouth. "I can see you all now." She lightly giggled. "Who would have known there were beautiful young women buried beneath such filth." She smiled at each one of us. "You're absolutely breathtaking."

My mouth parted; she who looked like a princess herself was calling *us* beautiful.

"Now, I have good news for all of you." She held our attention. "We have found wonderful places for you to live."

Inga gasped, then cried aloud, "But I want to go home."

"Yes," she moved over toward her bed. "I wish you could." She looked to me for help. "It's too dangerous, as you already know. The enemy hasn't stopped their bombings for months. It's just not safe to be on any roads."

Though the Polish language would have confirmed her words more clearly, I restrained, remembering her warning. "Please listen to her," I said in German. "We need to wait until the war is over, then we can go home."

Immediately, tears and cries burst forth from most of the girls. I had grown accustomed to this by now and sighed heavily. "That's enough," I spoke with a slight edge to my voice. "You have survived a terrible ordeal. There are eleven girls who did not make it this far. Do not stain their memory by being ungrateful. We must see this through…and please no more tears." I included the word *please* to soften my demand.

Once again, the girls stared shockingly in my direction. It really was only the three younger ones who had dissolved into despair, but they needed to be reminded of how far we'd come. Yes, everything about the lives we knew in Poland was gone—it was a terrifying reality—but nothing could change that now and crying about it didn't help.

Frida watched me as Helene moved around to comfort the girls.

"Well." She nodded in my direction with an awestruck look then peered around the group once more. "As I mentioned earlier, we have found homes for each of you. Good homes, and until the war is over and it's safe to return to yours, we will teach you how to live here."

I stared forward unsure if this news really was good or not. Homes, *plural*, meant we would not be together. "Is there not a place we can all stay together?"

She shook her head subtly. "I'm sorry, but with seven of you, there isn't a place big enough, but we can limit the separation to four homes. Ours, my sister Helene's, my cousin, and a friend."

All eyes frantically moved from one girl to the other. I could practically read their minds…they were contemplating how difficult it would be to get back to Poland on their own.

Frida smiled compassionately. "You will love Dresden, it's a lovely, vibrant city." She patted Olga's arm. "We have arts and culture and so much to offer a young woman of today."

"Don't you fear the enemy bombing here if they are bombing all over?" Olga asked in return—a question, I'm sure, several of us were wondering.

"Oh, do not fear," Helene spoke up. "You are possibly in the safest place in Germany." Then she whispered, "I heard Mr. Winston Churchill's aunt lives here, and he would never dare destroy such a dynamic city as ours."

"Winston Churchill?" Inga asked.

"Yes, the British Prime Minister. The one who is sending his planes all over Germany."

"But not here?" Karina whispered.

"No, not here."

This brought a touch of relief to us all, though I still feared being away from my newfound sisters.

As silence filled the space, the girls looked at me, and I recognized the need for me to demonstrate trust. I turned to Frida and Helene. "We thank you for your kindness," I said as I sat on the edge of my bed. "We will do what is asked of us."

Frida smiled again. "Helene, here, has a room for two of you. Is there anyone who might have a preference?"

Ruta raised her hand. "If you don't mind, I would like to be housed with Inga." This was no surprise to any of us, Ruta had cared for the youngest member of our group for quite some time. Frida continued, "That would be delightful. You will enjoy being in Helene and Josef's home."

Frida glanced around again. "My cousin, Giselle, and her husband, Leon, have two children and are looking for someone who either knows how to care for children or wants to learn."

I looked at Katia at the same time she raised her hand. It was a perfect match for her mothering skills.

"Thank you, Katia." Frida nodded. "Now, additional friends of ours, Herr and Frau Schneider, have room for two as well. I think Olga and Aneta will be a good fit there and Aleksandra and Karina will come home with me and Dr. Meier. This way we can keep an eye on Karina's progress."

Frida waved her hand toward Helene. "We will be back tomorrow. I believe a few of you will be discharged in the morning. The rest of you who will remain, please do not worry, we will visit you every day."

I sighed openly. I knew Karina would be one of the later ones. Since her rebreak yesterday, they had told me they could not cast it until the swelling reduced, something that might take a week. Aneta's ankle had also not healed correctly, and Inga's allergic reaction would force her delay as well. Though our separation would be temporary, it would be a hard adjustment.

Frida looked down at me with sympathy in her eyes. "Please believe us, Aleksandra, we will take good care of you all." She paused as if she prevented herself from speaking further. "Get some rest, I will see you tomorrow."

CHAPTER EIGHTEEN

When I said goodbye to Karina the next day, we both cried. If the staff would have allowed it, I would have remained if only for my sister's comfort, but they wouldn't—especially since my leg was no longer infected and healing as it should. Though the stitches wouldn't be removed for another week or so, it was certain a nasty scar would always be present.

When Frida, Helene, Giselle, and Frau Schneider arrived to retrieve us, they each brought clean clothes for us to wear. When I slipped out of the nightgown I had been wearing and into an olive-green button-up blouse and black pleated skirt, I hardly recognized myself—it felt so good to feel feminine again.

The other news that brought a smile to my face was to learn that all four homes were within walking distance of one another, so we would never be far from each other. This brought a great deal of relief to me. I could see Katia and Ruta every day.

Stepping out of the automobile in front of a beautiful brown brick apartment building, I paused at the sight before me. Apartment buildings were not new to me, having lived in a city filled with them, but I'd never seen anything this lovely… and for quite some time, nothing so well maintained.

The steps leading to the front door were crowned by a thick arched frame and the door itself appeared engraved with artistic elegance. I counted the windows upward…there were six pairs of glass leading to the roof, and on each side of the flat windows, rounded windows extended outward. I marveled at the idea that I found a building's features so fascinating.

I took a breath and hid my anticipation. When Frida stood next to me, I forced a smile for her benefit. I had never lived in a flat. At first, it was the farm, then the house we moved into when my father was elected.

"Are you ready?" she asked, reaching for my hand.

I nodded. Anything was better than the truck, the grass, or the cold concrete of an abandoned building.

Taking each step abnormally slow, I inhaled the sweet scent of the tiny blue flowers that littered the ground near the structure's foundation and, from somewhere nearby, the aroma of freshly baked bread.

Frida led me to a flat on the third floor. #12. When we stepped inside, I couldn't get my legs to move, the inside was more beautiful than the outside. Even with my father's wealth, we did not have carved molding on the ceiling or silk window coverings.

Frida nudged me forward into a lovely living space where a sofa and two chairs upholstered in sapphire blue welcomed me. Every wall within the room was adorned with a painting. Glancing from one to the other, I saw that the frames were nearly as intricate as the art itself.

"I work at the Staatliche Kunstsammlungen," she said as she placed her purse on a chair.

I blinked. I honestly had no idea what she just said.

She interpreted my blank stare correctly, for she quickly followed up. "The state art museum."

"These are stunning." I waved my hand.

"These are replicas." She chuckled. "The originals, of course, are in the museum, though the most valuable have now been dispersed as a precaution."

"A precaution?"

"If the war extends to Dresden, at the very least, the art will be preserved."

I gaped in her direction.

She quickly spoke over herself. "But it won't. We are entirely safe here. As I said, it is merely a precaution."

I grinned at her frequent attempts to soothe my concerns. "What do you do at the museum?"

"I am an acquisitions assistant. I've been studying art and sculpture at the university for a couple of years. Liam was so good to acquire these for me as a wedding gift."

"He seems like a good husband."

"The very best."

"Do you have any children?" I wondered…since I had never seen them with any.

"Not yet." Dr. Meier smiled as he came from around the corner. "Though hopefully soon," he announced, as an obvious blush crept across his wife's face.

"We have only been married a year," Frida answered. "We bought this flat with that very plan in mind, so we are most fortunate we had the space when we came across you." She led me down a hallway where a sculpture of the goddess Aphrodite graced a niche in one corner. I recognized her immediately. I had been privileged to take a Greek Mythology course at my school before the Germans arrived.

"This will be your and Karina's bedroom." Dr. Meier joined us, placing an arm around his wife's waist. There were two single beds on opposite sides and a wardrobe painted with white daisies in between. On each bed lay several sets of clothes—blouses, skirts, stockings, and shoes, all in varying styles and colors.

"Oh," I gasped.

"I believe they are adequate," Frida said as she lifted one up to me. "We guessed your sizes so if they aren't right, please let us know."

"They will be fine. Thank you."

I marveled about how the eleven days in the forest had changed my perspective on everything.

"Go ahead and rest, then join Frida for something to eat when you are ready. I must leave for the hospital."

I held up my hand. "Please tell Karina I miss her already."

"Of course." Dr. Meier smiled, then reached for the door handle and closed the door behind him. I sat on the bed numbly trying to take in my new life. The room, though simpler than the rest of the house, was decorated in gentle pinks and creams…a calming atmosphere perfect for two troubled girls. *Will we learn to love it here?*

My earlier concerns crept forward, and I wondered whether the people of Dresden would actually accept us. I wondered if they would be as kind to us if they knew how we really got here, or where we came from. Though I tried not to dwell on the likely despair, I often found myself wondering what heartache my own family had faced since my disappearance. After Ivan was forced into conscript, Mama was nearly inconsolable. Now, with me gone, I could only imagine her devastation.

Several hours later when I joined Frida in the kitchen, she had some paperwork laid out on the table and meticulously studied its contents until I approached.

"Please," She patted the seat next to her. "Join me."

I smiled and slid onto the metal chair. It squeaked a bit from my graceless effort.

"I don't mean to be presumptuous, Aleksandra." Frida put her pencil down and turned toward me. "But do you or any of your friends happen to have any identification papers?"

"No." I shook my head slowly. "Well, Ruta and Olga do, but the rest of us don't. We were given new papers for our travel to Berlin but lost them in the crash."

She tilted her head sideways. "Why were you going to Berlin?"

I didn't want to say. Everything the soldiers and Günter had spoken of made me feel uncomfortable and afraid.

She leaned forward while she waited for me to speak.

I chewed the inside of my cheek again—a bad habit as of late.

"I hope that you feel like you can trust me by now."

I nodded slowly.

"If my sister and I are going to help you, we need to know more about your situation. We need to arrange papers for you. They can be requested at any moment."

I bit my lip, then proceeded slowly. "The soldiers appeared at our school one day…um, on the 19th of August."

She nodded, encouraging me to continue.

"All the girls in my school were questioned and some of us were sent to another room for an…examination." My cheeks grew hot, and I swallowed hard. Frida's eyes went wide. "It was awful." I cleared my throat. "The nurse didn't stop it from happening, then when it was over, my Kennkarte was taken from me and replaced with a one-page passport. She told me my new home was Lebensborn."

Frida's hand covered her mouth. She tried to control her expression, but I could see she was upset. "Then what happened?"

"The soldiers forced us into a truck. There were eighteen of us."

"Eighteen?" She stood up when her kettle whistled. "Where are the others?" she asked while placing two mugs on the table in front of me.

I lowered my head. It all seemed so surreal. I had not spoken of this in its entirety before; even with Günter, I shared only bits and pieces. "They didn't make it."

After she poured the hot water, she added a cinnamon stick and two orange wedges to each. I watched the steam swirl with fascination. "Continue," she whispered.

I wrapped my fingers around the warm mug but didn't drink it. "The soldiers said we would arrive at our destination by morning, but that night, we learned the British bombers had destroyed parts of the road on our route and the soldiers had to take a detour. Two days later, we were fired upon, and our truck veered off the road and down a mountain."

"So, one day of travel and two days detoured would make it the 22nd of August when your truck crashed?" Her eyes lit up. "We didn't find you until the 30th! You were wandering in the forest all that time?"

I tilted my head. "Sort of."

She reached for a plate of crackers and cheese, then placed it in front of me. "Please go on, I didn't mean to interrupt."

I related the story of the camp, the severely injured, the dead girls, and the dead soldiers. I told her of our lack of water and the animal we ate, insect bites, even finding the railroad tracks, everything… except for Günter.

"Oh, my." She gasped several times during my account but never interrupted me again. When I finished, I took a long sip of my now lukewarm tea and nibbled on a square of cheese.

"I can hardly believe the seven of you made it this far."

I pursed my lips. "There were nine of us that set out to follow the railroad tracks."

One of her eyebrows arched severely. "Where are the other two?"

Tears bubbled on my bottom lashes. The guilt I felt for not having found Hanna and Yetta tormented me. *I shouldn't have left them.* I should have tried harder to find them, and I shouldn't have let Günter lead us away without them.

I couldn't respond and she didn't push me to.

Frida took both of my hands into hers. "You are a wonder, my dear." She shook her head. "I am not certain I would have survived any of that, much less all of it."

Now looking back…I, myself, was surprised I found the strength to do so.

"I'm sorry," she said. "I'm sorry you had to go through this." Then she reached for another delicate handkerchief and laid it in front of me.

"Thank you." Though I didn't move to pick it up.

"We will do everything we can to make sure you are safe here."

I managed to let a small smile surface, but it didn't last long. "May I ask you a question?"

"Of course." Frida nodded. "I will answer anything you ask."

"Do you know what the Lebensborn program is?"

My new friend stood up and refilled her mug with hot water. When she faced me again, her eyes appeared glossy. "Yes, I do."

Taken aback, I wasn't sure how to proceed.

"What do you need to know about Lebensborn?"

Though the topic made me shudder, I wanted truthful answers. I believed Frida had always given me this. "Is it true that if you are part of Lebensborn, you are being taken somewhere to give birth to German babies?"

Frida sat down once more. For the first time since we met, she seemed shaken. Her hands trembled when she picked up her spoon and dipped it in the sugar bowl.

"Yes. The program was created to further the Aryan race."

"But I am not German."

"But you are all blond and blue-eyed..." She added quickly, "I don't know if that was the specific purpose you were taken for but it's possible. I have heard rumors...stories that the program has expanded beyond volunteers and into occupied territories."

"Kidnapped women?"

She stirred her tea for an unusual amount of time. "It would not surprise me. The government is troubled with the German losses from the first World War and now fears this one could jeopardize our race. They are passionate about their bloodlines."

"How do you know so much about it?"

Frida's hands clasped tightly in front of her. "I joined the program four years ago."

"You did?" My brows furrowed. When Günter first told me about his sister and her friends it angered me...and now, like then, I found it difficult to imagine anyone would willingly choose to be part of something so appalling.

She must've read my mind because her pale complexion turned a rosy pink. "I was only twenty." She sighed and faced me fully again. "Since you have shared your story with me, I will share mine with you, but please...I ask you not to repeat it. My husband knows of my involvement, but we don't speak of it."

I watched her carefully. It almost sounded as though I heard regret in her voice.

"Give me a minute, this is not an easy subject to discuss." She closed her eyes and took a long breath before she opened them again. "I grew up in Munich, a city south of here, and in a very different world than the one I live in now."

My mouth parted but I quickly closed it as she continued.

"I was a member of the League of German Girls—the *BDM*—a branch of Hitler Youth. From a very young age, we were taught the importance of preparing for motherhood. Part of our training included the belief that we had a duty to produce a child for the Fatherland."

She didn't look at me.

"My instructor spoke of an opportunity for women like me to do something honorable for our country...to be involved in a comradeship regarding our National Socialism. She said nothing was more important than conceiving a racially valuable German baby. The Lebensborn brochure she gave me opened with a quote by Herr Himmler, which said, "*Every mother of good blood shall be holy to us.*" Her eyes met mine and pleaded. "I wanted to do something for Germany...something honorable. My father and brother both represented Germany in service and I wanted to do my part."

I nodded. I understood patriotism quite well.

"In my application to the program, I had to prove my Aryan race on an ancestral chart and go through a medical inspection...possibly similar to what you did."

I cringed but said nothing.

"Once accepted, I was sent to a castle in Tegernsee, uh, a town about fifty kilometers south of my home. Once there, I joined about thirty other girls also in their late teens, early twenties. We all understood our purpose for being there and we never shared any personal information about ourselves, not even with the men."

"The men?" Goosebumps appeared on my arms.

"Yes, tall, attractive men with blond hair and blue eyes were selected to impregnate us."

"You, you got pregnant?"

Frida took another deep inhale. "Yes. I was with one man for several nights each week. I got pregnant within a month and gave birth to a little girl nine months later."

"Wh—where is she now?"

She shrugged. "I don't know. I agreed as part of the program that I would give up my child to be adopted through the Reichsführer-SS."

Pain filled her eyes.

"You have to understand, Aleksandra, I truly believed that I played a critical role in Germany's hope and future."

"But if there were women willing to have sexual relations with these men, why would there be a need to kidnap us from Poland?" Irritation rose in my tone.

"From what I understand, Lebensborn has many facets. The willing... women from Germany, Scandinavia, Austria, Yugoslavia, or Poland. And the unwilling women from those same countries. These are the women who are coerced, forced, or kidnapped, as in your case, and either brought to the men who occupy their country or brought back to Germany. When the babies are born, they are taken from the mothers and placed with German couples. Even young children with the correct features are being abducted from their homes as infants, toddlers, and primary age."

I felt nauseous. Within a matter of minutes, she confirmed all my suspicions.

"I'm sorry, Aleksandra." She rubbed my arm. "Now you can see why I didn't want you to say anything to anyone." She squeezed gently. "They could have detained you and called the SS."

"What changed you?" I whispered.

"Changed me?"

I nodded. "If you believed so much in Hitler's dream, why didn't you call the SS and report us yourself or leave us to die? Why get us to the hospital or care for us now?"

She took a sip of her drink. "Liam. He is the reason for everything."

"How?"

"I met my husband two years ago. A friend introduced us. He had just begun practicing medicine and I was finishing my education."

I shrugged my shoulders. "How could meeting him change you? I've seen how nationalistic Germans react to me."

"There's no doubt Liam loves the Fatherland." She smiled for the first time since our talk began. "But...he believes in *life*, not death. He helped me to see how every life is valuable in the eyes of God. The way our country has treated people who do not fit their ideals, well, that is not our belief."

She kissed my hand. "I am sorry our soldiers have destroyed your home and taken you away. I'm sorry you have seen such wanton destruction and killing, but if you will allow it, Aleksandra, I would like to show you there are still good people in Germany, too."

My heart stirred. She spoke the truth—I could feel it. Leaning over, I wrapped my arms around her neck and pulled her close. When she embraced me back, it was the first time since leaving Poland that I felt safe...truly safe.

CHAPTER NINETEEN

Six days later, Karina came home to the Meiers'. Her arm, wrapped in a hard cast, didn't seem to bother her at all. In fact, she used it like nothing ever happened. No tears, no pain, no crying at night. In fact, her whole body seemed to be stronger from the nourishment and rest. When she finally joined me in our room, she was overcome, as I was, with the generosity of our hosts. The clothes they had given us fit perfectly down to the shoes on our feet.

That night, Frida had arranged for all the girls to come over for a special dinner. We were nearly beside ourselves with excitement. Though I had seen Katia, Olga, and Ruta twice in the last week, it was difficult to go from seeing them every minute of every day to occasionally.

Katia began her job several days ago, helping Giselle and Leon with their two children, six-year-old Helmet, and four-year-old Klaus. Inga had arrived home to where Ruta lived the same day as Karina, and Aneta arrived back with Olga the day before. Tonight marked the first time we would all be together in almost a week.

"Oh, Aleksandra!" Katia ran through the door and straight for my arms. We hugged for several seconds before she leaned back and inspected me. "I don't think I've seen you smile like this…ever."

I laughed. "Well, we do have something to smile about now, don't we?"

She chuckled. "Oh, yes we do." She held out an arm for Karina to join us and when the other girls stepped inside the flat moments later, it didn't take long before we were all linked in a tender circle.

"Okay, ladies," Frida called to us from the kitchen. "We have arranged for a nice meal all together, then shortly afterward, we must take care of some business."

I had already known this was the main purpose of our gathering. Frida had told me just today that she had finally secured our papers and we would be an official part of the Dresden community soon, but in typical Frida fashion, food always came first—even in our daily afternoon visits, she always provided some type of delicacy with our conversations.

Helene, Giselle, and Frida led us to a spectacularly adorned table in the dining room. The enormous crystal vase in the center displayed a variety of breathtaking flowers but I could only identify the baby's breath and poppies. The deep red blooms with black and gold centers were my father's flower of choice to win my mother's affection after their occasional quarrels. Seeing them here, once again, brought their memory to the forefront. Though my heart had splintered so often in the last month, I no longer felt the agonizing pain. It never truly went away, but the numbness finally superseded the sting. I wasn't sure if this was a good thing or not. The less I dwelled on it, the better, since there wasn't anything I could do about my current circumstances.

Seated next to Karina and Katia, we smiled at our good fortune. It had been quite some time since I personally had seen such lavish porcelain dinnerware. My family's finest china, among our other luxurious possessions, had been seized shortly after the occupation. Though we were allowed to remain in our residence, we lived with minimal niceties and always with the expectation that could change any day.

The purple-painted flowers and evergreen vines on each plate, corresponded with each individual cup and saucer. Additionally, the sparkling silver and fine linens rounded out the splendid presentation, making us feel as if we were dining as royalty.

Once seated, the girls and I were only momentarily distracted by the bounteous display of food, which I had come to know as delights traditional to Germany. *Fettbemme*, a slice of rye bread topped with pork, gherkins, and a dash of salt was often served with my afternoon coffee, but today it complimented the *Holunderbeerensuppe*—an elderberry juice and lemon soup I had only tasted once before but easily fell in love with.

"There is something different about the soup this time," I said to Frida who sat at the end of the table. "I don't recognize these white lumps."

"Yes." She smiled and lifted the spoon to her lips. "My sister likes to add semolina dumplings when she makes it."

"This is delicious!" Katia slowly savored her bite. "I have always loved parmesan cheese."

"Thank you." Helene blushed as the compliments continued. Not one bowl had leftovers, though we tried hard to save room for the main course.

"This is Giselle's family recipe for the *Sauerbraten mit Rotkraut*," Frida said as the three women dished out beef patties soaked in a combination of what smelled like vinegar and wine, boiled potatoes, and red cabbage.

"Ohhh," Inga giggled. "My mama made sauerbraten often. It was her childhood favorite." Speaking of her mother no longer brought Inga to instant tears. *Had we all come to accept our new lives so easily? Yet, it really didn't come about easily at all. I frowned. How could I have forgotten the hell we went through just to get here?*

I glanced around at each of my friends as they smiled, conversed, and ate heartily…they were happy, clean, and cared for…a world away from what was intended, and truly the only thing I should be grateful for.

Chatter amongst the girls increased as the meal went on. Each shared details of their living arrangements, their new acquaintances in the apartments they lived in, and anything else they could think of. When dessert finally arrived, everyone went silent.

"This is called *Quarkkeulchen*." Frida smiled as she placed a palm-sized plate before each of us. "This is my specialty." She glowed as she pointed out each of the ingredients. Three small, pan-fried patties of potato dough were sprinkled generously with cinnamon and powdered sugar. A scoop of cherries, still steaming hot, graced the side.

"Oh, my," Karina cooed. "This looks too good to eat."

Ruta leaned down and inhaled it dramatically. "I cannot remember the last time I had fresh cherries." She looked around at us and laughed.

"Do not get used to such luxuries," Helene spoke up. "This is a celebration of your new lives here in Dresden, but we do have some shortages and cannot eat this grandly too often."

"Thank you." I was the first to say it, but everyone followed suit. Though we did not face the same shortages the average Pole did, we were not ignorant of them and, as long as the war continued, I imagined additional deficiencies would transpire.

Once the dishes had been cleared, washed, and properly returned to Frida's cabinets, a stack of papers was placed on the table. Each of us took our seats in preparation for hearing what these dear women had arranged for us.

Frida stood up first. "As you all were made aware of the first day you arrived, it is essential we keep your backgrounds confidential." She glanced around at each of us. "Though Dresden is a city of new ideas and contemporary philosophies, we are still in Germany where, unfortunately, some deep-seeded prejudices still reside."

Helene quickly interrupted. "Please do not misunderstand. We don't believe your lives are at stake, we are just taking extra precautions."

Frida nodded. "Yes, we are only being vigilant. Therefore, we must invent a new background for each of you, including a new hometown and family name before you begin work or school."

Helene took over again. "A few of you are sisters, but all are related somehow, such as cousins. You already refer to yourselves as family, so this won't be a challenge. What might be difficult is referencing the place you come from. We have selected our hometown of Munich." She picked up several pieces of paper and handed them out. "These will tell you what you should know about the city if ever asked."

"But what if we mess up or say something about Poland?"

"Many Germans have traveled to Poland; it is perfectly okay to say that you visited there on holiday but refrain from mentioning any life there," Helene added. "If you think you might struggle with this, keep to yourselves, your sisters, and us."

Fear crept into the conversation.

Frida spoke up quickly. "The issue is not necessarily that you are Polish. The concern is that you don't have your Kennkarte, instead, you were given special papers for transport to Berlin and for Lebensborn."

I glanced around nervously. A couple of the girls appeared confused. Katia and I had never openly spoken of Lebensborn.

Frida continued, "We do not know if the SS has a record of your transport or obligation or not, we are only being careful by changing your family names and providing official papers."

"But what if they are discovered to be forgeries? Can't we be arrested?" Olga asked.

Frida smiled in an effort to ease her strained expression. "Please do not overwhelm yourselves, all will be well. I assure you, these papers are expertly constructed." She brought everyone's attention to the papers on the table again. "We have found jobs for each of you based on your interests. Everything will proceed as planned and, in no time at all, you will fall in love with Dresden as we have."

Several days ago, Frida had tried to convince me to come work with her at the museum, but I knew little of art or sculpture. I didn't want to embarrass her. That's when Dr. Meier suggested I assist at the hospital. Though I didn't have much experience in that area either, I found myself intrigued by the idea of helping others. Especially after our own healing process and the nurses who helped us recover. He also suggested that with my skills in languages, this would be a service to the staff who mostly only spoke German or Russian.

"Ruta," Frida spoke up. "You and Aleksandra will be working at the hospital. You will be trained to be assistants to the nurses beginning tomorrow morning."

Ruta smiled wide. I knew this would make her happy.

"Here are your new identification papers." Giselle handed them to each of us. I quickly perused it. If the papers were truly forged, they were very good replicas, and then I remembered that Frida was familiar with meticulous replicas in the art world…hopefully she didn't risk too much to make the arrangements for us. If anything happened to her or Dr. Meier because of us, that is one risk I couldn't live with.

I slowly read the document in my hands. *Aleksandra Vogel.* A new family name…a German name. Yet once again, I was willing to undertake this role if it meant survival. Anything to get through the war and return to my homeland and to my family.

"We have arranged for Karina and Inga to attend school." She peered over to Aneta. "I wish you would reconsider and join them."

Aneta shook her head swiftly. "No, I won't."

Olga placed a hand over Aneta's and patted it lightly. She must know the specifics of her refusal. I knew, for me, I had no desire to ever step foot in a school again.

"Very well. You will be working at the Field Gun factory with Olga. You are only to be a runner and not work around the machinery. You begin Tuesday morning."

Aneta smiled her thanks.

"Katia, here are your papers, but you will continue your employment with the children." She glanced at Giselle and winked. "I have heard wonderful things about your first week there and they look forward to a long, happy relationship."

"Thank you." Katia smiled, first at Frida then Giselle. "They have been very kind. Thank you again for all that you three have done for us. We cannot thank you enough."

The rest of us echoed her words. It was true; we would not be here without them. Looking back, though I didn't realize it then, we were in such dire straits that I doubt we would have survived another day. This brought my thoughts to Günter. It was because of him that we made it to Dresden when we did and because of him that it was done safely. I hoped with all my heart, that he had reached safety himself. He never spoke of crossing the Allied lines but maybe that is why he was headed to France. I prayed that wherever he was, he was okay.

"Well, ladies." Frida clapped her hands. "You all have what you need to begin your new lives." She paused and grinned at me. "Never forget where you came from girls. You have faced and overcome extreme challenges. You are survivors and some of the strongest women I have ever met...continue to show that same strength as we move forward with the next chapter in your lives."

I returned her smile. How did I get so lucky to have someone like her in my life?

After hugs and more hugs, kisses, and goodbyes, the other girls left our flat to return to their own, but not before we made promises to get together every Sunday, or any other day we might be able to, but no one knew exactly what our new occupations might require of us...me included.

CHAPTER TWENTY

W HEN RUTA AND I met on the corner the morning of our first day of employment at the hospital, she appeared as nervous as I felt. Dr. Meier had recommended we put our hair up into a braid or a bun, wear a skirt below our knees, a light-colored blouse, and solid shoes.

"Are you ready for this, Aleksandra?"

"I guess so." I fidgeted with the small pack that carried a simple lunch for my meal break. "I am anxious about working someplace I know little about."

"I know what you mean."

"But you have been around a doctor your whole life."

"Yes, but not a hospital. I will be learning just like you."

I linked my arm through hers as we walked to the trolley stop. Though the hospital was only a couple of kilometers down the street, we wanted to make sure we weren't tired upon arrival, but in all honesty, we were tired of walking unnecessarily…we felt we had done our fair share in the forest.

Upon arrival, we were assigned to shadow two separate nurses in different wards. Hers was a tall, thin woman named Helga who seemed friendlier than my short, stout, and grumpy Nurse Ingrid.

"Here's your ward dress, wear it at all times while in the hospital." She tossed a white apron-like cover at me, then waved at me to follow her. "How much experience do you have in recovery?"

"N—none, actually." I was rarely intimidated by anyone, but this woman had me shaking in my stockings from the moment I met her. She was at least a foot shorter than me, round in the hips and her dark eyes and sharp nose reminded me of a bird…a very angry bird.

She stopped so suddenly that I nearly bumped into her as I fumbled to get my uniform tied in the back. Turning around to face me, she pulled her lips into a deep frown. "None?"

"No, ma'am, but I am a quick learner."

"Scheiße!"

I understood the first curse word but didn't hear the rest as she turned back around and stomped in the direction of a row of beds. There were only three occupied at the moment. All men and, according to Ingrid, most had varying work-related injuries.

"This man needs his dressing changed. He was in an explosion and both hands were burned."

She marched to the second bed. "This man slipped and fell on a blade and nearly cut his foot off. Dr. Weber was able to save it, but it too must be changed once a day and he is also in need of a cloth bath."

My eyes went wide. I had never done any of these things before.

"And here is Herr Turner." She placed both her hands on her hips and stood at the end of his bed. "He thinks he is dying of dysentery or typhoid…" I had heard of them both and not in pleasant ways. She grunted. "Oh, wait, it's tuberculosis this week, isn't it?"

"I *am* dying!" He argued and then fell into a fit of coughs.

She rolled her eyes and looked at me. "He's allergic to everything. Dogs, cats, rabbits, anything with fur, and a wide range of foods. Every time he has an allergic reaction, he shows up here as if he's on death's door."

"He's been here before?"

She laughed a deep gurgled laugh. "He's been here at least once every month for years."

"Oh." I glanced back down at the man who appeared frail but not completely unhealthy and pulled my lips tight to prevent the nurse, or patient, from seeing my grin. It might have been too late, her brows furrowed tensely. "He only needs to have a special lung treatment, then he can be released."

She leaned in so only I could hear her. "You will get used to his ridiculous ailments."

I nodded.

"Now, I have paperwork to complete, I will be in the adjacent office, and once you are finished come and find me."

"Finished?"

Nurse Ingrid's nose wrinkled. "Did you not hear what I said?"

"Y—yes, I heard you."

"Then see to it. You have three patients to care for, stop wasting my time."

I swallowed hard as she stomped away. What was it she said about the first patient? I peered over at him; a slight perspiration built on my upper lip. Bandages…that's right, burns. A sharp pain pinched in my chest. *I don't know how to properly change bandages for a burn.*

"Nurse?"

I shook my head out of my stupor and turned to where the voice called me. "I—I'm not really a nurse," I muttered to the first man, the one whose injuries seemed so severe. "I am just an assistant and well," I hated to confess this, but… "this is my first day."

The man smiled. Though he was clearly older than me, he was handsome and the fine wrinkles around his eyes and mouth indicated he grinned often. "I understand."

I walked over to the side of his bed.

He winked. "What is your name?"

"Aleksandra Ja—Vogel."

"Ja—Vogel?"

"I'm sorry, just Aleksandra Vogel."

He nodded. "I can walk you through it. I have seen it done a dozen times now."

I smiled down at him in return. "Does it still hurt?"

"Yes, but not as much as before."

"Well, if you don't mind, I would appreciate the guidance."

He pointed to a nearby cupboard. "You will find a bottle of ointment, the bandages, and a stack of small towels in there. They keep it nearby. It must be done twice a day."

I walked over to the cupboard, collected the supplies, and set everything down on the small table next to his bed. Retrieving a chair, I sat down and began unraveling the old bandages slowly. My hands trembled as parts of the linen would stick and I would have to tug it free, fearing I caused pain.

"It's okay." He chuckled, though his voice tried to camouflage his duress. "I promise, Nurse Ingrid does not take this much care. You are doing fine."

As I neared the end, raw, red flesh peeked out from underneath. I fought my desire to wince. If I'm going to work here, I must get used to seeing difficult things. My mind flitted back to the truck accident and all the blood and death I witnessed then. I didn't recall flinching or wincing as we cared for all the injuries—we just did what had to be done. I took a deep breath. This will be the same…I will do what is asked of me regardless of how challenging it is.

As I wiggled the last of the fabric off what was left of his skin, the man gritted his teeth.

"Sorry about that." I rolled it up and set it aside. "I tried not to cause too much pain."

"It was my foolish mistake." He pointed to the table. "Start with the ointment."

I nodded and squeezed a button-sized amount of the gel in one palm, and, using the fingertips of my other hand, spread it gently on his injuries. Some of the flesh stuck to my own.

"That's what the towels are for." He pointed to the towel for me to wipe my fingers before I moved on. I nodded and did so. Trying not to think about the parts of him that were still coming off, I decided to distract us both in conversation.

"Now I told you my name, what's yours?"

"Werner Genau." He paused then chuckled darkly to himself. "I would shake your hand, but…"

I smiled. At least he can jest about it. "So, Herr Genau, I am new to Dresden. What do you recommend I do for amusement?"

His eyes lit up. A large chunk of skin slid off onto my hand, though he didn't seem to notice, as he began listing all the places I should go.

"You must see the Royal Palace and go to the Augustus Bridge over the Elbe. The view is stunning. And you mustn't miss Großer Garten Park, the botanical garden is quite picturesque…"

I smiled again as I finished up the last of his ointment. "It sounds as though you have seen it all."

He laughed, "Yes, I suppose so, I have lived here my whole life."

One of my eyebrows raised curiously. "How old are you?"

"Twenty-five."

"Why are you not a soldier?" The question came out before I could stop it. His face dropped slightly.

"I'm sorry, I should not have meddled."

"No, it is quite alright. I had polio as a child and walk with a limp."

"Oh." This was not what I expected him to say. Of course, I would not have known this with him lying in a bed.

"I am not fit for active duty, so I do my part and work at the munitions factory…or at least I used to."

I reached for the bandage and carefully unraveled it around his hands. "Was that the foolish mistake?"

He nodded. "I did not secure the machine properly when the Trinitrotoluene spilled from a cracked shell."

"Trinitrotoluene?"

"TNT."

"Oh." I was more familiar with the abbreviation. "How did it burn your hands?"

"A spark from the machine lit it and I didn't get out of the way in time. I'm lucky it was only my hands. If it had been the entire amount from the shell or several shells together, it could have been much worse."

It's true, I thought. I've seen the damage explosions can do.

"Please keep my thumb free from the other fingers," he said as he continued to guide me on wrapping the bandage. "I can still hold a utensil that way."

Once there was enough padding, he told me when to stop. I cut the excess free with a pair of scissors, then tied each end together into a small knot.

"What will you do now?"

He lifted the bandaged hands up. "What can one do without the use of these?"

I smiled partway in an effort to offer some relief. "I'm so sorry."

He smiled back. He had such a kindness about him. "Do you know of any place I can eat for a living? I do love to eat."

I laughed out loud at his attempt to make such a tragic situation light-hearted.

"See now, seeing you smile was more than worth it," he chuckled.

I pulled my lips tight, then whispered, "That wasn't very professional of me, I'm sorry."

"I am a survivor, Fraulein, do not feel sorry for me. I will find a way."

I paused before I collected the supplies and eyed him carefully. Survivors come in all shapes and sizes, I marveled. "Yes, I do believe you will." I returned the excess supplies to the cabinet and when I returned to his bedside, I carefully pulled the cover upward and gently placed his hands over the top.

"You did well for your first time, Nurse Vogel." He smiled and winked again, knowing I would not like that title.

"You may call me Aleksandra." I nodded. "And thank you for helping me."

He laughed. "I will look forward to it daily."

I moved on to the next patient and he, too, had to guide me through his needs and care. The wound on his foot where the blade had sliced through appeared red and swollen, much like the jagged scar on my leg, only he had the luxury of stitches early on…I did not.

I applied a different ointment, topped it off with the sulfanilamide powder, and redressed the injury. Afterward, I wet several cloths to wash down his arms, legs, chest, and back. Though he agreed to show me what to do, he spoke little outside of his directions.

The third patient, Herr Turner, was the liveliest. He was certain he was dying of every possible disease on earth. I had never known much about any of them, but I was quite pleased he turned out to be a source of information I hadn't planned on.

Once I located the breathing machine Nurse Ingrid wanted me to use, Herr Turner directed me to the dispensary to retrieve the medication.

"Albuterol, Fraulein, and can you please get me my metamizole pill while there?"

"I am only going to get what you are prescribed, Herr Turner."

"It is prescribed, I assure you. Look at my chart."

Looking at his lengthy chart, it took me several minutes to decipher it, and even then, it was confusing. I couldn't make out all the scribbles or directions and this frustrated me to no end. *Is this what Nurse Ingrid considered training?* Irritation bloomed as I turned back to the patient.

"I will have to get some help; I don't see it here."

"No, no trust me," he pleaded. "It is part of the medication I take. Metamizole…remember the name. Just check the dispensary."

I carried the clipboard with me to the medication room and fumbled around the space for several more minutes. Everything was in German, which should not have been a problem, but it all seemed so foreign to me.

"What are you doing in here?" A gruff voice rose from the doorway.

I circled around to find a man I presumed to be a doctor with a similar coat as Dr. Meier. He wore wired spectacles, and his black hair was cut so short it nearly made him appear balding.

"I asked you a question, young lady."

"I, uh, I am assisting patients and needed to get some medication."

"What do you mean assisting patients, who are you? I've never seen you before."

"Yes, it's my first day."

"First day and you are in the dispensary? Who is your charge?"

I swallowed. This was not going to go well. "Nurse Ingrid."

His cheeks flamed as he slammed down his clipboard against a counter. "Come with me," he insisted.

I followed him out and back to the office Nurse Ingrid had told me she would be working in. Once inside, the doctor did not hold back his anger.

"Is she one of yours?" He pointed to Ingrid.

She glared in my direction and stood to her feet. "Yes, sir. What happened?"

"She was in the dispensary and it's her first day!"

"What were you doing in there?" she asked as if this was all my fault.

I folded my arms in front of me and responded clearly. "You told me to see to Herr Turner's breathing treatment. Since you did not tell me where the medication was, I had to look for it myself."

The doctor mumbled something to himself as Nurse Ingrid took a step forward. "I, uh, I only left you for a moment." She stumbled on her lie.

"Take care of this, Nurse." He looked at me briefly, nodded his head, and walked out.

She stomped over to me with a huff and grabbed the clipboard from my hands. "Here." She pointed to the last entry. "Can't you read?"

"Of course, I can read," I snapped. "But I didn't see the machine medication and he also said he receives metamizole, and I couldn't find that on his chart."

"Because he doesn't receive metamizole," she hissed. "It's a pain medication which he is not allowed to have!"

My cheeks warmed; I had been fooled by them both. He was taking advantage of my ignorance and she was trying to make me look bad. I gritted my teeth; maybe I should go to work at the art museum after all. I couldn't imagine the humiliation there being much worse.

"Now see here." She pointed to another line. "Albuterol is all he needs for the machine. There is a box of vials in the cabinet above the machine. You put it in the dispenser, turn it on, and place it over his mouth and nose for ten minutes. Let him rest for another twenty minutes, then he can go home. Do you think you can handle that?"

I inhaled through my nose using all my strength to not smack her silly. "Yes, ma'am."

She moved to sit down once more, looking over at another nurse who happened to witness the whole scene.

Speaking in Russian, she complained. "These doctors can be so damned ignorant when it comes to finding us help."

I blinked. I understood her insults perfectly, though I had not conversed in Russian for over a month.

The other woman looked to me, then back to Ingrid but said nothing.

Nurse Ingrid continued her rant. "They think every pretty face that comes in here is capable of doing our job."

I jutted my chin out a little bit and spoke in the best Russian I could. "I am not taking your job. I am here to help you, but it might be wise for you to teach me first, so I don't make you look bad at *your* job."

Ingrid's mouth flew open. She did not expect me to understand what she said.

"Or would you like me to speak in English or Polish? I can do that too."

Her cheeks turned red as the other nurse chuckled to herself.

Ingrid waved me off with a sneer. "Finish with Herr Turner then take your afternoon break. We will meet again at one o'clock."

I smiled curtly, then turned on my heel and left the room.

CHAPTER TWENTY-ONE
17 September 1941

Over the next week, I only had to work with Nurse Ingrid twice. Nurse Huber, the nurse who cared for me during my recovery, offered to take over my training and Ingrid jumped at the chance to unload me—something I was most grateful for since Uta Lata Huber was more thorough, more detailed, and more willing…more everything actually.

Six additional men arrived in the last few days. Four were transferred in from surgery, and the other two had minor injuries from work-related mishaps. According to Nurse Huber, Dresden had quite a few military factories on the outskirts of town, but two other hospitals were closer in proximity, so we only received the injured when they reached capacity. Most of our patients were motor-vehicle accidents or illnesses.

Herr Genau continued to be a delight as I changed his dressings, now with no additional guidance. His initial help led me to know how to tend to the other patients' burns and I would be forever grateful to him for that. Day after day of his hospitalization, he moved his hands and fingers more freely, but he admitted the pain never fully went away.

"Nurse Vogel."

"Aleksandra." I groaned. This had been a daily banter between us. I refused to be called a nurse knowing quite well I was unqualified for that position, but Herr Genau teased me without remorse.

"Tell me about your home." He asked on the eighth day of my employment. I tried to school my expression and keep myself busy while I remembered the information from my notes.

"I'm from Munich."

"Hmmm." His gaze deepened. "I suspected something a little more… foreign."

I paused, then quickly went on to the ointment. "Well, my grandmother's family is from East Prussia." *Not a lie.* "And my mother has her native accent. I must've picked it up myself over time."

He nodded his head, though he didn't seem convinced. "Do you have brothers and sisters?"

"I have a younger sister named Karina."

"Karina, huh? How much younger, though I don't believe you ever told me your age…Nurse."

"Aleksandra…" I smirked. "And nope, I didn't."

He laughed. "I suppose it will stay that way."

"Yes." I smiled back. Truthfully, I wondered what the patients might think if they found out I was only sixteen, almost seventeen.

"Aleksandra, come quick!" Nurse Huber hollered to me from the doorway. "There's been an accident, an automobile collided with a trolley. We need your help!"

I turned to Herr Genau. "I'm sorry, I will finish wrapping your hands when I return."

"I understand." He waved. "Go."

I wiped my hands free of the ointment on my apron as I rushed out and into another room where attendants were bringing people in from three different ambulances.

"Where do you want me?" I asked Nurse Huber.

"Anywhere you can lend a hand. If someone has an open wound just apply pressure."

I glanced at the seven bodies, half of them being carried in by stretchers—all screaming and all in pain from various injuries. Dr. Meier was directing a man to be taken immediately into surgery.

"Here, Aleksandra," he hollered. "Come and see to this child."

A child? I cringed, then took a deep breath and hustled over.

"Here." He threw a stack of linens toward me. "Stop the bleeding." I glanced down at the child whose head wound seemed severe enough to be life-threatening.

I placed pressure on his head and tried to soothe his fears. "Please, little one, stop crying. We are here to help you." My thoughts immediately went to the night of the truck accident and Karina.

The little boy sniffled. Then everything that came out of his mouth shocked me. *He is speaking in Polish!*

My response tumbled out nearly too fast.

When the boy looked up at me with wide, shocked eyes. I slowed my sentence down. "Jestem tutaj aby pomóc," assuring the young boy of his safety in his native tongue.

His words were mixed with tears as he described what happened and how frightened he was.

"Proszy uspokój sie." Please calm down, I consoled, pressing the bandage on his head with one hand and wiping his tears with the other.

As the confusion around us continued, I assessed his condition. "Where else does it hurt?" We continued our conversation in Polish.

"Here," he whined and pointed to the side of his torso. "It really hurts."

Remembering how I distracted Herr Genau when changing his bandages, I thought to try it here as well.

"What's your name?"

"Jonas."

"How old are you, Jonas?"

"Eight."

"Are you in school?"

Despite the chaos nearby, it felt like little Jonas and I were in a bubble of our own. His cries had finally slowed as his attention diverted.

He frowned. "I used to be, but now we live here."

"What do you like to study the most?"

"Numbers."

"Oh." I lit up. "That was always one of my favorite subjects also."

A faint grin appeared.

"What do you want to do when you get older?"

"I want to work in a *Landesbank* like my papa."

"A local bank. What a wonderful—"

"That's enough, Aleksandra." Nurse Ingrid appeared. "We're ready to take the boy in for an examination. Step aside."

Although Jonas didn't understand her, he seemed to recognize her coarseness and shook his head wildly. "No! No, no, no." The boy's cries resumed. Then in Polish, he cried, "Please don't leave me!"

Ingrid waved to a couple of attendants to remove the boy's stretcher. He clung to my hand and refused to let go.

"*Mama! Tata!*" he shrieked.

"Move aside, Aleksandra. You're in the way."

"He's scared." I stood up but didn't let go of Jonas's hand. "Just let me translate the instructions for him. I can keep him calm."

"We are in Germany." She hissed. "We speak German."

"Or Russian?" I snapped.

She glared.

"He and his parents," I pointed to the man and woman he was brought in with, "they speak Polish, I can help." The boy's grip tightened around my fingers.

Her face pinched. "Useless feeders...Poles," she grumbled. "How can you be certain of that?"

"Jonas told me." *Useless feeders? What did she mean by that?*

"He goes with me, I'm the nurse." Ingrid attempted to pull the boy's hand out of mine. His screams attracted the attention of others.

"What is going on over here?" Dr. Weber approached.

"Aleksandra refuses to let go of the boy," Ingrid sneered. "He needs to be transported to a room for examination."

I glared in her direction. "That is not true. I was comforting him; he only speaks Polish and needs my help."

"You're merely an *Helferin*," Ingrid snapped. "An assistant! You have no—"

"Enough!" the doctor shouted. "Fraulein Vogel, let go of the boy. Nurse Ingrid, move him to an examination room."

She smirked like a childish classmate and directed the attendants to move swiftly despite the boy's cries.

"You will be alright," I assured him, once again, in Polish, then turned to the doctor. "Please check his side. He said it hurts, but I didn't see any open wounds."

Dr. Weber paused but didn't respond to my comment. Pointing to Ingrid and me he made his own demands. "After all this is through, I want to see you both in my office."

Ingrid nodded and hustled away. I watched her go with a fire brewing in my chest.

Dr. Weber pointed to the door. "Fraulein Vogel, I need you to assist the patients in the maternity ward, both nurses will be assisting me in surgery."

"Yes, sir." I didn't hesitate and walked swiftly toward the maternity ward, though my heart thumped twice as fast en route, stirred up over the quarrel.

It wasn't until I had nearly reached the other ward that a certain thought emerged. *Ruta!* Ruta works in the mother's ward. Though we were both employed at the same hospital, we were assigned different areas and rarely saw each other during the day. Knowing this, I sped up my walk and eagerly entered the area at the end of the building. At least something good will come from today's tragic events.

CHAPTER TWENTY-TWO

"Aleksandra!" Ruta cried when I entered. "What are you doing here?"
"They needed all the nurses available for surgery."

"Is it dreadful? The accident? They came and took Nurse Helga and Nurse Ana and told me to keep an eye on things here."

"Yes, it was awful. An accident between an automobile and a trolley. Five adults and two children."

"Oh, no."

"It reminded me of the night of our truck accident," I mumbled.

She lowered her head. I didn't know it then, but her two best friends died that night. "I try not to think of it," she muttered in response. "That's why I was so grateful I have been assigned maternity."

"It's quite nice in here." Glancing around the space, I was impressed with the condition and comfort of the ward.

"Nurse Ana says it's because Germany wants the women to have more babies. If they have a good birthing experience, they might choose to have multiple children."

I smiled tightly, remembering my conversation with Frida. It was true how much of a priority it was, though I had never discussed it with my friends. "Well, you are fortunate to be here."

She smiled and reached for my hand. "I get to help with new life, not death. Well…mostly not death."

My thoughts went back to the patients who just arrived. "Well, listen to this." I pulled her in close. "The boy I was helping, Jonas…he only spoke Polish."

Her mouth gaped open. "He's from Poland?"

I shrugged. "I don't know all the details, but it sounded like they had recently arrived from Poland."

"So, you spoke Polish with him?"

"I tried. Then Ingrid and I—"

"Ahhhh!" A miserable cry rang out from behind a partition.

I jumped at the sound. "What, what is that?"

"That, my dear friend, is Frau Peters. She has been in labor for ten hours now and the doctor said she is no closer to having a baby today than I am."

I stared at her blankly. She smiled. "I'm not having a baby. He just said her body is not ready yet. If nothing changes by tonight, he will have to surgically remove the baby and that can be so dangerous."

I went to the sink to wash my hands. "What can I help you with?" I scrubbed Jonas's blood splatters off my fingers and silently prayed he was in good hands. "I am not trained here, but I will do whatever you ask."

"I know." She smiled then wrapped her arms around me. "It's so good to have you here. I miss you so much!"

"I miss you too."

"Very well, if you will just see to Frau Peters and try to make her comfortable, that will help me enormously. I must stay with Frau Kaiser who is in the partition next to her. Her waters broke an hour ago, but since the doctor and nurses were called away, I am keeping an eye on her progress myself. Her pains are still ten minutes apart, so the baby still has some time to go."

"What if, Frau Peters's baby decides to come…well, soon?" I arched one of my eyebrows.

"I will find help and if nobody is available, you will have to assist me."

"You know how to deliver a baby?" I asked incredulously.

"I have been present for at least a dozen but never done one alone."

"Well let's hope it doesn't come to that."

She nodded as I stepped away. Crossing my fingers behind my back, I walked toward the first woman, praying heartily that that earlier cry meant nothing at all.

The moment I pushed the partition away, I saw Frau Peters was standing next to the bed. The way she bent over it with both hands clasped and pressed against her forehead appeared as if she was praying, but the cries were not directed to God.

I rushed to her side. "What has happened? Are you well?"

"Ohhh," she groaned. "It hurts. It hurts so much!"

I winced, trying to recall what Ruta recommended.

"May I help you back into your bed?"

"No, no I can't sit there."

"What can I get for you? Do you need some water?"

"Nooo! It hurts!"

I wiped my brow and stood next to her. "What hurts specifically?"

"My back." She pointed to her lower back.

"Okay." I licked my dry lips. "Are these pains the same as you were having earlier?"

"Yes!"

I sighed quietly. *At least they weren't worse.* "May I rub your back for you?"

"Who are you?"

"Oh, I apologize. My name is Aleksandra. I work in a different ward, but they needed my help in here today."

"Are you a nurse?"

"No, just an assistant."

"What if I have the baby?"

"Well, Ruta is still here, but from what I've been told, you're not ready yet."

"Then why does it hurt so terribly?"

"I don't know."

"Do you have children, Aleksandra?"

I couldn't imagine such a thought right now. "I do not."

Her body tightened as she cried out again. "Ahhhh!" Then she grumbled. "This will be my first."

I placed my hands on her lower back and through the thin linen robe, I began to knead her skin softly. "What a wonderful thing to look forward to," I said with a smile, even though she couldn't see my face. I can see why Ruta likes it in here.

"Yes," she exhaled.

"Am I reaching the right area?"

She nodded. "Thank you. That does help."

"You're welcome. I'm happy to do what I can."

Over an hour later, my hand ached severely, but I didn't dare stop massaging the poor woman's back. Her cries never lessened but it seemed that through the pains, she was more at ease than before.

"How are you doing, Frau Peters?" Ruta walked in.

"It hurts, it's awful."

Ruta looked at me with an element of alarm, but I quickly spoke up. "I don't think it's changed from when I started rubbing her back."

"You've been doing it this whole time?"

I nodded.

"Here let me take over for a moment so you can rest your hand. Frau Kaiser is getting closer. I've sent for anyone who might be able to do a delivery. Hopefully, not everyone is still in surgery."

I sighed and stretched my fingers. "I hope Jonas is doing well."

Ruta smiled at me. "I hope so too."

Ten minutes later, Nurse Helga walked in and Ruta left me alone with Frau Peters once more.

I retrieved a glass of water for her and pumped my hands before I resumed my massaging position when a wee cry came from the next partition. I smiled as Frau Peters looked over at me. Tears filled her eyes.

"Oh, Frau Peters," I smiled. "Listen to that sweet cry. You are going to be a mother soon and to a precious, precious little baby." My whole body tingled with anticipation.

"Ohhhh," she cried as she doubled over again. "It better be soon; I can't take this any longer."

"Maybe you should lie down," I suggested. "Maybe the baby will rest, too."

She rolled her eyes. "This baby has no intention of resting," she groaned. "And I just want this to be over!"

"I'm sorry."

I stepped over to rub her back again for an additional hour. When Dr. Weber walked in, he appeared tired and worn but came right to the side of her bed with a smile.

"I am going to check the baby again, Frau Peters," he said warmly. "Please move onto the bed."

As the woman did as she was told, albeit in a slow and grumpy way, I turned to Dr. Weber. "How is Jonas? The little boy from the accident. Is he well?"

"Oh, Fraulein Vogel." He peered at me as if he saw me for the first time, though he himself assigned me to help out here. "I didn't know you were still here."

"I am." I nodded with a faint smile. "I couldn't just leave her," I said pointing to Frau Peters. Another alarming cry came forth as she gripped her stomach and panted in short bursts through gritted teeth.

Dr. Weber lowered himself to check her progress. "Thank you for assisting her and yes, Jonas is doing quite well. Besides his head wound, he had several broken ribs."

I bit my lip. *He must be in so much pain.*

"Thank you for alerting us to that and for your assistance. He will fully recover."

"Oh, that's good to hear. Thank you."

"Well, Frau Peters," Dr. Weber chuckled. "I believe you are about to have a baby."

I smiled wide as I began to scoot backward out of the space. With the doctor, Nurse Helga, and even Ruta, it was apparent I was no longer needed.

"Fraulein Vogel," Dr. Weber called for me but didn't turn in my direction.

I stopped at the opening of the partition. "Yes, sir?" concerned I had done something wrong…again.

"How would you like to stay for the delivery of her baby?"

When he finally turned around and faced me, his eyes were twinkling. He must be at least forty, but the way his face lit up, he looked much younger, even on a day like today.

"May I, sir?"

"If Frau Peters does not mind, I do not either."

I looked to her for an opinion, but she only shouted in response. "I don't care who is here, just get this baby out of me!"

I pulled my lips tight to prevent a chuckle. I could only imagine how painful this was for her. I hoped that if I ever have a child, it would not be like this.

"What would you like me to do?"

"Take your place at her side, hold her hand, and use a wet cloth to keep her face and eyes clear. And most importantly, keep her calm."

"I will."

He turned and washed his hands in a nearby basin and when he dried them, he faced me. "You speak Polish?"

I nodded, taken aback. He must've heard some of my conversation with Jonas. "I do."

"Interesting," was all he said. I wasn't sure if this was a good thing or not, but now was not the time to fret over it.

"Nurse Helga," Dr. Weber hollered. "Please see that all is ready. Frau Peters is about to become a mother."

Within the next thirty minutes, and after a great deal of screaming, little Christoph Fritz Peters came into the world. With a mop of dark hair and a set of lungs very much like his mother's, little Christoph charmed us all. Wrapped in a tidy little blanket, he was placed on her chest and for the first time today, a wide smile graced her lips.

"Thank you," she said. "Thank you all for this wonderful gift."

When I said goodbye that night, a good four hours after my regular shift ended, I left the ward exhausted but with a calm I hadn't felt before.

"Oh, Ruta." I retrieved my sweater. "To have that kind of experience every day would be, well it would be like heaven."

She tugged her own sweater tighter around her as we stepped outside to a brisk night breeze. "They don't always have happy endings, Aleksandra."

"Yes, but they must outweigh the bad."

"Fraulein Vogel!" Dr. Weber stepped out of a small office just as we reached the outer door.

"Yes, sir."

"First thing tomorrow morning, I want to see you and Nurse Ingrid in my office."

I frowned. So, apparently, he hadn't forgotten about that part of the day. "Yes, Dr. Weber. I will be there."

"What is that all about?" Ruta asked as we walked toward the bus stop.

"I was arguing with Nurse Ingrid again."

"Again?"

I nodded. "It has become a favorite pastime of mine."

"But she has seniority, Aleksandra. You can be turned out."

"I don't do it on purpose…well, maybe I do, but she is just so rude and cold with people. She doesn't treat them with any kindness. She shouldn't even be a nurse if you ask me. She would have made a much better soldier."

Ruta laughed and wrapped her arm through mine. "Oh Aleksandra, I have missed your rousing spirit so much."

"Let's hope that spirit doesn't get me dismissed."

She kissed my cheek just as the bus arrived. "If you do, I think you just might single-handedly find a way to end this war. You are a gem, my dear friend, I love you."

"I love you too, Ruta."

CHAPTER TWENTY-THREE

THE NEXT MORNING, I prepared myself for a stern lecture and the very real possibility I would be unemployed within the hour. It was true what Ruta had said, I was merely an assistant—a *new* assistant at that—and if I was making trouble for the nurses, I would be the one they must let go.

"Come inside, ladies." Dr. Weber held his door open as both Nurse Ingrid and I stepped inside. Thankfully, I had arrived only a second after her knock, so we didn't have to converse at all.

We stepped inside as he took a seat behind a desk. Pointing to two broad leatherback chairs he motioned for us to sit. Somewhere in the room, the earthy smell of tobacco lingered, reminding me of the sitter pipe my father smoked every evening.

"I will get right to the point." He appeared a bit angrier than I remembered. "What happened yesterday in front of the entire staff and patients will not be tolerated. Any disagreement you might have must be dealt with in a private manner."

We both nodded at the same time.

"Nurse Ingrid."

She lifted her chin.

"Why is it that when I have seen you two together, there always seems to be contention? You are the senior nurse, how is this happening?"

"Aleksandra does not follow my instructions."

"What instructions?" I replied crossly with an equally frustrated stare.

She ignored me. "I ask her to do simple tasks and she does not complete them."

My mouth parted, but this time I held my tongue.

"For example?" He waved his hand for her to elaborate.

"Uh, well, she uh, that first day you found her in the dispensary, I did not tell her to go in there. I gave her other directions which she chose not to do."

"What directions did you give her?"

"To see to the needs of the patients, clean bandages, cloth baths…all the things an assistant should do."

"Did you teach her how to do these things?" He leaned back in his chair and steepled his fingers in front of him.

I fought my smile. *Of course, she didn't.*

"She should already be familiar with these basic tasks." Ingrid shook her head forcefully. "If she has been hired to work in a hospital, she should already be qualified for the position."

"Isn't that a decision for the doctors to determine?"

"Uh, well, w—we are responsible for people's lives." She began with a stutter, but her arrogance took over. "An unqualified staff member should not be working here."

"Yet you left her alone with your patients on her very first day."

She paled. "I assumed she had been trained."

He turned to me. "Fraulein Vogel, did Nurse Ingrid discuss your training experience that first day?"

"Yes, sir."

"What did you tell her?"

"That I had no experience, but I am a quick learner."

He glanced back at her and waited.

She fidgeted nervously with both hands. "I just assumed that the doctor who had appointed her had vetted her abilities. I trusted the doctor."

My eyes widened...*she is one very stubborn woman!*

"Is it not in your job description as the lead nurse in your ward to train the new assistants?"

"Yes."

"So, did you?"

"Did I what?"

He huffed as if he was losing patience. "Did you train Aleksandra Vogel properly on her duties as a nurse's assistant?"

She gasped, looking back and forth between us.

He didn't wait for her to answer. "It is my understanding, from other sources mind you, that she was given a list of duties but not thoroughly trained until Nurse Huber took over. Is that true?"

She didn't speak.

Dr. Weber's stare pierced with meticulous precision. "Well, I assume from your lack of response that the report is true."

He glanced over to me. "My deepest apologies, Fraulein Vogel, we have failed you."

Despite Nurse Ingrid's distance, I physically felt a surging heat emanate from her. She was clearly angry.

Dr. Weber continued, "I realize at times we must throw you into a situation that does not allow for proper training such as the emergency yesterday, but I saw the way you comforted that young boy…Jonas. You not only discovered that he spoke Polish, but you were able to calm his fears in his own language. I found that quite fascinating." He leaned forward in his chair. "Do you speak any other languages?"

"Besides German and Polish, I speak Russian and English tolerably."

"Hmmm." He rubbed his chin.

"Were you aware of these skills, Nurse Ingrid?"

She lifted her chin up higher. "Yes, but I did not think that mattered while attending to the patient's medical needs."

"Wouldn't that help if say a patient spoke a language other than German?"

"I suppose so."

"Well that alone would be reason enough for a doctor to employ her, wouldn't you say, Nurse Ingrid?"

He had proven his point quite effectively and she had been silenced.

"Now, go about your duties, both of you, and do not let me hear of another squabble in public again."

"Yes, sir," Ingrid answered and immediately jumped to her feet.

I answered shortly after. "Yes, sir."

Without a glance my way, Nurse Ingrid walked out.

I turned toward Dr. Weber before I departed. "I truly am sorry, Dr. Weber. I promise it won't happen again."

He lifted his chin. "I believe you."

When I turned to leave, he called to me once more. "Fraulein, if you have time today, could you please check in on the Polish patients? They are new to Dresden and could use a friendly face."

I smiled. "I would be happy to."

"Thank you."

Upon exiting his office, Ingrid was nowhere to be seen. Walking down the corridor, I stood a little taller knowing I now had two doctors that saw the value in me being here and when I stepped into the recovery ward, I was met with a handful of smiles. They, the patients, are the reasons I'm here…not Nurse Ingrid. She may have been quieted for today, but I doubted it would last. Though I no longer feared her like before, I had a sneaking suspicion she might continue to make my life as miserable as possible.

CHAPTER TWENTY-FOUR

28 September 1941

"I AM BEING DISCHARGED today, Nurse Vogel."

"Aleksandra," I countered. "That is good news, isn't it?" I reached the side of Herr Genau's bed, his warm eyes and kind smile had given me something to look forward to every day. Despite the malice Nurse Ingrid continually foisted when we were alone, I could often find a friendly face back in the men's ward with Herr Genau present. I glanced at the thin bands that now covered his hands, significantly thinner than the day we met.

"What will you do now?" I pulled a chair near his bed and sat down.

He sighed. "I have had a lot of time to think over that very question…yet I find I have not come to an agreeable answer."

I waited for him to continue, trying my best to come up with suggestions on my own.

"I have recovered some use of my hands, but I'm certain the factory will not allow me to return, I cannot be a soldier, I cannot play the piano, and I will never be able to paint as I did before."

"You played music? And painted?" After weeks of conversation, this was the first I had heard of this.

"I dabbled." He chuckled. "My mother insisted I learn the piano. Art was entirely of my own choosing."

"What did you paint?"

"Mostly landscapes, like the Elbe and the botanical garden."

"Oh, the garden is one of my favorite places in the city. I can see why you chose to immortalize it."

He lowered his head. "I suppose if I can't recreate it, I can still appreciate it." He glanced back up. "Can't I?"

My mind suddenly spun with ideas. I could barely contain the excitement that was building up. "Herr Genau, do you have a reasonable knowledge of artists and their work?"

He tilted his head curiously and grinned. "Not just reasonable... extensive."

I jumped to my feet with a surge of enthusiasm, causing him to flinch. I quickly composed myself. "Now I cannot promise you anything..." I paced in the tight space between the two beds, mumbling to myself, then peered over. "But I have a very dear friend who is in acquisitions at the art museum."

"The Staatliche Kunstsammlungen?"

"Yes, that's the one. I've been there myself to visit her."

Herr Genau's eyes lit up. "Would you make an introduction?"

"Yes, yes of course I will." I patted his shoulder. "Though you may not consider working in a museum as serving your country...you are." I smiled.

His forehead wrinkled and I recognized the need to elaborate.

"You are protecting and conserving the history of some of the greatest artists in Germany. Most definitely a noble cause."

Herr Genau reached for my hand, the one I placed on his shoulder, and squeezed it gently through his bandage. "You have become a good friend, Aleksandra, and I thank you for your kindness."

I grinned. I knew his words were sincere when he used my first name instead of the teasing one of *Nurse*. "I should be thanking you, Herr Genau. If it weren't for your assistance that first day, I might not have even made it a week."

He laughed, then let go of my hand. I went to the nearby desk and wrote down my address. When I handed it to him, I repeated my earlier statement. "I don't know if there will be a place for you at the museum, but at the very least you will have been introduced to a connection and, well, you will love to see the art in my flat at the very least."

"I was unaware you had a love of art."

"Me too." I chuckled. "Actually, it has grown on me. The artwork belongs to Dr. Meier's wife, Frida. She is the one who works at the museum."

"The Dr. Meier who works here?"

I nodded. "Yes, he and his wife took me and my sister in when we first arrived."

"Well, I look forward to meeting both your sister *and* your friend."

I chewed on my inner cheek as I calculated a hasty possibility. "Wait!" I slapped my skirt. "I have an idea!"

Now both of his eyebrows lifted.

"Why don't you join us for dinner on Sunday? This will give her a few days to speak to the necessary people at the museum." I tapped my finger against my cheek. "Although truthfully…between us, if there isn't an opening, she just might create one. Frida is resourceful that way."

Herr Genau laughed. "You have such an interesting life, Fraulein."

"Oh, if you only knew the half of it." I chuckled as I replaced the chair next to his bed and held out my hand to shake his. "It has been a pleasure knowing you, Herr Genau, and I will be most grateful to see you again so soon."

He met my hand gingerly. Though the burns had begun healing, they certainly would remain tender for quite some time. "It is I who am lucky that Nurse Vogel appeared at my side those many weeks ago. I have always believed there is a reason for everything."

CHAPTER TWENTY-FIVE

"Thank you for coming, Herr Genau." I reached for his coat when he entered the room. I had nearly forgotten his story about his polio impairment until I saw his slight limp when he walked forward.

"I think it's safe to call me Werner now…Aleksandra." He winked and easily handed his tweed jacket over. Though the autumn days here in Dresden were mostly temperate, the last week had brought in a frigid blast of cold air. *Could this be a precursor to a miserable winter to come?* I prayed it was not…I had a volatile relationship with cold temperatures.

"Werner," I said, grinning as I faced the smiles of the rest of the group present. "You know Dr. Meier…" The doctor stepped forward to shake his hand then remembered his bandaged fingers and pulled back.

"It's healing well, doctor," Werner spoke up and extended his hand. "I'm getting more and more use from them every day."

Dr. Meier nodded and met his hand gently. "That is good to hear." Then Dr. Meier turned to Frida. "This is my wife, Frida." They also shook hands, then Dr. Meier pointed back to me to take over the other introductions.

"This is my sister, Karina."

Her eyes grew wide. She had recently discovered the joy in appreciating men's good looks. She nearly forgot to let go of his hand while she stared with obvious adoration.

"And these two are my cousins, Katia and Ruta." For several months now, they joined us for our Sunday dinners.

"Nice to meet you both." He smiled. Then faced the whole group. "I feel as though I already know you all. Aleksandra speaks nothing but good things of her family."

I laughed out loud, then quickly covered my mouth. We spoke of all sorts of incongruous topics.

"Well, why don't we continue this conversation over food?" Frida motioned toward the dining room, and, with swift obedience, we followed.

Karina walked next to Werner and giggled. "You will love Frida's cooking.

She is better than my own mother."

"Where is your mother?" Werner's innocent question instantly put us on guard. I stiffened before I could remind myself to relax. After all, I had told him we were sisters, so this question would have naturally included me.

Karina's eyes flickered anxiously toward me. I reached for her hand to ease her concern. "Karina and I left our parents to come here and expand our education. Dresden has provided opportunities home did not."

"Now that I can understand." His smile assured me he did not seem to think anything was amiss. "Dresden is known as the *Jewel Box of Germany*."

"Yes." Frida jumped into the conversation. "Yes, it is, and I understand you, Herr Genau, have a flair for art." She pointed to the paintings around the room, though I doubted he missed seeing them upon his initial arrival.

"I do have a bit of an obsession." He stepped over to one and leaned in. After a few seconds, he turned around and asked, "Johannes Vermeer…an original?"

Frida smiled broadly and joined his side. "It is!"

My eyebrows pinched. "I thought you said they were replicas?"

She laughed over her shoulder. "Well, most of them are." She winked at her husband as I crossed my arms over my chest. "Oh, Aleksandra." She waved my anger aside. "Do not be upset. Only three are originals."

"Which three?" Karina joined in, as curious as I was, especially after us living here for nearly six weeks.

"Wait." I threw my hands up. "Let's make a game of it," I suggested and walked over to the counter to retrieve a paper and pencil. Joining the others, I said, "Let's put our guesses here and see who is right. Of course, you and Liam cannot play, but Werner, me, Karina, Katia, and Ruta can."

"That is a brilliant idea." Frida flashed her pretty smile, though in a way I think she was more interested in testing Werner's knowledge over anything. "So, this one as you all know now is Johannes Vermeer, the first original. Out of the other fifteen paintings in the house, you must identify the other two originals…but only after supper."

"Yes!" Ruta cried. "The smell of bacon is testing my fortitude right now."

Everyone laughed and went to the dining table where another decorative dinner awaited us. This time, it was *Rinderroulade* on the menu with its combination of mustard, bacon, and pickles, slathered in burgundy gravy and a roasted potato dumpling on the side.

Katia, who sat on one side of Herr Genau, was the first to speak. "Aleksandra told me of your injury. She said you worked at a munitions factory."

"Yes." He nodded. "Both of my brothers and I have worked there for three years now."

"I'm sorry you are unable to return." Her typical sweetness was evident in her every word. I smiled from across the table. There could not be a single person in this world that she disliked, she showed true compassion for everyone.

Herr Genau tilted his head in her direction. "Sometimes our plans do not happen the way we want them to," he said, holding up a bandaged hand as evidence. "But I believe as one door closes, another is opened."

She smiled in return.

Since our recovery, Katia had blossomed. Her hair resumed its golden shine from before, her complexion was clear and rosy, and though her clothes were simpler than what Frida had provided for Karina and me, it didn't matter...she was a vision, and *someone* seemed to notice.

"I believe," he continued with conviction in his tone, "that there was a reason Aleksandra was the one I met in the hospital and now she has introduced me to all of you." He shrugged his shoulders. "Would we have met otherwise? I don't know, but because of this favorable circumstance, I might have the opportunity to follow my first love after all."

Ruta swallowed a large bite from her bread, nearly choking on her inquiry. "And what is that, Herr Genau?"

"Werner, please call me Werner." Though he was answering Ruta, his eyes never left Katia, whose cheeks brightened under his gaze.

"If all goes well," he continued, "I might be able to work with art. Painting is my first love."

I saw Katia's glance move from his face to his bandaged hands as he lifted his fork to his mouth. "I'm sorry you can't paint the way you did before, but I believe you're right. God leads us in directions we might do the most good for others. He has led you here after all."

His fork froze in midair, and he beheld her with a look I had never seen from him. *Admiration, maybe.* I grinned, trying to keep my elation to myself as best I could.

After dinner, I noticed as the five of us meandered around the room examining the artwork, Katia and Werner were together the entire time. She could have been trying to gain an advantage from his knowledge but that wasn't like Katia to do so. *It must be more than that.* Each time I glanced in their direction, they were smiling, laughing, or deep in conversation. Something was happening and I could not have been more thrilled.

"Okay." Frida clapped her hands and gathered us all back together. "Have a seat and let us tally the results." This may have pleased her more than anything to have had her artwork at the center of everyone's attention. "I will point to a painting, and based on what you wrote down, tell me if you believe it to be a replica or an original. Remember, there are only two originals remaining besides the Vermeer."

We all nodded in agreement.

"Although," she drawled, her eyes narrowing playfully, "I do believe we will have Werner go last."

He chuckled. From the complacency on his face, it was certain he knew exactly which pieces were which.

In the end, I was right; well wrong in my choices, but right in knowing that Werner would choose correctly. He had chosen a garden scene by Nicolas Poussin and a painting of the Madonna by Sandro Botticelli.

"Congratulations, Herr Genau!" Frida clapped her hands and the rest of us joined in. "You truly are a skilled professional in regard to fine art."

"Thank you." He smiled. "At the very least, this has been a delightful diversion and a wonderful visit."

As we finished with our evening coffee, we learned that Frida had previously arranged for Werner to meet her employer the following week—something I truly never doubted. Frida had found seven girls a home and a future. She would find a way to offer a wounded man, hope. That's just who she was.

After Herr Genau had extended his goodbyes and promises to meet again, Katia lingered longer than usual. Standing next to me, her hands fidgeted nervously at her side.

"Might I walk you home, Katia?" I asked. She seemed relieved we would not be speaking in the company of others.

We stepped outside and she immediately reached for me. Her hands shook and her tears moistened my own cheek. I drew back in surprise. I thought she had a good time tonight.

"What is wrong?" I questioned, alarmed. I had not seen her crying in weeks. "What has you so upset?"

"I am a terrible friend." She sobbed. "I have wronged you, Aleksandra."

"Now that is quite untrue." I wiped the tears off her cheeks and led her to a short brick wall we could sit upon. "There is nothing you could ever do that would upset me."

She sniffled, then pulled out a handkerchief to wipe her eyes and blow her nose. "I—I..." She could hardly speak.

I squeezed her hand. "Tell me what has you so upset?"

She closed her eyes, then whispered. "I flirted with the man you favor."

My eyes widened. "What?"

"It all happened so quickly. We were talking at dinner, and I found everything he said so fascinating. Then as we played the game, I didn't even recognize I had stayed by his side the entire time and I just, oh, Aleksandra, can you please forgive me?"

"Wait." I blinked. "You are referring to Herr Genau?"

She nodded slowly and more tears spilled down her cheeks.

"Oh, Katia!" I embraced her tightly. "I do not see Werner that way. I never have—wait, did you think he came to dinner for me?"

"Well, yes," she mumbled.

I leaned back to make sure she could see my eyes.

"No, he actually came to meet Frida. Werner, um, he and I are merely friends."

Her eyes widened. "Are you certain?"

"I am very certain."

She took a deep breath while I continued, "He is handsome and charming and a very lovely person." I added, "but I never intended anything more than friendship." I grinned. "I promise."

"Oh my," she bit her lip. "I was sure I had made a mess of things."

"No." I grinned. "However, you should know, I've never seen him happier than I saw him tonight when he was near you."

"Truly?"

I nodded. "Trust me, Katia, I saw him nearly every day for weeks and I've never seen him smile as he did with you."

She reached around me and pulled me in for another hug. "I was afraid I had affronted you and I would never intentionally do that to you, Aleksandra."

"I know that, believe me, I know your heart, and you know what else?"

She seemed to hold her breath as she watched me.

"I suspect that something is happening between you two."

She smiled and blushed again. "I don't know." She frowned. "I spent so much time at the end of his visit fretting over what I had done, I hadn't considered anything else. Are you certain I haven't muddled it?"

"Oh, I doubt you could ever muddle anything."

She grabbed my hand and squeezed. "How did I get so lucky to have you as my friend?"

"I've asked the same question since the very day we met."

CHAPTER TWENTY-SIX

17 April 1942

"Herr Turner, you do not have scarlet fever, I assure you." I clasped my hands in front of me.

"Do you see this rash, Fraulein? It covers my whole body."

"Yes, it does. It's just your typical allergic reaction, sir."

"But my throat…it feels like it's closing completely. I will suffocate if you don't do something." He opened his mouth and, sure enough, his airway was swollen.

I raised one of my eyebrows in response. "Did you have shellfish recently?"

"Well, uh, um…"

"Herr Turner…" I reprimanded, full well knowing his weakness for Belon oysters. "You must stay away from those foods that you are allergic to, or this will happen every time."

"What about the pain in my side? It's much worse. I need something for the pain. Metamizole, perhaps?"

"Oh no, not this time. I'm not falling for that one, sir. The doctor will prescribe only what you need."

"I might die today, Nurse Vogel, and how would that make you feel?"

I gently patted the arm of his coat. "First of all, I will not be able to use that official title until I take the exams. Call me Aleksandra, please, and second of all, if you die, it is because you do not follow your doctor's orders."

He removed his hat and grumbled as he paced to and from the closest window.

"Go ahead and wait over there." I pointed to a bed at the end of the first row. "I will have Dr. Meier examine you shortly."

"Wait." He stopped in place and glanced back at me with wide, fearful eyes. "It could be rubella! My sister's son had a classmate who contracted rubella recently."

"We will know for sure in a few minutes."

I went to retrieve the man's very thick chart when Nurse Huber stopped me. "What is it this time?"

"Scarlet fever or rubella."

She chuckled. "Or a really good European delicacy."

"Yep, that too." I winked.

"So, Aleksandra, I have been instructed to bring you into surgery with me today."

"Really? Already?"

"You're ready." She rolled her eyes. "In fact, you're more ready than most of the girls here who are actually taking nursing classes."

I laughed. Work at the hospital had not only become something I looked forward to every day, but I had also become very good at helping people.

"How many patients do you have today?"

"Herr Turner makes it two."

"Slow day?"

"Slow week…" I smiled. "Thankfully. I just pray every day there isn't a widescale accident at any of the factories."

"Yes, nobody wants that to happen again."

"Again?"

"Before you arrived, there were several. The worst we saw was one at the anti-aircraft factory. They had a minor explosion in which a dozen people were killed and nearly thirty burned. I'd never seen anything like it. Their flesh was literally sliding off their bones."

"I think to die by fire would be the most horrifying experience."

She nodded. "Meet me in surgery after Herr Turner has been accommodated. See if Dr. Meier will increase his dosage of allergy medication. The last time he did that, the man slept a whole day."

I chuckled. "He's simply an odd one."

"Oh, there's plenty of those out there."

I smiled.

She glanced at me warily. "I don't hear of you talking about any male friends like the other assistants. Do you have a boyfriend?"

"No…" I snickered. "I just don't have time."

"Pshhh." She waved her hand back and forth. "You are young and beautiful; you need to be enjoying life."

"I enjoy life." I defended. "I read books, go to all of the museums, I've been to the cinema three times, and I go to the botanical garden every Sunday."

"Alone?"

"I go with my sister and cousins…occasionally."

"Not good enough."

"It's fine."

"I'm going to arrange for you to go on a date."

"No, no, no. Really, I'm fine."

"My neighbor is a kind man."

I laughed, "How old is your neighbor?"

Her face wrinkled into deep thought. "I believe he's thirty-something."

One of my eyebrows arched. "I am seventeen, Nurse Huber."

"Oh, yes, I forget." She laughed out loud. "Sometimes the way you work makes me think you are older. Never mind…I will keep looking."

I patted her arm sympathetically. "I will be in surgery shortly."

As Nurse Huber walked away, I thought about what she said. Before we were brought to Germany, there was a boy whose father owned the neighborhood market Mama and I visited. He was handsome, kind, and strong. I recalled the excitement I felt each time I caught a glimpse of him while we shopped. He often offered to carry our groceries home for us. Mama usually let him, but over time and seeing the way he looked at me, she eventually refused. Of course, at the time, I had hoped he would be the one to give me my first kiss. Yet here it is six years later and I'm still waiting.

Before today, my responsibilities involving the surgical room included preparing the instruments for use through identification and disinfecting. But this afternoon marked the first time I would be present for the actual surgery, a day I had looked forward to for quite some time.

The patient, a young woman of twenty-four, complained of loss of appetite, nausea, and pain in her lower abdominal area. When Dr. Weber examined her yesterday, he believed her to have abdominal swelling as well, which led us to suspect the presence of an inflamed appendix. Unfortunately, the extent of our medical devices could not confirm this prior to the doctor's incision and examination of the organ himself.

"See here, Nurse Vogel." I leaned in as Dr. Weber pointed to a swollen tube with obvious blockage. "If we do not remove this, it could build up and burst."

I nodded as I watched him continue to use the scalpel in a quick efficient manner. "Sponge." I realized that was my cue to swab the blood. "If an appendix bursts, it could spread the infection and ultimately kill the patient."

I made mental notes of everything he and Nurse Huber said or did. I would not give them a reason to regret my presence. It didn't matter that I did so little, everything I have done at the hospital has progressed like a puzzle. Each piece leads me to the next and the next and eventually, it all comes together in a bigger picture.

By the time I wrapped up my closing duties in my ward, I found myself once again mulling over Nurse Huber's words. What *would* it be like to go out with a boy, well, a man? To have his arms around me, to feel safe, to be kissed?

A flutter of curiosity overwhelmed me as I stepped out of the hospital for the night, but it was the appearance of a handsome soldier's face in my mind that caused the biggest buzz within my chest. Though I truly knew very little of Günter, the way he protected me and my friends that night would always hold a place in my heart—whoever I loved, whoever I married must make me feel safe…safe like he did…even if it had only been that one night.

CHAPTER TWENTY-SEVEN
22 November 1943

Two years in Dresden and still no word from my parents. After dozens of letters were sent to my home address in Poland, I refused to believe the worst. I wanted to trust they were alive and well and hoped they would find comfort in the knowledge that their daughter was safe and alive, but thus far, my efforts yielded no reply. I knew I had been careless in my correspondence, but I desperately yearned to know the status of my family and my hometown. It was possible the Nazis didn't allow letters to be sent from Łódź— I never had an occasion to write one when I lived there— or maybe the failure came directly from being in Germany? Either way, my longing for answers never ceased.

Though I searched the *Sächsische Zeitung* daily for Poland's current status, the newspaper mostly emphasized the accomplishments of the Third Reich—their invasion of France, Yugoslavia, Greece, the Netherlands, and even their triumphs over the Soviet Union. Bold black print confirmed the Nazi Party's drive to overtake Europe and they were nearly unstoppable in their pursuits...*or so we read.*

The Americans, who entered the war late in 1941, were fighting the Japanese, mostly in the South Pacific with some forces in Europe tied to the British and French troops, and, according to Joseph Goebbels, the chief propagandist for the Nazis, Germany was on its way to becoming the grand victor of the second World War.

Despite the growing desperation around us, Frida seemed correct when she said Dresden was safe, even with a constant influx of planes overhead. They were mostly the *Luftwaffe*, the German Air Command, yet on occasion, an aircraft with an unrecognizable exterior appeared...possibly British or American, but the anti-aircraft guns generally kept their flybys short.

I can't say precisely when I stopped looking up anymore.

The engine sounds blended easily with the hums of the vibrant city, and life went on as normal. Even the air raid sirens that reverberated regularly became irrelevant to the point we rarely blinked twice when they trilled. Life in Dresden felt far from what Łódź faced from the ravages of war and I found myself truly grateful that Frida's words rang true…

"Dresden's the Florence of the Elbe," Frida announced one beautiful Sunday morning as we walked to *Frauenkirche* for a church service. "From the architecture, culture, history, and art." She threaded her arm through mine as the baroque, bell-shaped dome came into view.

I had only started attending the Lutheran services with her recently when I stumbled upon the stunning structure in one of my wandering walks… only to learn this was the very church Liam and Frida were married in.

"But don't you worry as the war prolongs?" I bit my lip.

Frida took the first two steps toward the front doors and paused. "No, I don't." Waving a hand up toward the sculpted magnificence, she answered, "Look at this place, Aleksandra. It would be a political offense to even threaten such a treasure. We have nothing to worry about."

When we stepped through the doors to the breathtaking foyer where the intricate woodwork framed exquisitely painted glass, I wanted nothing more than to believe her.

"Aleksandra." Karina posed in front of the full-length mirror in our bedroom the following weekend. "What do you think?" She placed her hand on her hip and tipped her head down for me to see her beige-ribbon chaplet hat. "Do you like it?"

"It's lovely." I smiled. This Karina before me was the new and stronger young woman of Germany. Now sixteen, she enjoyed school, made new friends, and even had a boyfriend; well a friend who was a boy who happened to be everywhere she and her new friends went.

"Where are you going tonight?"

"We…" she emphasized the word with an arched brow. "We are going to a dance hall."

"Dancing?"

"Yes!" She turned around and squealed. "Peter told me all about this place where we can go and listen to music and dance," she cried. "It sounds delightful!"

I smiled. Though one might think a nineteen-year-old woman would seize the opportunity to forget about the war raging around us and the world falling apart and spend a night frolicking—I didn't. A typical gratifying night for me included curling up alone with a good reading book after work. Frida had recently introduced me to the local library.

In my previous life, though I studied well—heaven forbid I willingly picked up a book in my leisure time. I almost laughed out loud at my inner thoughts. *What has changed me?* The adventurous, rebellious, and even aggressive Aleksandra from before, found a more peaceful way of life and truly enjoyed it. Renia might not even recognize me today.

"I don't think so." I sighed.

"Oh, I thought you might say that." She winked, then opened our bedroom door and hollered, "she refused."

I peeked out to see who she was speaking to, and a handful of girls descended upon us. Katia, Olga, Inga, Ruta, and Aneta. All dressed for a night out.

"Well, we're here to make sure she doesn't," Ruta said, then chortled behind a sly grin.

Each took a turn trying to convince me to join them. Though I put up a playful fight, I knew it would be impossible. They would drag me out kicking and screaming in the end.

"Fine, I need to change first."

Olga walked over to the window, opened it, and looked down. "Okay, too far for you to escape, I suppose we can leave you alone for one moment," she snickered. "We'll wait in the living room."

I chuckled at her comment. If we lived in a ground-floor flat, I might have considered such a getaway.

All the girls left the room except for Karina. "Would you like me to help you pick something to wear?"

I nodded as she moved to the wardrobe. Her clothes had taken over most of it now, but I still had a few rarely worn dresses Frida convinced me to purchase in the last year.

"This would look lovely on you." She brought out a floral print dress that gathered at the waist, then dropped to a slim knee-length skirt.

I reached for it and placed it in front of me in the mirror. It had been a long time since I dressed up for anything.

"With your blue hat, it will be stunning." She squeezed me from behind.

"Thank you, Karina." Though I wanted to strangle her for making me go, I honestly looked forward to being with the girls. We still met almost every Sunday in the botanical garden, but each girl's life had begun to stray in varying directions. Ruta, Olga, and Karina had boyfriends, Inga and Aneta had made more friends their own age, and Katia spent much of her free time with Giselle's friends who participated in various causes around the city. The idea of us living different lives was exciting but equally disheartening.

"I'm ready." I stepped out to join the other girls as they visited with Frida and her fifteen-month-old son, Henry. I stepped over and tickled his neck and placed a kiss on each of his chubby cheeks. He was the most precious addition to our little family and stole my heart the moment he arrived. When Dr. Meier delivered his son, with Frida's permission, both Ruta and I assisted. It was the most incredible sight to behold.

"You look quite pretty." Ruta glanced over. "I don't think I've ever seen you in that dress."

"Because she's never worn it," Karina confirmed.

While the others laughed Frida placed a loving hand on my shoulder. "Our sweet Aleksandra loves to spend her free time at home or in the library and neither place requires this kind of attire."

"Thank you, Frida." I smiled.

The rest of the girls brushed it off and several reached for my arms. "Let's go. I've heard terrific things about this place."

"Okay." I shuffled forward slowly as if I were being led to prison, but I didn't say this out loud.

Katia leaned in on one side of me as we descended the stairs. "I'm so glad you're coming with us, I've missed you."

I chuckled, "I'm not the one who has become unavailable."

Her cheeks pinked.

"How is our charming Werner, anyway?"

She smiled. "He is doing well…very well."

I knew Katia was not the type to kiss and tell, but they had been spending a great deal of time together over the past year. They had to be progressing toward something more.

"Do you think he will propose?" I whispered again just in case she didn't want the others to hear.

"I hope so." She bit her lip and her eyes sparkled. "I never believed I could love someone so much. He is everything to me."

"Well, I'm sure if he were here, he would say the same thing about you." I wrapped one arm around her. "You deserve to be happy, I'm sure it won't be long before something wonderful comes to pass."

"And for you too, Aleksandra. I know the right person is out there for you, I just know it."

"I'm still a couple of years behind you, Katia, I can wait." I laughed and hugged her closer.

When we stepped into the café, we were immediately met with an energy that I rarely saw or felt at the hospital. Everyone inside was young, happy, and lively. No broken bones, burns, or screams of pain. In the center of the dimmed room, there were couples dancing…even kissing. Both young men in sharp attire and soldiers, donning their uniforms, flirted shamelessly with girls from one end to the other. I had no idea what to expect, but this was not it.

In the whirl of excitement, I reprimanded myself for fighting my friends and realized how close I came to passing this up. For the first time in what seemed to be ages, my body lifted with exhilaration and the anticipation of a night of merriment.

In one corner, a modest band struck up an animated tune as if it was just for us. Karina reached for my hand, and I easily let her lead me to the dance floor. "I've heard this song," she declared. "It's from a cabaret singer from France…a woman by the name of Édith Piaf. She's quite popular with the Germans."

I listened intently to the notes. They had an appealing flair to them, and I smiled at the way the music lightened my step.

Within minutes, willing dance partners appeared, and the pairing began.

"What's your name?" My new companion sported the short haircut and the angular jaw of a proud German man, and even before he smiled, a deep depression appeared on his chin. *Goodness, he was handsome!*

"Aleksandra." I nearly had to shout over the noise. "What about you?"

"Frederic." He probably would have shaken my hand had he not already held both of them as we swayed to the lyrical ballad. Though I hadn't danced in public often, Renia and I spent hours dancing in my bedroom to our favorite Polish tunes.

"Are you attending university?" he asked with genuine interest.

"No, I'm not a student. I work at a hospital."

"A nurse?"

"I will be when I pass my exam, but no, not yet."

"When is it?"

"What?"

"Your exam. When do you take it?" He twirled me under his arm.

"Next month."

"Well good luck." He smiled wide and my heart skipped a beat.

"Thank you! Are you on military leave?"

"Yes." He drew me in and out, then side to side. "But only for three more days."

"Are you from here?"

"No, I'm from Berlin. My unit is stationed just east of Dresden."

"Oh." My smile faltered. It had been two years since we walked to Dresden along the fated railroad tracks. The memory of that night, Günter, the soldiers' camp...*Hanna and Yetta.*

"Are you well?"

I peered up to find him staring at me. "Yes," I said, shaking myself back to the present. "Yes, it's just a little hot in here. I think I need a drink."

"Oh, allow me." He kept hold of one of my hands as he led me to a vacant table. With the manners of a gentleman, he pulled out my chair and waited for me to sit down. "What can I get for you to drink?"

"*Wasser*, please."

"Mit Kohlensäure?"

"Yes, gas, thank you." I suspected the bubbles might help settle my stomach.

I pulled out the linen handkerchief I had tucked into my dress pocket and wiped my face. It had been a long time since those nights of August 1941 reached the surface. Was Frederic part of the unit with Günter? *Maybe.* Do I dare ask?

"Here you go." Frederic placed a glass of water down on the table then sat in the chair next to me and lifted an amber-colored drink to his lips.

"May I ask you something?" I turned toward him.

He nodded and placed the glass down.

"I had a friend who was part of a military camp just east of here...like you. I wonder if you might know him."

"It's a large camp but it's possible."

"Large? How large?"

He smiled. "Now I can't give away all of our secrets."

"I, uh, I just recall him saying there was an abandoned village nearby, some burned-out structures and farms." I wasn't good at lying.

"Yes, yes that's the one."

My chest tightened. Could Frederic be part of the soldiers who were told to do awful things...things Günter refused to do?

"Who is your friend? Or is he a boyfriend?" He winked.

"No, nothing like that."

Frederic's smile broadened. "What's his name?"

"Günter."

"And his family name?"

I thought about it a moment. *He never told me.* "Uh, I don't know." I took a sip of my water.

He chuckled. "I'm sorry I don't know of any Günter, but I've also only been there three months. I was in Poland before that."

"Poland?" I nearly spit my drink across the table.

He nodded.

"Uh, wh—where in Poland were you?" I tried to force my words to come out casually.

"Warsaw. Have you been there?"

"No, I haven't." It was the truth. I hadn't gone that far away from home before.

"I was part of the initial occupation three years ago," Frederic spoke with pride. "The city was alright, but I much prefer it here." He winked. "I can't dance in Poland."

"I can't either," I mumbled.

He leaned his head to the side and held out his hand. "Then we shall do so here."

I nodded and stood up, recognizing the very different life I now led far, far away from my homeland.

CHAPTER TWENTY-EIGHT

3 January 1944

"OH, KATIA!" I lifted her left hand for closer inspection. "The ring is divine!" The striking gold band sparkled in the sunlight. I glanced over at a beaming Werner. His eyes lovingly beheld the woman at his side. "You did well, Herr Genau!"

"Thank you, Nurse Vogel."

I laughed out loud. It was the first time he had used this title and actually spoke the truth. I had passed my medical exams and earned the label of *nurse* officially one week ago. "I'm so happy for you both."

Katia hugged me, then paused, holding both my cheeks in her hands. "You might not be so happy when you hear the next bit of news."

"What?" I looked between them. A touch of anxiety developed in my chest. "What news?"

They looked at each other before Katia spoke. "Werner has been offered a curator position."

"But that's wonderful!" I cried out.

Her smile was tight. "Yes, yes, it is."

"What museum? Is it the Art Museum?"

"It is *an* art museum…. In Nuremberg."

"Nuremberg?" I bit my lip. "Oh." Fully aware this meant she would be several hours away, I hid my discouragement.

Werner wrapped an arm around his new fiancé's waist. "The Germanisches National Museum has offered me the assistant curator position." He kissed her on the cheek. "Katia encouraged me to accept it, though I knew I could not leave without her."

I smiled, watching the two of them. They belonged together.

Katia reached for me in a loving embrace and whispered in my ear. "I will miss you Aleksandra… Jaworski."

"I will miss you Katia Zieliński." I whispered back. "Does he know?"

She nodded. "He knows everything."

My heart swelled for her…swelled for them both. When she returned to Werner's side, my gaze dropped to his hands…the very hands I had wrapped for weeks. They clung tenderly to my dear friend and now his future wife. Though the streaked, fleshy scars remained, he had found a way to put them to good use.

I glanced back up to see him looking at me and, in that brief moment, we both seemed to recognize the unique twist in fate as our lives intersected.

There was no doubt in my mind that he and I met for *this* very purpose. Katia and Werner were always meant to be together.

That night, I wrote my parents another letter. I tried not to let my emotions cloud my words. Even though I was delighted for Katia and Werner, the idea of saying goodbye to yet another dear person in my life weighed heavily on my heart.

Mama i Tata,

I have wonderful news. I passed my exams to become a nurse and now I'm no longer an assistant but can administer to the patients with a great deal more responsibility. I enjoy the recovery ward, but the more I learn in the surgical room, the more I enjoy it.

Most of the nurses I work with are kind. There is only one who has sought to make me miserable. Two weeks ago, SS officers arrived at the hospital saying they had a report that I secreted a Jewish girl…which I would never risk. They confiscated my identification papers and put me in a room to be interviewed. I was detained for five hours. It wasn't until Dr. Meier interceded and not only spoke on my behalf but allowed our residence to be fully searched that they released me. Another nurse quietly confessed that she overheard Nurse Ingrid make the telephone call to the authorities that morning.

I'm certain you recall how the Germans treated the Jewish people in our hometown; it is just as troubling here, if not worse. If they find you have hidden a Jude in your home, you will face the same punishment as they… and be sent to a death camp. The same camps we had heard about years ago. I am angry with Nurse Ingrid but must be careful...for she is devious in her behavior.

I paused and retrieved an eraser. "I cannot write anything that would have them worried about me," I mumbled, then preceded to remove the detention story with the SS. This will only make them fret unnecessarily. I brushed the remnants of the eraser off the paper and filled in the space with words of positive accounts.

I have now helped nearly a dozen different patients from Poland. A family from Poznan, two brothers from Lubin, and a child from Opole. I don't know what I would do if I were to meet someone from Łódź ...I might embrace the person right then and there.

I ache to hear from you, to know that you are both well. We do not get much information in the press about Poland other than the military news. Tata, how is your health? And the dogs...do they miss me? Above all please do not worry about me. I am safe and happy and love Dresden. I never thought I could love any place other than my beloved Łódź, but it is beautiful here and the only thing that is missing is you.

Please write if you are able and address your post as follows...I will explain one day my reasons.

Aleksandra Vogel

3 Rosenstraße No. 12
01109 Dresden
Germany

CHAPTER TWENTY-NINE

July 1944

"Nurse Vogel?"

"Yes, Dr. Weber."

"I need you to translate for me. A young woman just arrived in the women's ward, and she only speaks Polish."

"Of course, sir, anything."

Dr. Weber had asked me to assist in this manner several times in the past couple of years and each time he did, I was thrilled to do it. Sometimes the request was for Polish, several times for Russian, and once it was for English for a British prisoner of war. It was the first time I had ever come face to face with a member of the Allied forces...the German enemy.

Though his injuries were severe, my interaction was intentionally kept brief the moment the German soldiers arrived to detain him. Apparently, he had ejected from his plane before it crashed outside of Dresden and was brought here by a farmer. The soldiers didn't even wait for a complete diagnosis before they apprehended him and transported him away.

This afternoon, when I arrived at the women's ward, nobody needed to point out the young Polish girl. I immediately knew who she was from the way she appeared. Most likely something quite close to how I did that first day here in Dresden. Broken, alone, and terrified of what my future held in a foreign country.

When I approached her, I smiled and spoke in Polish. "Hello, I'm Aleksandra. What's your name?"

Her eyes broadened with relief, and she reached for my hand. Rubbing it between both of hers she rattled off almost too quickly for me to follow. Though Polish would always be my native tongue, I no longer spoke it daily and only when I was alone with my friends.

"Slow down, please. I don't speak the language often enough."

"Nata, my name is Nata."

"Hello Nata, how old are you?"

"Fifteen."

"Okay. It appears you have an awful cut on your head." I placed the clipboard down on the bed and examined the wound on her left temple. "Do you hurt anywhere else?"

She pointed to her knee. The way the bone protruded through the thin fabric of her skirt could have indicated a break or merely a dislocation, but she wasn't shrieking in pain as one might expect.

"May I?"

She nodded.

I lifted her skirt up just above her knee for a better look, then I felt the bones through the swelling. Dislocation would be my guess. I glanced behind me; Dr. Weber hadn't appeared yet, so I quickly continued my questions in private.

"How did you arrive in Germany?"

Now her tears began, but she spoke through them.

"My family was traveling from Poland to Austria."

I tried to picture the route in my head, it would not have been an easy journey, especially knowing how severe the fighting had grown in the last few years. One could be certain there were more roads, bridges, and causeways bombed than three years ago. Plus, being Polish didn't help.

"Where is your family?"

"I don't know." She sobbed. I handed her a linen to wipe her face. "We were all together, then bombs came from the sky, and we were separated." She buried her face. "A tree fell down and I don't know what happened after that. I must've hit my head and fallen asleep. When I awoke, nobody was around."

"Nobody?"

She shook her head. I knew immediately I would need to contact Frida. We could let this girl think she was alone.

"How did you arrive at the hospital?" This piqued my interest since she surely couldn't walk with this type of injury.

She shook her head. "I don't know. I fell asleep again, then woke up here."

My eyebrows pinched. Her head injury might be worse than I thought, perhaps she was going in and out of consciousness.

"I would like to help you if I may?"

She kissed my hand.

"Where in Poland are you from?"

"The city of Łódź."

I gasped.

"What do we have here, Nurse Vogel?" Dr. Weber arrived behind me. Nata released my hand and drew backward.

It took a moment for me to catch my breath, reeling in her last words.

"Nurse?"

"Yes." I wiped my forehead and reached for my clipboard. "Her knee is injured, though it may only be dislocated and not broken. Then the gash on her head could use a few stitches. The blood has dried but it is still deep. From what I can gather, she was injured and possibly lost consciousness. She doesn't recall much, not even how she arrived here."

"I see. Will you please advise her that I need to check her injuries?"

I nodded and faced the girl. "Lekarz musi sprawdzić twoje obrażenia."

Fear shrouded her dainty features, but she still allowed Dr. Weber to examine her.

"I believe your assessment is correct, Nurse," he said with a hint of pride in his tone. He had always been one of my greatest advocates. "Please explain to her that I need to put her knee back in its rightful place and… it will hurt."

I relayed the information as I moved to her side and asked her to lie down, then wrapped both of my arms around her torso as Dr. Weber maneuvered the knee back into the joint. Though she cried out, it was not as much as I had expected. She might have a high threshold for pain or still be in shock.

"Nurse Vogel," he called. "Finish up with her sutures and she can be released within the hour but must not walk on the injury for a day or two."

"Doctor, I don't think there is anyone here for her." I bit my lip. I couldn't just let her go when she's so far from home without family.

"Then you must contact the Nationalsozialistische Volkswohlfahrt. They will know what to do."

My heart thumped nervously within my chest. The NSV was the social welfare run by the Nazis. Nata is Polish, she would surely be taken to one of those camps I'd heard about. "May I make a suggestion, sir?"

He nodded.

"Because she might be experiencing fleeting unconsciousness, maybe we should keep her overnight for observation first."

I glanced over to Nata with her frightened eyes. Thankfully, she couldn't understand what we were discussing, or she might have started crying again.

He rubbed his clean-shaven chin while he mulled it over. With one hand, he pointed to the empty beds in the room. "Since our occupancy is relatively low at the moment, I imagine we can accommodate her for one night."

Keeping my relief contained, I nodded. "Thank you, sir." This borrowed time would allow me the chance to speak to Frida and together we might come up with a plan.

After I explained to Nata the process of stitching her head, she proved to be a wonderful patient. She held completely still while I threaded seven sutures to close the deep gash in her head. I then washed the area with alcohol, applied a topical salve, and covered it with a bandage. The knee needed no other attention other than rest, for it would most likely be sore for a few days but should heal fully over time. As for her family...I had no idea how to fix that problem.

Before I left for the night, I returned to her side.

"Nata?" She appeared quite sleepy. "How are you feeling?"

"Better."

"Have you had any more trouble remembering or going unconscious like before?"

"Not like before." She sighed, "I just wish I knew where my parents went."

I nodded and patted her hand. I understood that more than she knew. "You can trust me to help you."

She smiled weakly. "Thank you, Aleksandra."

"I will see you tomorrow."

That night when I met with Frida, we had to act quickly to formulate a plan. At least with me and the other girls, we had more time to prepare. With Nata, we only had until tomorrow.

Needless to say, Frida did not surprise or fail me. She arranged to have another bed brought into our shared room temporarily until we found her a home where speaking Polish would not be a problem.

The following evening when we stepped through the door of the Meier residence, Nata's expression seemed vaguely familiar to mine that first day.

"Nata, this is my sister, Karina."

Karina didn't hesitate and stepped forward for a sound embrace. Nata was surprised but welcomed the gesture, especially when Karina spoke in Polish.

Because of the need for discretion, I had not fully informed Nata of our background or what awaited her here, but once we were in the privacy of our home, we had nothing to fear.

"We…" I pointed to both of us. "Are also from Łódź."

Her mouth gaped open, and tears formed in the corners of her eyes.

"We came from Poland three years ago."

"I cannot believe it," she squealed. "Truly?"

"Yes." I smiled at her excitement.

"Oh, I am amongst my own people." She clasped her hands in front of her.

I continued, "We are anxious to hear of any news of home. What can you tell us?"

It took her a few moments to form any words. Tears fell freely down her cheeks. Karina retrieved a handkerchief. Nata happily accepted it but stared at the delicate lace in disbelief. "This is lovely," she said while fondling the fabric.

"You will find many lovely things here." I smiled.

She shook her head and continued to sniffle. "Łódź is…it is in a dreadful state."

My breathing increased while the worst scenarios came to mind. "Has it been destroyed?"

"Not destroyed…not the buildings really, but the people…the people are downtrodden, hopeless. There is nothing but sorrow and grief."

Karina came to my side with this news and buried her head in my shoulder. I could feel her weeping under my touch.

"That is why my family tried to leave. There is nothing for us there. Even the ghetto has been cleared. No more Jews, Romani, or such. It's only soldiers…" She placed her hands over her face. "Soldiers who hurt."

I reached for her with my other arm and pulled her close. She didn't need to elaborate. As I rubbed her hair, I hummed the tune of "Ta Dorotka"—a traditional Polish lullaby.

When both girls had stopped crying, I stepped away to prepare some tea for them both. When I returned, I placed the tray on the table before them. "Have something to drink. The warmth will make you feel better."

"Thank you, Aleksandra. You have been so kind."

I picked up the teapot and poured the hot water into a cup. "I used to have tea every day after school with my neighbor. She was the one who taught me English." I laughed. "She had learned it herself by watching British television for many years, then she would have me practice on the baker on Łąkowa Street. He—"

"Łąkowa?"

I nodded.

"Pan Kowalski?" she cried with a lift in her voice.

"You know him?"

"Yes, he is in my neighborhood."

I set the cup down. "Polesie?"

She nodded vigorously.

"Do you happen to know Szymon Jaworski, my father, the politician?"

She gasped lightly, then pulled her lips tight. When she looked away, I panicked. "Nata, tell me."

"I know your family," she mumbled.

"And…?"

She met my eyes again. "They are alive."

I gasped, letting out all the air I'd been holding in. *They're alive!* I felt faint. Grasping for the edge of the sofa, I stumbled to sit before I fell to the floor

"They live in the flat below us, one floor down."

"No." I shook my head. "That can't be them. We lived in a house on Moltke."

"I'm sure it is the same Szymon Jaworski…the official. My father says the people are angry with him. They feel betrayed."

"How?" My voice rose slightly.

"He helped the Germans. He worked with them."

Karina watched the exchange with wide eyes.

"Papa didn't work *with* them," I snapped. "The Germans threatened to kill his family…to kill me, my brother, and our mother."

Karina sat next to me, this time it was she who wrapped a comforting arm around me. When I glanced back up at Nata, she was crying. "I'm sorry, Aleksandra, I didn't mean to upset you. Maybe it isn't the same man. The one I know…he—he cannot walk."

I gasped, then broke down crying myself. "Neither can my papa."

Nata knelt on the floor before me and took my hands into hers. "His wife pushes him outside in a special chair. The dog seems to make him happy."

I released our hold to wipe my eyes. "The dog? Only one?"

She nodded.

"Do you remember the dog's name? Or what he looked like?"

She wrinkled her nose. "A light brown dog with black ears. Um…Wilt, I believe." She tilted her head in thought.

"Wilk," I whispered.

"Yes," she said. "That's it. Wilk." She stood back up. "I'm truly sorry if I upset you."

"No," I shook my head. "You have brought me the best news I can imagine. My parents are alive. They are well." *And not refusing my letters…they are being sent to the wrong address.*

"Do you know how they live?"

"Our neighbors have your mother mend their clothes. I believe she might be a seamstress."

A seamstress? I was astonished she had been laboring like all the women we had once hired to do that very work for us.

"Do you know anything of their son? My brother, Ivan?"

"No. I wish I could tell you more. They mostly keep to themselves."

I stood up and hugged her tightly. Thank you, thank you for telling me this."

When I drew back, the look on her face paralleled mine. I knew precisely what she was thinking.

"We will do our best to help you find answers too, Nata."

Her smile appeared slightly more relaxed. "Thank you for taking care of me. I don't know where I would have gone."

"You are safe here." Frida smiled broadly as she swept into the room with her typical grace. "And you will adore your roommates." She smiled and pointed to Karina and me.

I grinned in response, wondering just how many times Frida has said those very same words all these years…most likely many more times than I might ever know.

CHAPTER THIRTY
12 February 1945

PLACING THE ALBUTEROL vials back into the cupboard, I locked it before I slipped the key into my apron pocket next to an envelope—the newest letter to my parents that I had failed to post before my shift began.

Recently there had been a rash of mysterious thefts in both the ward and the dispensary, so the doctors asked the nurses to be more vigilant in their rounds and make sure the patients were not left unattended at any time during the day or night. Although, both the hospital and Dresden in general, remained unscathed by the growing anxiousness of the population as the Allied forces made their way across the western border and toward the Rhine River, there were still some who behaved rather neurotically with the news.

Turning around to face Herr Turner, I smiled. He rested comfortably in his usual bed and the light rise and fall of his chest indicated the medication was infiltrating his lungs properly. In the four years I had known him, he had come to be an unusual friend. Though his dramatics never ceased, he often brought a smile to my face at the most unexpected moments and generally after Nurse Ingrid had reprimanded me for one thing or another.

"Rest well, Herr Turner," I whispered as I neared the end of a twelve-hour shift and closed the drapes on the window closest to him.

"Nurse?" A throaty call came from the newest patient nearby.

The man had undergone surgery to remove his left foot, which had grown infected with gangrene as he fled through the forest, and he was just awaking from the sedatives. For the last three days, he had been in and out of consciousness and mumbled so incoherently that nobody had understood him...although twice, I suspected his words to be of Polish origin, his papers proved otherwise.

"Nurse?" he repeated as I peeked toward the doorway. Despite my long shift, my replacement hadn't yet arrived, so I picked up his chart and moved to his side.

"How are you feeling…Herr Müller?"

"Symanski," he mumbled.

My eyes shot to his as they flitted open. He winced as if in agony but held my stare. "Pardon me?" I leaned in.

"Symanski is my given name." He coughed and groaned again. "Müller is for the Germans."

My mouth parted, but nothing came out for several seconds. When I finally spoke, it came out nearly as hoarse as him. "Why do you say this, I am German."

"No." He shook his head vigorously. "You are Polish, I see it in your features."

My breath quickened and I drew back. "Y—you are mistaken, sir, I am from Munich. A city south of here."

His lips pulled into a frown. "No, Fraulein, do not insult me. I have spent fifty-eight years in Poland. I know these things and you are Polish."

"I—I, uh, I am Nurse Vogel f—from Munich."

He tried sitting up but flinched, surely from the throbbing that assaulted his left leg.

"Please keep still, Herr Müller, you don't want to irritate the wound."

"Symanski!" He yelled a bit louder. "If I must die here, I want the last thing I hear to be my family name spoken from a fellow Pole!"

I glanced nervously about. Thankfully, the few patients present remained asleep. "Y—you will not die; you will survive this ordeal."

He wiped his sweaty forehead and smirked. "You have forgotten."

"Forgotten what?"

"What they have taken from us."

My heart stilled. *I could never forget.*

"You can change your location, Fraulein, but you cannot change your genetics."

Bungling through his chart once more, I read the last entry with blurred sight. "You must be suffering from delirium, sir." I could hear my voice quivering. "I will get you something for the pain."

Before I could step back, he gripped my arm. "Do not forget about your people, Nurse. Do not forget your heritage."

Tears built in my eyes as I made my way toward the dispensary. I fumbled with the keys until I found the right one and opened the door. Leaning against the closest shelf, I exhaled as a volley of tears slid down my cheeks. "I have not forgotten about my people," I whispered. "I miss my people."

The sound of footsteps coming in my direction had me standing back to my normal height and swiftly brushing the wetness off my cheeks. The footsteps stopped.

I held my breath for only a second. I had nothing to worry about, I was a certified nurse now and could enter the dispensary as needed. I held still. Why hadn't the person entered yet? Or walked away? As the seconds stretched, I imagined it only to be Hannah, my replacement, or just another orderly coming to retrieve medication, but when Nurse Ingrid's red, pinched face appeared in the doorway, my breath hitched.

"I knew it!" she hissed. "I knew you were not who you say you are."

I folded my arms across my chest...partly to stop their trembling and partly to show I did not fear her. "What are you talking about?"

"I heard everything, *Polish* girl."

"I am not Polish. I am German." I managed to keep my lips from quivering.

Her mouth lifted in a shrewd grin. "You can deny it all you like, but now I have proof. I will have your counterfeit identity exposed...you little *Schlampe*." She stepped inside. "You will finally get what you deserve."

"What proof?" It would be her word against mine if she was going to try and use the conversation with the delirious patient.

"This!" She lifted a folded piece of paper.

I squinted until I recognized the handwriting...*it was mine*. My hand flew to my pocket. I must've dropped it outside the door when I retrieved my key. In that brief second, I tried to recall all that I had said to my parents. I never used my real name...then gasping as if the air in the room had evaporated, I recalled how careless I had been in talking about how much I missed Łódź and assured them of my return once the war was over.

Fumbling, my fingers clutched the sides of my apron as I backed out of the room and turned on my heels and fled—a sure sign of my guilt, but I could not face her any longer. My resolve had been weakened by the memories of my past. I didn't even retrieve my sweater on my way out and ran the entire distance to my home.

Once inside, I rushed to my room only to find Karina and Nata present. I backed away as sweat and tears distorted my vision and tightened my throat.

"Aleksandra?" Karina called.

I ignored her and ran to the living room where Frida met me and reached

174

out to stop me in place. The advancement in her second pregnancy did not impede her nimbleness. "What has happened?"

I trembled in her hands until she led me to the couch and forced me to sit by her side.

I lowered my head into my palms and sobbed as Frida rubbed my back. She let me cry for several minutes before she asked again. "Please tell me what happened, Aleksandra."

I sniffled and took several cleansing breaths before I spoke. "I have been found out."

"What do you mean found out?"

"Nurse Ingrid, the nurse who has caused me such grief…she knows I am from Poland and suspects my papers are counterfeit. She won't hesitate to report my fraud." I peered over to see Frida's lips tightly pursed.

When she finally answered, she spoke with a surety I lacked. "You have nothing to fear." She lifted her chin. "I will speak to Liam about this, we *will* protect you."

"The last time she apprised the authorities, soldiers came to the hospital."

She patted my hand. "You are not scheduled to work tomorrow and with the *Carnival* festivities, the authorities are otherwise detained. I assure you, Aleksandra, they will not have the time or resources to seek out a solitary nurse on a day like tomorrow."

I marveled at Frida's confidence even while I shook uncontrollably beside her. "You are certain?"

"The process will be days before they can manage to give up even one soldier who would otherwise be handling the crowds and, by then, you will not be found. Trust me, love, I have lived here my whole life. I have seen the entire city turn out for Carnival."

It was strange for me to believe I could put this all behind me and enjoy music and pastries and costumes with the looming threat of losing my freedom. "What if they force me back into the Lebensborn program? Or take me to one of those camps we've heard of."

"My dear…" Frida patted my hand. "We are family, and family protects one another. We will take advantage of the time we have and concoct a new plan."

"Aleksandra?" Karina stood in the entryway. "Are you well?"

I glanced over and schooled my features. She was the last person I wanted to alarm.

I nodded. "I had a difficult time at work today, but I will be fine."

Frida smiled back at Karina as Nata joined her. "You will have a lovely time tomorrow and forget all about your worries. Make sure you are up and dressed early, we want to view the floats before the parade."

That night, I struggled to fall asleep. The sinking feeling in my stomach told me that my time at the hospital was over. I could not return unless Ingrid was silenced and that was unlikely. *How could I have been so foolish?* I was not aware she was nearby when Pan Symanski questioned me, though I thought I had defended my nationality well enough. But what ultimately exposed me was the letter. I had been warned by Liam and Frida before about my personal correspondence, but in light of their new address, I needed to write.

Turning to my side, I listened to Karina's soft breaths in the darkness. I had taken a terrible risk by not posting the missive first thing in the morning and I have now brought misfortune upon myself and possibly my friends.

Turning in the other direction, I could not settle my body or my thoughts. When Dr. Meier returned home, he and Frida's whispers through the thin wall that separated us did little to assure me…especially when I heard the words…*we must send her away.*

Lying flat on my back, once more, tears tickled my skin as they leaked out. *What would the authorities do if they discovered my papers were falsified?* They didn't notice the subterfuge before when Ingrid accused me of hiding the Jewish girl, but now that a second complaint would be registered, they may look more closely. Then what would happen if they discovered who doctored my papers? We could all be sent away and Henry would become an orphan. Pulling the pillow over my face, I tried to keep my whimpers silent. I may have just sentenced this entire family to death.

CHAPTER THIRTY-ONE

13 February 1945

"Goodnight, my handsome prince."

"Night, Ante Alek. Tank you for take me to Carval." Henry's little two-and-a-half-year-old body sagged when his head hit the pillow. The boy, who was a spitting image of his father, had me wrapped around his pinky finger the moment he entered this world.

"Thank you for coming to Carnival with me, little pig." I kissed his cheek. Traces of cinnamon sugar stuck to my lips from the pretzel he had eaten earlier. I removed his little pink snout off his face and the pointy ears off his head as he snuggled deeper into the blanket. My heart swelled with happiness for him and his parents, then sank just as I thought of my own mother and father. Three and a half years ago, I left Poland and no matter what I have done to move on, the hole in my heart remained. I missed them terribly.

"That boy is going to break hearts one day, Frida." I slipped into one of the sitting room chairs as she snuggled closer to Liam on the couch. Her large protruding stomach made any position uncomfortable except for the one right next to her husband. He draped one arm around her and rubbed her belly with the opposite hand as the chime on the mantel clock struck ten o'clock.

"Yes," she mumbled nearly asleep herself. "That is entirely my husband's fault." She giggled lucidly. "For being so devastatingly handsome."

I chuckled.

Nata occupied the chair opposite of me and rested her head sluggishly against her arm. Her eyes were closed, but she wasn't quite asleep. "I go home," she mumbled in broken German. "If I wait, you not move me." She had taken over Katia's position now helping Giselle's children and while her German was coming along…I had already heard more than one Polish word surface from the oldest son's mouth. I chuckled at this discovery.

An air raid siren shrilled in the distance.

I looked to the Meiers, who did not even jump. We had heard the alarms so often now they had become commonplace. Removing my own pink pointy ears off my head, I fingered the plush fur and reflected on the day.

Despite the lingering fears concerning Nurse Ingrid's threats, it had been heavenly, enjoying the traditional celebrations of *Fastnacht* in the city center. Just as Frida had anticipated, Dresden's streets overflowed with patrons of all ages, delicious food, wild revelries, and endless parades. The costumes all ranged from storybook characters like Hansel and Gretel or, in our case, the Three Little Pigs, to jesters, or witches and devils with their peculiar wooden masks.

"Stay, Nata," I encouraged. "Giselle already knows you walked home with us tonight. She won't mind. Besides, I think that third mug of *Glühwein* she had, might've made her quite sleepy. She won't even know you're gone."

Both Meiers laughed hazily in response.

"And you can sleep in Karina's bed," I suggested, stifling a yawn of my own.

Nata lifted her head. "Where is she?"

"She's with Peter…" I snickered. "Which means she might not come home at all."

"She better," Liam vowed. "Or that boy won't be allowed anywhere near this place."

Frida playfully slapped his hand. "Oh, Liam. You remember what it was like to be young and in love, don't you?"

He nuzzled his face into her neck as she giggled.

I watched their interaction and grew serious. "Frida, Liam?" They slowly peered my way. "Have you given any further thought to what I should do or where I should go?" Glancing at Frida's stomach, I winced. "I can't go back to the hospital, and you will need the extra bedroom for the baby."

Frida's eyes went wide. She appeared fully awake now. "Aleksandra, don't." But Liam hushed her gently. This really had been an ongoing discussion. We had overstayed our welcome by a couple of years as it was. Karina had already made plans to move in with Helene, and now, my foolish actions had accelerated my departure as well.

"Please don't." Frida's voice squeaked.

Liam squeezed her shoulders. "Stay calm, dear. You know that she must leave until this mess is sorted. We talked about this."

"No." She had quite the mother's authoritarian voice when she wanted one. "You said Nurse Ingrid might be swayed with the right coercion." Then she looked to me. "The infant will be in our room for several months, then can share with Henry."

When I met Liam's eyes, concern crept into his features. I swallowed hard. "You mentioned an uncle in Leipzig, Liam."

"No!" Frida struggled to her feet while Dr. Meier tried to keep her seated and relaxed.

"It's only temporary, love, until this blows over."

I turned to the wonderful woman who had cared for me as much as a mother would. "I cannot risk bringing trouble to your family. You have your children to think about."

Tears instantly spilled down her cheeks. Liam tenderly cupped his wife's face and brushed her eyes with his lips. They had shown me over the years how truly wonderful love can be. Turning in my direction, he whispered, "Aleksandra, we will discuss the details in the morning."

My heart caught in my throat. "I—I will miss you b—"

BOOM! BOOM! BOOM! BOOM!

A succession of explosions rocked the room so rapidly, that we nearly fell over. Terror put a stranglehold on my body until I forced myself to move. Scrambling for clarity, I beat the others to the window and yanked back the long drapes to see fire light up in the distance. **BOOM! BOOM! BOOM!** Another round of loud assaults seemed to collide with structures in the distant darkness. Bursts of random light sprouted against a blackened horizon. I searched Liam's face for a reason as he held Frida's shaking body next to his side. Nata was instantly next to me, gasping for air.

"We are being bombed!" I yelled as another round of earsplitting booms continued. Henry's door flew open with a bang and his screams were heard before his footsteps. Frida ran toward him with her awkward, clumsy gate and threw her arms around him. A curly, pink tail from his costume protruded from behind. The floor groaned and shook and when Liam rushed to get to his family, he lost his footing and fell to his knees. Clambering toward them, he crawled forward and pulled both of them into a protective, huddled ball.

I faced the window once more to witness another rapid chain of explosions light up buildings as far away as the palace and as near as the building two streets away. I cowered as the window rattled and a large crack split the glass in half. Balls of glowing fire appeared before me in all pockets of my vision. I pinched my arm. Am I dreaming? Did I fall asleep in the chair?

The next explosion caused the glass to shatter.

"We have to get out of here. It isn't safe!" Liam hollered above the crashing sounds. I ran toward the others and tried to help when a rumbling sound shook us violently where we stood. I only caught part of Frida's horrified expression. Had we been hit? Was our building going to collapse? Liam lifted his wife to her feet as she clung desperately to Henry. "We have to go now!" Liam pointed to the door.

The floor continued to roll and rattle as we made our way to the front. Liam grabbed his keys that hung from a small hook at the entry and sheltered his family as we and many of the other residents of the building stumbled our way out of our apartments and toward the stairwell. I grabbed one of Nata's hands and forced her to clutch the hem of my blouse while I pushed through.

Bodies were smashed together in the rush, and many were being forced backward. With every step we took, more and more people descended upon us. With a hugely pregnant woman and a child, we were being overtaken. Though Frida tried desperately to cling to both her husband and child, she was losing her grip. Liam reached for the screaming Henry clutched in Frida's arms and pushed him into mine. "Take Henry!" he yelled. "I will see to Frida!"

A nearly inconsolable Henry wrapped his tiny arms around my neck as I tried to get through the narrow entry to the stairs but failed. Losing sight of Liam and Frida, I panicked until I remembered the fire escape. I glanced over to the opposite end of the hallway. One man had already opened the window and was helping a woman through. If we could get there before it became mobbed, we could get down the side easier than fighting the crowd.

BOOM! BOOM! BOOM!

Henry and I were thrown against the wall, and Nata lost her grip. "Stay with me, Nata!" I screamed and reached for her again. She met my fingers as we raced toward the window. I pushed Henry's face into my chest and regained composure. "Henry, do not let go of me. Do you hear me? Do not let go!"

I could hear his whimpered response and, after forcing Nata through the window first, I maneuvered through with Henry. The man and woman who had gone before us had reached the level below and began lowering the ladder. I turned around to see a crowd of people now headed in our direction and hustled to rush down the steps to avoid getting trampled.

Thankfully, as I climbed down Henry did as he was told and wound his arms tightly around my neck. Every move I made had to be swift to keep the people who followed us from overtaking us.

Once I took the final leap to the walk below, I squeezed the frightened boy tenderly. "You are doing so good, Henry. Keep your head down."

"Mama," he cried. "I want my mama!"

I leaned in and whispered in his ear. "We are going to see them very soon." I pressed one hand over his eyes to shield them, though it seemed impossible to protect him from a sky that seemed to light up like the fiery pits of hell.

With Nata at my side, I moved toward the front entrance and looked anxiously at each person who ran out. After several minutes, Liam exited carrying a very weak Frida in his arms. We caught their attention the moment a hand gripped my shoulder. I nearly jumped out of my skin.

"Karina!" I screamed. "I thought you were with Peter."

She hugged me briefly. Her body practically convulsing. "He's here." She glanced at Henry and Nata. "Where are Liam and Frida?" she cried.

"Over there." I pointed to the front steps as they descended.

Liam shouted in our direction. "To the car! It's down the lane!"

I nodded and gripped Henry tighter. "Stay with us, Karina."

With Peter right behind her, she gripped my elbow as I jogged through the growing masses of people. Many now were sitting or lying in complete exhaustion on the walkway. "Get up!" I shrieked, though I didn't even know them. "Get out of here!" I screamed.

For some strange reason, they must've believed they would be safe now that they were outside of the building. Though the tall structures concealed some of the attack from below, I had seen the worst of it from our windows. Certainly, the horror I had seen was only the beginning. Even now, you could hear the enemy's engines roaring through the air. This was *not* over!

BOOM! BOOM! BOOM! The blasts continued unceasingly, and somehow in the hollow of the night, they echoed and shook with unimaginable force. I glanced around at the buildings that surrounded us and prayed we were not the next target.

Karina, Peter, Nata, Henry, and I reached the automobile first, but within seconds, Liam and Frida appeared. She frantically reached for Henry and sobbed. "This was never supposed to happen..." Her cries multiplied. "Not here! Not Dresden!"

With trembling hands, Liam managed to get his car unlocked and both his wife and child inside the front beside him. Karina, Peter, Nata, and I dove inside the backseat as the automobile roared to life. It was not built for four people in the back, but that did not matter at this moment, we just needed to get out of there as quickly as possible.

Shifting the car into gear, Liam tore out of the alleyway and swerved erratically in his attempts to maneuver the roads. Though several other cars joined ours in similar attempts to escape, most people were on foot. Pedestrians were now running wildly in all directions and became our biggest obstacle.

Liam mumbled incoherently to himself on which direction to get out of the city as Frida shouted conflicting directions. Peter huddled against one door and buried his head in his arms and Nata coiled up on the floor between Karina and me. I peered back through the rear window and watched in horror as the deafening sounds of large bombs dropped rapidly from the sky. The outline of teardrop-like bombs dropped one right after another, easily ripping open the roofs of buildings. Then, as if this was calculated, a second wave of smaller missile-like flames followed the big ones and torched each structure from the inside out. I watched in horror as this process repeated over and over and entire buildings exploded on contact behind us, crumbling to the ground within seconds.

"I have never seen anything so awful." Karina sobbed, then thrust her head into my shoulder to shelter herself from the scene. I didn't blame her. Peter continued to mutter incoherently by her side without lifting his head. Though at times he appeared older than his seventeen years, his fear made him seem very childlike.

"Verdammit!" Liam cried from the front seat. He had wound around several buildings and ended up only a short distance from where we started.

"Stay away from the factories, they're probably trying to target those," Frida cried with a whimpering child still huddled against her.

I shook my head. "I'm not so sure." I pointed in the direction of the anti-aircraft factory and gun factories on the outskirts of town, and each remained untouched in the blackness. "They seem to be targeting the city."

As more and more buildings lit up in the rear window, the warmth from the flames began to seep through. I touched the glass. The heat that stung my fingers was hotter than touching a jamb stove directly. I pulled it back and wrapped my arms around Karina tighter. Though we knew it was night, the fire lit up the sky as if it was midday.

Liam continued to maneuver madly in all different directions. Sometimes he was on the walkways and alleyways and other times in the gardens. It didn't seem to matter which way we went, explosions continued in every direction.

"If I can just get to the bomb shelter, we will be alright."

"*The* bomb shelter?" I cried from the back. "There's only one?"

Liam grumbled. "I told Jörg over and over we weren't equipped for this kind of attack. We were too vulnerable." He was speaking of his best friend who worked for the government. I had met him several times when he came over for supper.

"No, Liam!" Frida cried as she covered Henry's eyes. "Everyone will be heading to the shelter. There won't be enough space for all of us."

"Where to then?"

"Go toward the Elbe. Cross the Augustus, just get us out of this city."

Liam pressed the gas harder and worked his way away from the town center, but it was obvious the bombers, whoever they were, didn't really seem to have any specific targets. They were hitting anything and everything.

The longer we were in the car, the more obstacles we had to face. As Liam turned down one road filled with people, he rotated his steering wheel to the left and drove through a park. The booms never stopped, and between the thunderous crackles, screams filled the air. I placed my hands over my ears in an attempt to drown out the awful sounds.

Another bomb went off to the left of us and the impact rattled our car, raining rocks upon us. One such rock hit the back window and it shattered, spraying glass all over us. I had the foresight to close my eyes, but I could feel the shards land in my hair and on top of my clothes. When I moved to shake them off, needle-like pinches cut my skin.

"You're bleeding!" Karina shouted when she lifted her head.

I pointed back to her and Peter. "We all are." Small streaks of blood seeped from each of us.

"But you're covered, Aleksandra."

Frida glanced back and tore her sweater off and threw it at me. "Use this," she cried. I unbuttoned my blouse as carefully as possible keeping the largest pieces inside though my fingers were sliced several times, then threw it out the back window and put Frida's sweater over me. It didn't remove all the glass, but it seemed to help.

"Careful, Nata. Stay down." She hadn't moved from the floor, but I feared she might now with the glass falling upon her.

Liam turned briefly back toward us. "Wait until we get somewhere safe, then I will pull over and we can brush the glass out. Just keep still for now."

When he looked forward again, a man stepped right in front of our car. Liam slammed on his breaks but still hit the man. His body draped over the hood.

"Scheisse!" Liam shouted. Everyone gasped at the sight of this man with half of his face crusted and burnt.

Liam put the car in neutral and braked.

"No! Liam! No!" Frida screamed, trying to reach for him as he opened his door. "Do not get out!"

"I cannot drive with a man on the hood," he hollered back. "And I cannot run him over."

Frida begged and cried as Liam stepped out of the car and removed the man, placing him to the side. When I glanced around, I recognized the street. The hospital was nearby. *Our hospital.* Liam must've realized this at the same time and looked over in the direction of the building. Though I didn't see his expression, I was certain his heart was as heavy as mine as hordes of people descended on the clinic. Some were being carried while others walked but catching sight of their scorched injuries was unavoidable.

I gripped Karina closer as another round of bombs sounded in the distance. So many all at once, I wasn't sure they would ever stop. We cowered at the sound. When I glanced back up, I saw dozens of people running and falling to the ground. Outside, Liam was frozen in place. A woman appeared next to him with what appeared to be her own flesh cradled in her hands.

"Liam!" Frieda shrieked. "Liam, get in!"

He shook off his shock and moved back to the car but in that instant, he flung the back door open and pulled me out. My shoes no doubt hit Nata in the head. Screams erupted once more both from the front and back as Liam shoved me forcefully into the driver's seat.

"What are you doing?" Frida screamed.

Liam grabbed my hands and placed them on the wheel. "Drive!" he yelled, "Go, get out of here!"

My eyes widened in shock. I had only learned how to drive a month ago.

"No!" I screamed in unison with his wife.

"No, no, no!" She cried and clawed past me to get to him. Karina reached over and pulled Henry into the back seat with her and Peter.

Liam reached past me and held his wife's face in his hands. Getting very close, he sobbed. "Frida! My love! I am a doctor, I cannot leave, I cannot turn my back on these wounded people." He cried through every word.

"But you are *my* husband!" she screamed. "Get in the car this instant!"

He shook his head. Tears streamed down both their faces. He backed out and slammed the door. Through the window, he yelled. "Go! Aleksandra!" His palm slammed against the window. "Take them to safety!" he hollered again. "Go to Leipzig! I will find you. Drive now!"

I released the brake and pushed the clutch, thrusting the automobile into first gear, then pressed the gas.

Frida clawed at me and fought to get to the key, but her oversized belly prevented her from reaching it. I placed one hand out to gently push her back, but she convulsed and thrashed wildly, screaming so unintelligibly, one would think she herself was burning to death.

Karina tried in vain to calm Henry down in the back, but at the sight of his mother's outburst, he shrieked nearly as loud. The inside of the automobile was as frenzied as the scene around us.

Racing down the road toward the bridge with the same fervency that Liam did, I shook violently as my hands gripped the steering wheel. *He told me to go,* I justified. Tears streamed madly down my cheeks. *He told me to get his family to safety!* I didn't look at Frida, and I tried hard to block out her cries until we reached another road, then another, and another.

By the time I hit a road where there were no longer flames in front of us and only behind, Frida's screams had reduced to agonizing cries as she wilted against her door. Her body showed all the signs of hopelessness.

What was I to do? I screamed in my head. Liam gave me no choice. We would have all perished if I had remained still. I battled every possible scenario in my head. Could I have grabbed Liam and forced him back into the car? The man was stronger and taller than me! Should I have fought him and jumped in the backseat again, compelling him to drive once more?

Though the booms never ceased, the more distance we gained, the explosions no longer rattled the car. In the darkness, both fire and flame seemed to grow like spilled ink on a canvas, but mercifully, it was now only seen from the rearview mirror.

And I continued to drive and drive and drive.

CHAPTER THIRTY-TWO

Kilometer after kilometer passed but I didn't stop. I didn't want to see the glowing yellow anywhere in my sights, though it seemed impossible to avoid.

I finally pulled over to a side road and turned off the car. Frida scrambled out first, but we all followed and faced the direction of what used to be our beloved city. Above the trees, a glowing halo ascended. Dresden was one massive inferno.

New sounds erupted overhead, bringing our eyes to the sky…the horrifying roar of engines sounded from above. The enemy wasn't finished. Frida fell to the ground and hit the dirt screaming. "No, please no."

I tried to stop her from hurting herself. "The baby, Frida. Think of the baby."

She looked at me with horror. "My husband, Aleksandra!" she whimpered, her voice hoarse and strained.

Henry continued to sob in Karina's arms as I looked at the sky. The outline of more aircraft passed the limited light of the moon and stars above. In the distance, more explosions erupted…it was a second wave of bombers. *They aren't going to stop until everything in Dresden is destroyed. Nobody will survive this attack.*

"Why did you leave him?" Frida shrieked. I had never seen her so angry. Her eyes were swollen red. She stood and pulled at her dress and her hair with a fierceness I had never seen. Facing me, she sobbed, then charged at me crying out loud. "Why did you leave him? Why?" Shaking me, I acceded to her accusations in a wave of cries of my own. "Why?" She fell to the ground once more as if her spirit had departed, leaving the shell of her body.

Sobbing, I knelt down. "Because he told me to, Frida. You saw what he did. He told me to save his family!" She beat the ground with her fists until she could no longer move. I inched closer to her and tried to put my arms around her. She shrugged them off at first, then finally let me hold her. I leaned my head against hers and wept. "Liam knew we would die if we stayed, and he wanted you to live."

"He should've come with us. He should've come!" She looked back over to the orange sky and the destruction we left behind.

Cradling her head, I whispered, "You are the one who told me he valued life above all. You know he could not see what we saw and not do something."

She wailed.

"You know more than anyone the kind of man he is."

She looked at me with eyes practically swollen shut from crying. "But there were so many, Aleksandra. Too many to help."

My eyes flitted back over to the deadly glow in the distance. Anger surged through my veins. *Why? Why did he do that?* Liam should be with his family. He should not have gotten out of the car.

We sat on the ground paralyzed in grief, unable to make sense of the attack. We were exhausted yet charged.

Once Frida gathered her senses, she reached out for a weary and traumatized Henry and held him in her arms as best she could. We sat in total silence for what could have been hours, time seemed to swallow us whole.

Peter never left the car while Karina and Nata joined us on the ground. Karina leaned her head on my shoulder. "Why Leipzig?" she asked. "Why did he say to go there?"

Frida wiped her nose. "Because that's where his uncle lives," she mumbled. "He knew we would be safe there." She stared down at Henry who had finally succumbed to his exhaustion and shock and, despite all, slept peacefully in her arms.

I stood to my feet. "Then that's where we must go." I reached down and lifted the sleeping child from his mother's arms and held him until she climbed back into the front seat and placed him in her embrace once again.

Turning back to Karina and Nata, I hugged them tightly. It was sheer luck Karina arrived home at the same time we were leaving. If it had been a mere ten seconds later, we could have missed her. I kissed her cheek. I could not bear the thought of what could have been.

Opening the back door, I turned my attention to Peter. "We are going to Leipzig. I am not sure how to get there, but if we keep Dresden behind us, we should be safe."

Peter's head lifted abruptly. He stepped out of the car with a strange determination. "I have to go back."

"What?" Karina and I questioned at the same time. "You can't go back."

Karina choked out and ran to his side.

Though Peter covered his face for most of our escape, he could not have missed the horror that we had fled from.

"I cannot leave my family there." He pointed to the orange blaze off in the distance. "I cannot run away."

Karina leaned forward and gripped his shoulders. "You aren't thinking clearly, Peter. The city is destroyed. There can't be many survivors."

Frida wailed from the front seat.

I stepped toward the teenagers and whispered. "Peter, please be smart. Let's get to Leipzig first, then we can arrange to get you back there once it's safe to return."

"No!" He shouted, "I am going back now."

Heat singed my cheeks. "*We* are not going back. We are going to Leipzig." I tried to keep my voice even, but I could feel it faltering still. "If you insist upon returning, you must find a way on your own."

Peter let out a long string of cuss words and turned his back to us as he started swiftly down the road we had just traveled.

Karina ran after him. "Please, don't do this, Peter."

He didn't turn around.

"Please, please come back." The heartache in her voice ascended above all the other sounds, but Peter continued on. She finally dropped to her knees and sobbed.

Within seconds, we could no longer see his silhouette. I had no idea where we were or how far we had come. Our only focal point was the bright flames that rose in the night sky. I didn't even know if the road we were on would take us to Leipzig, I only knew we would keep that horror behind us.

Karina struggled to her feet and ran back to my arms crying. "Why? Why would he leave me?"

I shook my head, confused at the sudden turn of events. They had been romantically linked for almost two years; this was not a passing fancy. First Liam and now Peter. I knew German men were raised to have a strong allegiance to their country and their family, but none of this made sense to me...*none of it.*

I lifted her chin and wiped her eyes. "If the situation were reversed, Karina, and your parents were there, would you go back?"

She blinked several times, then buried her head against my neck. We had met the very day both of us were taken from our parents. The answer was not an easy one.

"Come, help me try to get the glass out of the car." I led her back over to where Nata leaned silently against the car. I gently brushed the glass from her hair. "Are you alright?" The worst possible question to ask, really.

She shook her head no.

"Are you injured?"

She shook it again. I pulled her in for a gentle hug. Between the three of us, we tried to carefully clear the back seat of the bigger pieces of glass as best we could. Inside the hatch at the rear of the vehicle, I found a couple of folded blankets. I laid one over Frida and Henry and the other down on the rear seat so Karina and Nata could rest. When I took the driver's seat once more, I peered over at the mother and child. She, too, now had her eyes closed but looked anything but at peace.

Will she ever forgive me? I wondered, then turned on the car and maneuvered back onto the road. Wild thoughts filled my head as I drove, but without a doubt, one burrowed in deeply—*None of us will ever be the same after tonight.*

CHAPTER THIRTY-THREE

IT TOOK US seven hours to travel the one hundred kilometers to reach the town limits of Leipzig, though I truly wasn't aware of how close it should've been as I drove, and I most certainly traveled in circles for a considerable portion of the night.

We stopped three times at closed and darkened petrol stations along the way until we found one in which the family offered to help. We were practically running on fumes and our tires were severely worn. The man had awakened to the sounds of the booms and he and his wife and two sons stood outside watching the glow in the distance when we arrived.

Though their place was a fair distance away from the destruction, they were not so far removed from the war and surely knew what was happening. Through conversation, it was discovered that Klara, the wife, had grown up in Dresden and still had family there. When she recognized our escape came from the city, she questioned us with a vehemence. I understood her desperation, but it was hard for us to speak so openly of what we had just witnessed—the pain, too recent, too raw. Frida hadn't even acknowledged the presence of others at all from her coiled position in the front seat.

The husband, Moritz, filled our vehicle with petrol while his eldest son removed the remaining jagged shards of glass from the window with a hand tool. He then located a piece of plastic and wound it around and through the back doors.

"This will need to be repaired when you reach Leipzig," he said as he tied it awkwardly. "But it will prevent the cold air from seeping through."

Cold air? Such a foreign thought after feeling like we had just stepped out of a fiery furnace.

Then the men replaced all four of our tires as well. The rubber had nearly melted to the rims from the heat in our flight. Their kindness could not have come at a better time. Without them, we might have become stranded on the side of the road.

Once we were settled and ready to depart, I gripped the map Moritz had provided for me. Moving toward a headlamp at the front of the car, I spread it out. "You are certain I am going in the right direction?"

"Yes, here." He took a pencil and drew along the route I must follow. "Once you turn onto this road, stay on it and it will lead you directly into Leipzig."

I nodded and shook his hand. "I'm sorry, I can't pay you for this."

Moritz waved his hand. "No, you have been through too much. And here, take this in case you do not find your family right away." He handed me a handful of silver coins—over a dozen fifty Reichsmarks. When I turned them over in my palm, the eagle and swastika appeared.

"I can't accept these." I moved to return them when he closed my fist over the coins.

"Please," he whispered. "I would like to think someone somewhere is helping Klara's family."

I nodded and my thoughts instantly went to Liam, praying that he had avoided the worst and really was able to help the wounded after all. "Thank you!"

Klara returned to the car with two more quilts and a paper sack. Inside the sack, she had placed some fruit, bread, cheese, and a bottle of milk. She glanced over to Frida who sat very still in the front seat holding a still-sleeping Henry. "I would see that she gets to a clinic very soon," she whispered. "She doesn't look too well."

"I will, thank you. Thank you for everything."

CHAPTER THIRTY-FOUR

THE CITY OF LEIPZIG was nearly as distressed as Dresden—without the fire and brimstone. Even with the distance, they knew...they knew their beloved neighborly city had been reduced to rubble in a matter of one night.

Through the journey, I didn't allow my mind to linger long on the possibility of losing all the places that meant something to me...the art museum, the library, the botanical garden, the Frauenkirche, Frida's art, our home...all of it. But worst of all... in the quiet of the early hours as I drove, my heart physically ached for those I loved—my dearest friends, my sweet sisters in survival. I could only pray that they somehow survived.

With the attack on Dresden, it had now been confirmed to us there was not one place in all of Germany safe from the Allied air raids. Anyone could face the horror that we did, and because of this, I could never fully relax, regardless of our arrival at Liam's uncle's home the following morning.

There was no hesitation in their acceptance of us. He and his wife, along with their kind neighbors, rushed to assist us, already believing there would be an influx of refugees headed their way.

Though you could not see any of the destruction from Leipzig, the tales of the horror spread swiftly. The German papers reported the savage assault derived from both the British and the Americans. Their blatant disregard for life had resulted in two hundred and fifty thousand casualties and most of Dresden had been demolished. Frida was inconsolable, and within a day of our arrival, she went into early labor.

A midwife had been summoned to assist in the birth, but she was quite relieved when I offered my assistance. During my years of training at the hospital, I had assisted in at least thirty deliveries and, miraculously, one entirely on my own.

By the following morning, Frida had given birth to a baby girl who, against all odds, entered the world with near perfection. Luisa Nicole Meier. The name Frida and Liam had chosen together only days before their separation.

Over the next few days, I gained control of my wits and put my nursing skills to good use. Despite my superficial wounds from the glass, which numbered quite high, we all had a significant number of burns that we didn't realize we had. Burns on our hands, arms, and legs with Karina having the only severe one on her elbow. Even our hair was singed at the ends and Henry had a bald patch at the back of his head.

I cared for them all...Karina, Nata, and little Henry in one room of the uncle's home, and Frida and Luisa remained in another room under the direct care of the aunt.

After a week of rest and recuperation, all of us were getting noticeably stronger physically, but our emotional health had plummeted. Karina was withdrawn and angry, Nata had spoken very little since our arrival, and Frida had shut me out almost completely after the delivery. Only Henry enjoyed my companionship, spending most of his days cuddled in my arms. A precious, tender mercy in light of the darkness we had endured.

Liam's uncle, Karl, tried to suppress the continued news of Dresden for Frida's sake, though it circulated heavily each time we ventured out. He then encouraged us to remain inside. He insisted it was for our continued recovery, but I recognized his attempts to lessen the pain. I know he meant well, but curiosity got the best of me. I wanted to know anything and everything.

One night, after tucking the others into bed, I heard him speaking with his wife, Gretta, through the home's thin walls.

"Dresden will never be the same," he said. "Everything that spoke of its culture, class, and tradition was destroyed...even the historic church with the antique bell dome is gone."

I gasped. *The Frauenkirche is gone?*

"Do you think Liam survived?" Gretta asked.

After a long pause, he said, "No. My correspondent has reported the hospital is almost entirely in ashes."

I felt dizzy. *Liam gone?* No, maybe he survived and is simply trying to get here. Maybe he realized he could not help everyone, and he left to find us. *And the hospital?* All those dead and injured people...two hundred and fifty thousand of them!

My heart ached and my cheeks burned. *I can't stay here.* I slipped out of bed and tiptoed out of the room. Grabbing a borrowed sweater, I stepped out of the flat and to the walkway. The night was cool, crisp, and dark.

I never believed I could feel so much relief in the dark, though my eyes shot to the skies watching for the outline of an airplane, and my ear tilted upward for the sputter of an engine. *Nothing.*

This is what it had been like for Dresden, too…before its demise.

I pulled my sweater tighter around me and sat on a stone bench across the street beneath a dim lamplight. *What am I to do now?* I had grown to love Dresden—my life and my work. Frida and Liam had given me a life of peace…a future filled with hope. Now I was here, and I truly was grateful I was not alone—Karina, Nata, Frida, Henry, and now little Luisa were here, but where was Ruta? Olga, Aneta, and Inga…did they get out in time? I knew Katia was safe. She and Werner were in Nuremberg, but my friends…my dearest, sweetest Polish friends…where were they?

I looked over at the wastebasket beside me and a copy of the *Leipziger Volkszeitung* lay on top. The headlines showed a graphic photograph of the dreadful skyline—buildings burnt and collapsed. I picked it up and could not pull my eyes away. Another photograph showed a large pile of bodies, heaping with men, women, and children. Tears slid down my cheeks. *Why? Why was I spared once more?*

Anger stirred within. I had never felt so much revulsion toward anyone in my life, even more than the German soldiers who came to my home and threatened my family, even more than that doctor who examined me at my school. I thought I could never hate more than that, but here I was, so filled with anger toward those who had committed this evil crime. A horrible, bloody, and deadly travesty…and only a fragment of a senseless war that has been raging on for over five years now. I was tired; tired of seeing the awful consequences of pride and greed and all the innocent who suffered because of it.

CHAPTER THIRTY-FIVE

2 April 1945

AFTER SIX WEEKS of hiding in Liam's aunt and uncle's home, it was time for me to contribute to the household expenses. I was determined to find work, save money, and leave Germany altogether.

The hospital I applied to work for merely took my word for my nursing licensure due to their desperation and immediately put me to work. Though I had four years of medical experience, nothing prepared me for what I was about to encounter. The Allies had pushed through France and the western part of Germany and were pressed at the edges of Leipzig, which meant we had a daily influx of wounded soldiers of all nationalities.

I had not forgotten my anger toward the British and the Americans. As more and more information came forth about the assault on Dresden, more was revealed about the unscrupulous attack on the innocent residents of the city. Men, women, and children awakened in terror from their beds, although some never awakened. A scene that never left my mind, no matter how hard I tried to forget it.

Despite that animosity, I worked as a professional, giving the utmost care to anyone who required it. This war had opened my eyes to the evils of man, and I had seen both sides prey on the other. The Germans in their occupation of other countries, and now the Allied forces in their destruction of cities through air bombs. I just wanted it to be over...*all of it!*

Though there were field hospitals spread out closer to the fighting, many of the wounded who could survive the transportation were brought to us. Instead of the factory burns, the minor broken bones, the dog bites, the babies, and Herr Turner's endless ailments...there were missing limbs, gaping holes, blood transfusions, blindness, infection, gangrene, and anything awful you could imagine. And the constant heart-wrenching pleas for help...

"Please, I need something for the pain."

"Nurse, my legs, I can't feel my legs."

"Please, please send my wife this letter."

"Nurse, just sit with me. I know I'm dying."

One week in, and after a particularly grueling day, I took the stairs to the rooftop. Sitting on a sole bench that overlooked the city, I soaked in the quietness of the night without the incessant screams and cries of pain. Although the booms in the distance reverberated, I had come to the belief they might never go away.

"Oh, pardon me, I didn't see you here." A man spoke from behind.

"It's fine." I startled a little, but didn't turn my head to his approach, still hypnotized with what little peace I could find. He stepped in front of me.

"Do you mind if I have a seat? I see you have found my hideaway."

I grinned. "No, please sit. I just wanted to come...you know..."

"Yes, yes I do, that's exactly why I'm here, as well." He reached out his hand to shake mine. "Dr. Schmitz. And you are?"

"Oh, I'm sorry." I motioned to stand. "I shouldn't interrupt your privacy, sir."

"It was I who interrupted yours, please stay, it will be nice to commiserate with another."

I chuckled. That's exactly what I was doing. A particularly loud boom sounded in the distance and a light sparked through the darkness. I didn't even flinch.

"Your name?"

"Oh." I shook my head and met his hand with mine. "Aleksandra Vogel."

"Nurse Vogel, huh?"

"Yes, sir."

"Oh, no, no *sir* here. We are comrades, after all, attempting to patch up the same men just so they can go out and fight again in the name of honor." There was sarcasm present in his tone, but he did not smile.

"You have not been here long, have you?"

"No, why?"

"I would have seen you before today." He smiled. His thinly wired glasses slipped just a bit as he turned in my direction. I stole a closer look. He was older, possibly thirties, and had kind eyes.

"Did you come from the DRK?"

"No," I replied. He referred to the *Deutsches Rotes Kruez*—the nurses who worked on the front lines. "I came from Dresden."

The silence was thick. You couldn't say that word without invoking a somberness.

Another boom, only closer.

"What will you do when the *Amis* arrive?"

This time, my eyes shot in his direction. "What do you mean?"

He raised one eyebrow. "Have you not heard?"

"Heard what?"

"They will come upon the city by next week."

I gasped. *Where have I been?* I didn't think I lived under a rock but… possibly. I knew Liam's uncle and aunt kept anything related to Dresden out of the home, but I didn't realize I was this clueless about an Allied occupation. "Will they, uh, will they make us prisoners of war?"

He tilted his head curiously. "No, not us, we are not soldiers. We are medics, we have no allegiance either way…well, none that we are foolish enough to admit."

"I hate them," I mumbled.

Through my peripheral vision, I could see him nodding. "Understandable, Fraulein."

My mind wandered. *What will I do when I face these men?*

He continued, "So, will you remain on duty while the Amis take over our hospital?"

I shrugged.

"Of course, those who only speak German may not be of any use."

"I speak English."

"You do?"

I turned to him. "Yes, but it has been a while since I have used it."

His mouth curled into a half grin that was quite charming. "Well, then I will be sure to remain by your side when they come barreling in."

"They really are coming?"

"Without a doubt."

CHAPTER THIRTY-SIX

16 April 1945

A LOUD COMMOTION shook me from my post. I had fallen asleep on the chair beside an amputee's bed. He had screamed himself to unconsciousness before we could get a dose of morphine in him.

Back at the hospital in Dresden, my shifts were generally no longer than ten hours; here, I would be lucky if I left within twelve. I glanced up to see a stream of soldiers in unfamiliar uniforms enter the ward.

The Americans are here.

A surge of anticipation of the unknown filled my bosom. If this was it… this was it. Above all, I wanted the war to be over and, though my resentment over Dresden remained close to the surface, I truly wished for the end, regardless of who won.

The soldiers all carried guns but none of them were aimed at any one person. They split into two rows and saluted two men who wore similar uniforms to the others but displayed different identifying markers on their hats and shoulders. One had two silver parallel bars, the other a bronze-colored leaf…most likely their commanding officers. They disappeared inside the administration offices.

At first, the room was dead silent, then several of the men around me began cursing in German at the newest occupiers. Recognizing the harm that would cause to their recovery, I stood up and maneuvered through the beds. "Please, please calm down," I pleaded. "Your injuries cannot handle such excitement."

Though the grumbling continued and the tension was high, we waited to see what would happen next. Would they line us up and lead us out? Will they have us imprisoned? Killed?

When several American soldiers entered carrying some of their own wounded on stretchers, they approached the only spare beds in the space. The eight empty beds were flanked on both sides by Germans and a shouting match ensued. Without hesitation, I rushed to stand between them and, once again, petitioned for peace. Turning to the Germans, I ordered them to be still and remain quiet. When I turned and faced the Americans, I used my best English, though it was rusty, to order them to hold their tongues as well.

"Please understand this is confusing, you have held guns to each other for years, and this anger does not go away in a day."

I circled back again to the Germans. "Regardless of where your pride remains, they have taken over this city, and they can imprison you, or worse. Please be quiet and allow your wounds to heal. Be still."

I had not realized that everyone in the room froze at my command until a man in a sharp American uniform stepped forward and in a loud, clear voice he addressed me in German. "Go about your duties, Fraulein, I will handle this." He waved me aside.

I pointed at him emphatically. "Then handle it with empathy, sir. These men have been through hell."

He stared at me under thick bushy eyebrows and a scowl formed. I didn't wait for a reprimand and went back to my chair and sat down. Several soldiers on both sides of the room watched me curiously for several minutes afterward. They were both most likely trying to ascertain my role in the conflict...*friend or foe.*

Truthfully, I was neither.

After the American wounded were placed in the empty beds several men saw to their immediate needs. They could be the doctors who came to treat them. Everything happened so fast.

Next, the officers stepped out of the office with our administrator close behind. One officer stepped forward in front of all the men. His hat was different than the others and he was tall and intimidating. The man with the bushy eyebrows stood to his side and demanded everyone's attention in both languages.

"We are members of the United States Army. I am Major Samuel T. Jones." The interpreter translated in perfect German. "The United States has commandeered use of the city of Leipzig as their forward operating base as we go forth to liberate additional German cities in an effort to end this war as swiftly and safely as possible." A few mumbled cuss words resonated from the room. "We understand you see us as the enemy. However, we entered this war to stop evil dictators, like Adolf Hitler, from destroying the world." More grumbles. "You are not in danger unless you become a threat. If at any time we feel like you might harm an Allied member of the Armed Forces, you will be detained. If you resist, you could be dispatched."

I glanced around at the soldiers' faces. Aside from the man who spoke, they were all so young…late teens and early twenties, then it occurred to me that I was only twenty but felt like I had lived a lifetime since leaving Poland.

"We would appreciate your cooperation in cohabitating at this hospital, but if you feel you cannot continue as such, we will remove you, patient or staff." He pointed to a man in a white lab coat. "This is Dr. Kimball. He will take over as lead physician here. All doctors and nurses will report to his staff. He will see that your health and wellness regimens are continued with very little interruption. Thank you."

I peered back over at the American soldiers as they moved around their wounded. The injured men all had varying wounds from what I could see. Several, possibly, even life-threatening.

"Nurse." The lead doctor, Dr. Kimball, pointed to me and waved me over. "What is your name?"

"Aleksandra Vogel."

"You are a nurse, are you not?"

"Yes, Nurse Vogel."

"Would you please show my staff around the hospital? I presume you have surgery rooms, exam rooms, and dispensaries?"

I blinked.

"What about etherizing rooms and a mortuary?"

His English words were complicated, and I struggled to keep up. The man with the bushy eyebrows stood next to me but did not look me in the eyes. He then said the German equivalent to which I nodded and pointed the way. Though I knew many conversational words, I had not learned English medical terms from my neighbor or the baker.

Throughout the tour, the handful of men, no women, asked random questions about the facility, and though I tried my best, mistakes in communication were made, though it quickly became apparent to me that their field medical experience exceeded that of my own.

Thankfully, the men were patient with my words and kind in their interaction. I wasn't sure what my expectations were to begin with when asked by Dr. Kimball, but I had not envisioned the Americans to have such decent manners.

When I returned to the main ward, most of the soldiers who had accompanied the commanding officer had all departed. I sighed my relief. Maybe now we could just move forward and operate as normally as possible.

I glanced around to see a huddle of nurses near the back of the room. I had worked with two of them and knew them to be competent and knowledgeable. I didn't understand why they were now being so suspicious and secretive. Truthfully, their actions were foolish. Though most of the foreign soldiers had departed, a least a dozen or so remained.

"What's going on?" I approached the four women.

Nurse Hahn faced me. "I will not care for any Amis," she hissed. "They cannot make me."

I pressed my fingers against my temple, losing patience by the second. "Yes, they can, Petra. They can make you or remove you."

"They killed my brother, Aleksandra." The pain was evident across her face. "I will not heal their wounded. I would rather die."

I pursed my lips as the other nurses agreed with her. "Look, they have three doctors of their own…"

"But they will require our assistance." She cut me off. "They said so themselves, and I am certain they will bring more." She crossed her arms over her chest and nearly shouted. "I will poison them, Aleksandra…watch me, I will die before I'll help an enemy."

I glanced around; we had attracted the attention of several American soldiers who were now walking in our direction.

"Please, Petra, Ilse, please calm down."

"Why are *you* not angry?" Ilse, the other nurse snapped in my direction. "I know you've come from Dresden, Dr. Schmitz said as much. I would think you would be vengeful for that tragedy alone." I inwardly groaned. I did not want my history to become gossip for the group. Why did I tell him that?

"I'm as angry as anybody else." I looked to see the soldiers who were descending upon us. "But I am tired of all this death and destruction, aren't you?"

The soldiers stepped in front of us. "What's going on here?" They spoke in English, of course. The four nurses beside me looked at each other confused.

I faced the soldiers. "We are discussing who can assist with your American doctors. I know some English, so I will do my best. They only understand and speak German." I then turned to the nurses and told them in German that I will handle the Americans and they will need to look after my patients as well as their own. I also pleaded with them to behave.

"Alright." A soldier with dark skin nodded his head and smiled. I had never seen such perfectly white teeth before. I couldn't draw my eyes away from them. I had also never seen a man with black skin. I didn't smile back.

"Please introduce me to your wounded." I stepped forward to walk with them.

"I'm Sergeant Driggs." The Black soldier held out his hand. I stared at it longer than I should have but quickly met it before he pulled it away. He had a strong grip, which should not have surprised me for such a broad-shouldered man. "This is Sergeant Rich."

I nodded. The second soldier had light skin and green eyes. He was closer to my height than the first man and had terrible body odor, something one might believe I'd grown used to by now. I wanted to pinch my nose as we walked but I didn't.

Normally, with such a greeting, I would have responded appropriately such as *nice to meet you*, but that was not the case here.

We walked back to the beds where the American soldiers lay, and the men stopped at the first bed. I retrieved a stack of empty clipboards and some observation sheets and brought them over to a nearby table. Grabbing one, I picked up a pencil and stood at the end of the bed ready to take notes. Sergeant Driggs pointed to the soldier. This is PFC Zachary Wilson."

"PFC is his name?"

"No, that is his rank—Private First Class."

"Oh." I looked to the paper. "Do you need that besides his name?"

"Yes, please."

I nodded and wrote it down at the top, then hooked the clipboard to the end of the railing.

We moved to the next bed. "This is Specialist Scott Ochoa."

I didn't question this time...His rank must be "specialist". I continued this process as we moved down the row until all the men with black skin had a clipboard assigned to them, most of the men had the rank of private. When I reached the first bed with a white soldier, Sergeant Rich took over and gave me their names and ranks. Though this process seemed odd to me, I just did what was asked.

Once finished, I turned to both men, thanked them for their help, and introduced myself to the closest medical doctor. "My name is Nurse Vogel.

I have been assigned to help with your men. I speak English but not really well. I'm sorry, doctor."

He shook my hand. "I'm not a doc, just the medic, ma'am, and your English will do just fine." He had a strange inflection in his words.

"If you can tell me what you or the others have assessed, I can put it down in their charts."

"Well, I wouldn't expect you to do it alone, little lady."

I blinked. I thought he understood that I was the only nurse that could speak English or even chose to be here without a vendetta. And why did he call me a little lady? I was nearly as tall as him. "I'm sorry it's just me."

"No," he chuckled. "I mean, I will help y'all."

The curve of my mouth could not be construed as a real smile, but I was relieved that the burden didn't fall entirely on me.

Over the next hour, I took notes as the man, who told me to refer to him as *Smithy*, recited the soldiers' known injuries. There were a few that would need additional examinations and at least two of the eight who needed surgery as soon as the rooms were prepped.

And though the newcomers' arrival had been unconventional, it seemed everything from that point on was fairly normal, and I took a great deal of comfort in that.

It was nearly ten o'clock that night when I finally departed the hospital after a long fourteen-hour day. As I trudged from the trolley stop down the block to my flat, I reflected on the afternoon's events. Though I had wrongly envisioned the American soldiers to be more like crazed savages with an appetite for blood, I wasn't about to disregard my own bitterness.

I may never forget what happened in Dresden or who is responsible.

Opening the front door, I paused…I will do my duty and save lives as my oath requires, but nothing more, and if all goes well and the end of the war really is coming…I might be able to return to Poland by the year's end.

And that thought was worth any amount of displeasure I might endure.

CHAPTER THIRTY-SEVEN

OVER THE NEXT few days, I worked side by side with a handful of American medics and two doctors. They never complained about my broken English but as time went on, I tried harder and harder to recall my lessons and do better. The German nurses stopped speaking to me altogether, which was fine since I didn't have a spare minute to talk anyway, but I didn't like being the subject of gossip either.

Dr. Schmitz, two additional doctors, and six nurses resigned. Well, I'm not sure if it was considered an official resignation since they all left one evening and never came back. Before he departed, Dr. Schmitz tried to convince me to join them as well.

"Nurse Vogel, you are turning your back on your people."

I clenched my teeth. *I wouldn't be here if I hadn't been taken from my people by German soldiers.*

"You must make a stand." He continued, "walk out with me. Leave this place and let them fend for themselves."

"Thank you for your advice, Dr. Schmitz, but I must remain to help pay for my family."

"I will find you another job in another city. A city still occupied by the Nazis."

Within a day, the American wounded went from the original eight to seventeen, then the count reached twenty-three. Soldiers who were mostly recovered or had superficial wounds were moved outside into a dozen tents that had been erected in the nearby field. The very large green military tents were adequate enough so that the external conditions would not affect their injuries, but I remained inside assigned to the more serious patients.

The Black American soldier, Sergeant Driggs, was present nearly every day. Though I was unfamiliar with the hierarchy of the American army, I sensed he was a leader of some sort from the way the Black men acknowledged him from their beds. Yet, it was the one referred to as Specialist Scott Ochoa with whom he spent the most time. He was indeed the more seriously wounded in the group.

"Nurse?"

"Yes, sir?"

"Specialist Ochoa, here, seems to be in pain. Is there something you can do for him?"

I stepped over to the opposite side of the bed and touched the man's forehead. He was feverish. He had gone in for surgery the first day he arrived, and we had to remove a portion of his stomach from a gunshot wound. The damage was severe, but Dr. Kimball was highly skilled and did his best to repair the awful injury.

I felt the bandages around his torso and blood seeped through to my fingers. "He is bleeding through his sutures," I said as I glanced upward. The Black man's deep brown eyes met mine only inches away. My breath caught. I had never seen such long eyelashes on a man before. He had the most beautiful eyes. I blinked. "I think we need to take him back into surgery. He might be bleeding internally."

Concern flashed across his face, but he tried to conceal it—yet I recognized that emotion all day, every day.

"Will he…" He glanced down to his friend who was writhing uncomfortably now. He pointed for me to step away from the bed.

As we met away from the patient, he leaned in. The scent of gun powder mixed with something like apples surfaced. At least it wasn't the foul smell of body odor like the other soldier. He whispered, "I'm worried that he might not be strong enough for surgery again."

I respected his concern for his friend, but I had seen many soldiers die in the last month. We just didn't have all the resources to fix everyone. "If we don't take him in soon, he may not make it through the night. There is an infection somewhere and we need to find it."

The muscles in his jaw tightened. He was clearly anxious.

I started to walk away when he grabbed my wrist. I looked down at his grip and he quickly let go. "Please Nurse, he's not only under my command…he's my cousin."

My mouth parted in surprise. I understood the value of a cousin. Despite the fake identities and relationships we had created in Dresden, my friends *were* my family, and I would do anything to save them, too.

"I will alert the doctor and have him prepped for surgery." I started to walk away then turned around. The man's head hung low. He looked up as I approached again, worry etched into every line on his face. Placing my hand on his arm, I did what I had vowed not to do…I soothed his fears. "I promise, Sergeant Driggs, I will do everything in my power to help your cousin recover."

He nodded and thanked me.

I circled back around and found the attending physician. When he examined the soldier, he came to the same conclusion that we needed to get him into surgery immediately.

Once again, darkness had fallen before I stepped out of the hospital's front doors. A man sat forlornly on a nearby bench. It wasn't until I passed by that he stood up, nearly frightening me with the motion.

"Nurse?" Sergeant Driggs fidgeted before me with his hat in his hands. He did not have that same solid confidence from that first day we met.

"Mr. Ochoa is recovering," I said, recognizing what he was waiting to hear.

He ran one hand through his short black hair and exhaled audibly. "When I didn't see him in his bed, I, well…" The nearby lamplight hit his eyes as he tilted his head toward me. They glistened as if he'd been crying. "I assumed the worst."

I smiled. Though my feelings for the soldiers hadn't changed, they were still human, and I understood his current fear more than he might ever know.

"He's in a private room. He's too fragile to be around the other patients and well, he is…"

Sergeant Driggs watched me intently.

"He is…how do you say?" I mumbled the word, "in Gefahr."

"In danger?"

My eyes went wide when he knew what I had said in German. "du sprichst Deutsch?"

"Some." He smiled then the wrinkles appeared on his forehead again. "Do you think Scott will live?"

"I think he has a very good chance; the surgery went well. We found the problem, but we won't know for sure for a couple of days." I noticed a chain wound through the man's fingers and a silver cross dangled at the end. I pointed to it. "You believe in God?"

He nodded vigorously. "I am nothing without Him."

I stared at him with a touch of bewilderment. *How can someone who believes in a merciful, loving God drop bombs on women and children?*

I cleared my throat. "Goodnight, Sergeant Driggs."

"Goodnight, Nurse Vogel."

CHAPTER THIRTY-EIGHT

AFTER FOUR DAYS in a private recovery room, Specialist Scott Ochoa returned to the general ward and when Sergeant Driggs was finally able to see him for the first time, he did not contain his excitement. Though he was careful in his proximity to his cousin, relief was evidenced all over his face.

I watched the happy reunion with tears building in my own eyes. We had heard nothing of Liam or my friends, though they in turn knew nothing of us. A group of people with ties to Dresden had begun compiling a list of names—known dead, injured, and missing. The papers had agreed to post such a list and I searched it daily. So far, *nothing*.

When Sergeant Driggs looked up and caught my eye, he smiled wide… the same stunning smile that had shocked me the first time I saw it had not lost its potency. I swiftly looked away and resumed my duties with the other patients.

An hour later, Sergeant Driggs appeared behind me. I knew it was him from the same apple scent that wafted over to me. He must love apples. "I cannot thank you enough, Nurse, for all you've done for my cousin."

I kept my back turned while I restocked bandages in a cupboard. "It wasn't just me, sir. Your Dr. Kimball performed the surgery. He is somewhat of a miracle worker."

"Yes, well he wouldn't have known there was a problem if you hadn't noticed the complications."

I finally turned around to see kindness in the man's eyes. Despite his genuine appreciation, I tensed up. "I value life, sir." I couldn't control the edge in my voice. "I prefer it over death." I started to walk away.

"Wait, please." Sergeant Driggs touched my shoulder, then quickly let his hand fall. "I just wanted to express my gratitude. Might I take you to dinner or out for coffee?"

I spun around, unsuccessful at withholding the malice from my eyes. "Your gratitude will be more graciously received if you make that same offer to your doctor. I am not interested."

Before I reached the door, Sergeant Driggs was at my side. "Wait. Did I do something wrong?"

I inhaled slowly and remembered that picture from the newspaper of the bodies piled up. "Not you personally, I suspect." I slowed my words to keep my temper from flaring. "But whatever you and your army stand for has caused me and the people I love more grief than you could ever imagine."

"Ever imagine?" The sergeant quickly retorted. "Do you even know what your beloved Hitler did to all the people he put in those camps?"

"He is not my beloved Hitler!" I steamed. "He is not even *my* leader."

"Regardless." His voice raised. "You live here, you work in a German hospital, caring for German soldiers who carried out some of the vilest, most inhumane acts in history."

"And the bombing of the innocent women and children in Dresden was not vile or inhumane?"

He flinched, then quickly resumed his argument. "Before we arrived here, we went through Chemnitz." He crossed his arms over his chest. He appeared daunting in that position. "Have you heard of it?"

I continued to stare but said nothing.

"It's a town where one of those camps was created. One that detained Polish and Hungarian Jews…all women."

My eyes widened and I couldn't stop my gasp from escaping.

"And do you know what kind of conditions we found those women in? Can you even imagine as you live here in your comforts—well-fed and well-dressed." He pointed to my patent leather half-boots under my skirt.

"You know nothing of my circumstances," I snapped.

"The women were thin, malnourished, sick, and dying. They had been worked to the bone, some assaulted repeatedly by the guards, and others left for dead in the very spot they fell."

Tears filled my eyes. My thoughts went to Erela, my Jewish friend from Łódź, and the suffering she and her family may have endured. My cheeks grew hot, and I felt faint. Without saying another word, I rushed out of the hospital and didn't stop until I had reached a nearby park two streets away. In my solitude, I dropped to the nearest bench and wept. I could not stop the sobs from coming.

"Nurse Vogel?"

I recognized the voice but did not lift my face from my hands. I sensed the sergeant take a seat next to me. He must've run to keep up with me, though I never heard him.

His sigh was heavy and burdened. "Please, please forgive me. I was completely out of line back there. I'm so sorry."

I shook my head. I wanted to be alone—to suffer in private.

"I should've never said anything." He inhaled deeply. "This war has made us all so angry...so resentful. I should not have mentioned the camp. I hadn't realized how much it affected me until it all came out...and you were the faultless bystander who took the brunt of it."

I sniffled.

"I'm sorry, Nurse Vogel. I've been away from home for so long, I don't know how to properly converse with a woman. My mama would've taken a switch to me if she'd heard me back there."

I wiped my nose. *A switch?* I didn't even know what that was, but it probably wasn't good. Looking over at him, I saw that same kind regard from before. He truly appeared repentant.

"Where is home?" I whispered.

"Good 'ole Georgia, ma'am." A similar twang like Smithy's materialized. I hadn't noticed it before, or he only used it on occasion.

My eyebrows pinched. "In the Soviet Union?"

"No." He chuckled. "Sorry. Georgia is one of the forty-eight states in my country. America."

I nodded. I knew they had varying territories but didn't know all the names.

"What do you miss the most from Georgia?" I wiped my eyes.

"Oh, hands down my mama's cooking. I haven't quite gotten used to these sparse rations all these years and then, I'm sorry if I offend you, but this bland German food...there's no flavor...no spice."

I grinned. I wasn't sure what he was used to, but we did have a shortage of many things. Yet again, we didn't put a lot of spice in our food either.

"Now there," he smiled back. "I'm hoping that smile means you don't entirely hate me."

I shook my head. "No...not entirely."

"Thank the Lord." He stood to his feet. "May I walk you back to the hospital?"

I watched his hand extend toward me. It was a large strong hand with smooth brown skin. What I really wanted to do was go home, but that was childish, even for me. I knew the staff had grown quite dependent on my English and I didn't want to explain the reason for my half-day to the family. Though Frida still rarely spoke to me, Nata and Karina had returned to their old selves; prying into my life as much as possible, though there was nothing to tell.

"Yes, thank you." Though I didn't meet his hand, I stood up. "Would you tell me more about that camp you liberated?"

He took another deep breath. "I'm not sure you want to hear the details. It was awful."

"I want to know."

"It's called the Langenleuba-Oberhain Camp. It was mostly filled with Polish and Hungarian women but there were some Slavs and Muslims as well. The camp had rows of quarters like something we have back in Georgia, the old slave quarters on plantations."

"Slave quarters?"

"Yeah, someday I'll explain that to you, but not now."

I didn't miss his insinuation there would be a *someday* with us, though I highly doubted it.

"The women were surprised to see us and happy, but weak. They mostly wore tattered and torn overalls and wraps over their short or missing hair, and you could see their bones—cheekbones were defined because of how hollow their faces were from lack of food, and shoulders and ribs protruded. They had missing teeth, sunken eyes, and cracked and bloody lips." He did not look me in the eyes at this point. The memory of the horrors could be seen in the lines of his face. "When my fellow soldiers and I shared our rations, the women fought over them. I didn't even know the last time they might've eaten."

We walked slowly as he continued to describe the sorrow he had seen and the frustration he felt because he couldn't fix them all. He barely had any food but gave them all he had, even chocolate bars. By the time we reached the hospital again, he had told me everything…or everything he was willing to share.

"I really do hope you forgive me for my childish tantrum earlier, nurse. I am truly sorry."

"Aleksandra." I held out my hand as if we were meeting for the first time and in a way we were, for I saw him so much differently now.

"Thank you, Aleksandra. I'm Jackson, but everyone calls me Jack."

I nodded, though again I doubted there would be another visit that would allow for such a personal exchange.

He apologized and I accepted. It was over.

"Goodbye, and thank you," I said, then stepped inside.

That night as I dressed for bed, I struggled with the emotions that warred within me. The man I saw today, the one who showed compassion for the women he had saved could not be the same man who would fire upon innocent people in Dresden. Could there be something I was missing? Something I didn't know? The contradiction frustrated me to no end. *Could I be wrong?*

CHAPTER THIRTY-NINE

1 May 1945

"H E'S GOING HOME today, Sergeant." I met Jack at the door as he entered. Once again, his smile lit up the room like the noonday sun.

"Really? He's strong enough?"

I nodded and smiled back. Since the day of our fight and subsequent truce, we had spoken in passing nearly every day without an argument of any kind. "Dr. Kimball did his final assessment, and he will be transferred by airplane this afternoon. He's waiting to say goodbye."

Jack didn't hesitate and tore off in the direction of his cousin while I resumed my duties. When Specialist Scott Ochoa was carried out on a stretcher for the last time, Jack was by his side.

I stepped over to say goodbye.

He responded quietly. "Thank you, Nurse Vogel. You've saved my life."

I chuckled at the exaggeration. "I have merely seen to your needs. You are the one who fought to survive. Good luck in America."

Within minutes of his departure, Jack was by my side again. "I don't know what I'm going to do without him," he said as I heaped a pile of freshly laundered linens on top of the table and proceeded to fold them. "He's been by my side since the day we were sworn in." Then he laughed, "Well actually, he's been by my side since he could walk."

I smiled. "He will get the help he needs in America. I've heard there are hospitals there that can do all manner of new medical techniques. I'm sure he will be in good hands."

"Yes, you're right. I'm just being selfish."

I laughed. "When it comes to family, selfish is allowed."

He smiled again and watched me carefully. "Any chance I can convince you to go to dinner tonight? You know, to help me cope with his absence?"

I laughed again. He really was smooth. "No, I have plans." This was the truth. It would be the first time in two months that Frida, baby Luisa,

Henry, Karina, Nata, and I would spend time together outside of the home. We had plans to go to a May Day Festival. I had been looking forward to this for a week.

"Tomorrow then?" He was relentless.

"No."

"Wednesday?"

I chuckled. "You will not give up, will you?"

He shook his head.

"Very well, Sunday," I conceded. "It's my day off."

Dr. Kimball came running from his office and with shaking hands and pale skin, he stood before us. "Can I…" he stopped to catch his breath.

Jack and I exchanged glances of concern. I had never seen him so anxious or winded.

"Are you well, sir?" Jack moved to his side.

He nodded but struggled to put his words together. "I—I need your attention p—please." He stuttered when he called for everyone to look his way. I didn't know what to think, I had never seen him so muddled.

"I—I have just received word…Adolf Hitler is dead."

Dead?

My hand flew to my mouth as very audible gasps and cries filled the room. What did this mean? Was the war over? I glanced to Jack whose eyes were as wide as mine. Once the news sank in several soldiers jumped up and shouted their joy over the news. I peered around to see several German soldiers weeping. The extraordinary contrast of emotion stunned me.

I went to the side of each of the German beds and offered my condolences to the patients who wept. I didn't know much about Hitler except that his people loved him, and they fought for him.

Jack appeared at my side once more after I had made my rounds. By his expression, I could see that he wasn't sure how to react around me.

"The news caught me by surprise…" I disclosed. "But I don't care either way if it means the end of this terrible war."

He smiled. "I hope that's exactly what it means and now we have something to celebrate on Sunday." He winked and then joined his fellow soldiers in their congratulatory reveling.

CHAPTER FORTY
6 May 1945

WHEN I AWOKE Sunday morning, I lay in bed for an extra hour wondering how I could reach Sergeant Driggs and cancel our date before he arrived to pick me up. At the very least, I should have agreed to meet him somewhere other than here. Things had only started to heal within our little family, and I didn't want them to assume I had a boyfriend or a reason to place my attention elsewhere.

The night we went to the May Day Festival was the day Adolf Hitler's death was announced. Since then, it was revealed that he had been holed up in a bunker with his lover, Eva Braun, and both committed suicide.

Talk of his demise seemed to be on everyone's mind, but for me, it seemed to be one more step toward hope and that we might just get through this agonizing war after all.

That same night, Frida even let me hold Luisa, which she hadn't done before. She still didn't look me in the eyes, but Karina and Nata assured me this was progress and ultimately the night ended up being one of the best nights in a very long time...or at least since the day of the Dresden Carnival which, by all accounts, was the last perfect day in my memory.

"Do you want to go with Nata and me to the cinema today?" Karina rolled over in bed and saw me staring at the ceiling.

"I can't," I droned grumpily.

"Why not? You don't have to work."

"I...um...I have a date."

"What?" Karina sat straight up. "How come you are just now telling me? Do I know him? What's his name? I bet he's a doctor, isn't he?" As she nattered on and on, I realized I couldn't really tell her who he was. How would she react, knowing he was an American soldier? If Frida knew...what little rapport we had improved upon would be gone forever.

"Oh, my…" I groaned and placed my hand over my eyes.

"Well?"

"What?"

"Who is it?"

"Um, it's nobody really, just a man I met. It's nothing at all, this will probably be our first and last date."

"Wow, you are just a joy to be around, it will probably be your *only* date," she retorted sarcastically.

I snickered and threw my pillow at her head.

She, in turn, responded with hers and for the next few minutes, we whacked each other repeatedly until we fell over in laughter. *Oh, how I missed those days.*

"Well at least let me help you find something decent to wear."

"I have clothes."

"Not many."

This was true. We lost everything in Dresden.

"Why don't you wear my blue slim skirt and matching jacket?"

"Not the one you just purchased?"

"Yes. I want you to have more than one date and once he sees you in that…well…"

I laughed. "Suppose I don't want a second date. I can wear my brown high collar and pleated skirt."

She pretended to gag. I hit her again with my pillow.

She jumped up to retrieve the clothes and placed them before me. It was such a lovely ensemble that I conceded rather easily. It was true that the flaring peplum of her V-neck jacket flattered my hips and helped to pro-portion my height, though I really had no intention of going out with Jack more than once…since this was, after all, his apology date.

I had left the flat early enough to catch him before he came to the door. I hadn't thought things through clearly when I gave him my address.

I stood on the nearest corner and the moment the tall, handsome soldier appeared down the street I waved for his attention.

Once again, my heart stirred at the sight of his brilliant white teeth and striking brown eyes.

"Well, Nurse Vogel," he chuckled. "I almost didn't recognize you outside of your white uniform."

My nose wrinkled at his playfulness. "I don't wear it all day long. I do have other clothes."

215

"And stunning they are." He smiled again and lifted his arm for me to take.

I hesitated.

"I have been taught quite persuasively to be a gentleman, Miss Vogel. Please allow me to show you just how."

I nodded and threaded my arm through his as we walked down the street. When we arrived at a café to eat, as promised, he opened the door and held out my chair. He even handed me the menu first.

As I perused it, whispers materialized all around us. I ignored them at first, assuming the patrons were dissatisfied with the food or the service, but then the grumblings multiplied to the point they could not be ignored.

"What can she possibly be thinking letting a man like that anywhere near her?"

I didn't take my eyes off the menu, but it no longer held my focus—the conversation behind me had my full attention.

"What right does this scheisse Ami have, wooing one of our Frauleins?"

"And a Blackie, too!"

I lowered the menu to see Jack staring at me. His face was hard to read. Did he hear the same things I did? Certainly, he must.

"Would you like to go somewhere else?" I whispered.

He shook his head. "Not unless you want to. I'm used to this."

I stared at him with an admiration I hadn't felt before. He did not let his differences control the situation. When the waitress appeared, I smiled first at him and then at her. "I'd like the schnitzel please…with the mushroom gravy."

"Brötchen, for me," he said.

When the waitress brought our drinks, Jack leaned back, seeming oddly relaxed. Though the murmurings and onslaught of insults continued, he simply ignored them and proceeded to ask about my life.

"That day that we had that rather…well, heated conversation…" He smiled. "You said that Hitler was not your leader. What did you mean by that?"

I nervously glanced around the room. I wasn't sure why unless I was about to tell him the truth and why would I do that? I barely knew the man. When he scooted forward and clasped his hands together on the table, I could see that he was a good listener, waiting for me to share.

"I'm from Poland," I said quietly.

His eyebrows raised curiously. "That makes sense."

I tilted my head. This man is an American, he doesn't know Europe as I do. "How?"

He held up one finger. "Your accent." Then a second finger. "You speak Polish…"

I didn't know he knew that.

His third finger went up. "You were surprised and angered over the camp and the condition of the Polish women." Then his fourth finger joined the others. "…and you're beautiful."

I almost sneered at that last item. "German women are very beautiful."

"Some," he agreed, "but most are not humble or kind."

"I happen to believe some of the kindest women I have ever met are German." I thought of Frida and Helene.

"I happen to know one…but she's Polish." He winked.

I couldn't hold back my smile; he was quite the charmer. I wondered how many women he had flirted with in each of the towns he passed through.

"Tell me about your home, Aleksandra. Your *real* home." He wasn't smiling this time and I was touched by his genuine interest. Over the next couple of hours, we conversed as if we were the only two people in the room. I was certain the stares and the grumblings continued but I no longer heard them.

At the close of the night, he walked me back toward the flat, but I stopped him a good street away. "My family might not be so ready to meet an American soldier," I explained. "They are…well…" I couldn't quite find the words to justify it myself.

"I understand. I will watch you go in from here." He took my gloved hand and kissed it gently. "Thank you for today. Maybe we can do it again."

I chuckled. "Do you have more apologies to make?"

"If it gets me a date…maybe…"

I smiled and stepped away. "Goodnight, Jack."

"Goodnight, Aleksandra."

CHAPTER FORTY-ONE

THE NEXT DAY, Jack met me after work with a bouquet of flowers. A bundle of tiny, blue blossoms I had come to know as forget-me-nots. He walked me home, stopping short as we had agreed the night before, but it seemed neither one of us wanted the conversation to end, so we found a bench at the nearby park and talked for several more hours.

The day after that…the war was over—*at least in Europe.*

When the news came into the hospital that the Germans had surrendered, there were mixed emotions from both the patients and the staff. Similar to a week ago when we learned of Hitler's death, whooping and hollering erupted from some with a contradictory rush of tears from others. Though the German soldiers no longer argued with the Americans, they struggled with the belief that they had lost…again.

After the first World War and Germany's defeat and subsequent reparations, many believed Hitler would be the one to help them reclaim their place in the world. But they were coming to the realization that it would never come to pass. Not only that, but it had come at the expense of many, many German lives and the defeat now had greater implications with greater consequences.

On our third date, Sergeant Driggs took me to see *Der Stumme Gast.* The Silent Guest—a crime film starring René Deltgen and Gisela Uhlen. When the height of the suspense peaked in the film, I found myself clinging to Jack in a way I had never touched anyone before, and he didn't seem to mind. In fact, once the intensity had subsided, his arm stayed comfortably around my shoulders and when he walked me home, he held my hand.

"What do you think you're doing with this fair lady, colored boy?" a voice from the shadows asked.

Jack moved slightly in front of me as two soldiers approached. From my limited view, I could see they were American soldiers as well.

Why would they confront one of their own?

"We are just passing through, guys. I don't want no trouble."

"You brought trouble when you thought you could be with a white woman."

"We are friends on our way home," Jack said.

"Well, you just turn her over to us and we'll see her home properly."

Jack's frame stiffened in front of me, he was bracing for a fight. His hand reached behind and nudged me farther away from him right at the moment one of the men took a swing at him. He dodged it effortlessly and even got a punch in himself, but then the other man somehow got him from behind and held him tight while his friend, who recovered quickly, began punching his stomach.

I stepped over to the one who punched and whipped my purse across the back of his head and continued swinging until he turned his attention to me. When he grabbed my arm, he squeezed with such force, I thought my hand would go numb. In the seconds that followed, all I could hear was a clash of bodies. When the dust settled, another man appeared. He had entered the fray and between him and Jack, the two offenders were rendered helpless—now lying on the ground with varying degrees of injuries.

Jack reached for my hand and pulled me out of sight as the man who helped him followed closely behind. Winding through an alley and past another building, we stopped to catch our breaths.

Jack stretched out his hand to shake the other man's. "Thanks, man. I appreciate that."

My mouth gaped open when he stepped into the light…he was a white man, too. I was more confused than ever.

The man smiled, first at Jack then nodded at me. "My pleasure," he said, before taking off in a different direction.

I stumbled my way to a bench and sat down, pulling my purse to my chest, I shook my head. "I don't understand what just happened."

Jack took a seat next to me and rubbed his palms on his pants. "It's complicated."

"Help me understand," I pleaded.

"In America, people with black skin were sold into slavery…my people…my ancestors."

"Slavery?"

He nodded solemnly.

"Eventually there was a civil war between territories, those who fought to keep their slaves and those who fought to liberate them. It was a bloody war."

"Like this one?"

"Worse."

I gasped.

"Eventually slavery was abolished, but hatred towards my people hasn't changed much. In fact, I wouldn't be fighting in Germany right now if we hadn't lost so many white soldiers early on. The leaders put us into service duties, they didn't believe we could fight as well as a white man."

"When did it change?"

"Three months ago. I was one of four thousand volunteers to go to the front."

I choked out my next words. "You volunteered? Why would you do that?"

He turned to face me and reached for my hands. His thumbs caressed them gently. "Because despite what has happened to my people, America is my home...my country...and I would defend her to stop evil men from conquering her."

For a brief moment, I saw the same look in Jack's eyes as I had seen in my father's, and my chest warmed with admiration. Once again, my mind alternated between truth and lies.

I went out with Jack the following three nights, though we were more careful about our surroundings. Each night we made an effort to stay in public spaces and around more people, regardless of the continued whispers and comments. I found the particular attention to our courtship odd, but much better than risking the empty alleyways and facing more men who were intent on hurting Jack because of his skin color.

Though life in the city attempted to return to normal with the official end to the European war, there seemed to be more confusion and chaos than anticipated. A clear division transpired between those loyal to the Third Reich and those having their eyes opened to the atrocities committed in the name of nationalistic pride.

Newspapers that were now free to print the news outside of the Nazi rules and propaganda were filled with photographs and stories of the liberation of the death camps all over Germany; and the very worst one, Auschwitz-Birkenau, was located in Poland—*my* Poland.

I recalled the time that the butcher had told my mother and me about the poison gas and the Jews, but it was hard to believe that such atrocities were actually taking place. Now the stories that surfaced included showers that were used to gas the Jewish people in masses and the use of crematoriums for just as appalling reasons. It seems the butcher was right after all.

Sickened by the stories that flooded our homes and our lives, I looked forward to the quiet moments I could spend with Jack. He made me feel cared for, loved, and even wanted. He never spoke of anything war related unless I was the one to bring it up. He was by far one of the humblest men I had ever been around.

"Are you cold?" He asked one night as we sat on our favorite bench in the park.

I shivered on cue. "No."

He laughed as he shrugged out of his jacket. We hadn't planned on being out this late, but I didn't want to go home, I wanted to stay with him. Placing the overly large jacket across my shoulders he completed the process with his arms firmly around my body. He pulled me close, and I laid my head on his chest.

"What do you think is going to happen to Germany next?" I asked.

His lips tenderly brushed my forehead as he spoke. "I'm not sure. The Allied leaders will all come in and figure it out. But it will be divided, that's for sure."

"Divided? What do you mean?"

"Well, you have France, Britain, America, and the Soviets. They all believe they have the best rebuilding plan, and all are vying for a piece of it."

"Why the Soviets?" I had no lost love for our neighbors to the east. They probably did more harm to Poland than the Germans did.

"They are part of the success. They will make a claim."

"What will happen to all the Jewish people, the ones who lost everything? Where will they go?"

He seemed deep in thought. "They will be helped, assisted. The United States has offered sanctuary to them, but now I suppose they get to choose where they want to go. They get to live where they want. They can go home."

Home.

I can go home.

Why had I not thought of that until now? Then as the warmth of Jack's breath heated my neck, I realized…I wasn't ready to leave him yet. The very thought surprised me.

"What about the Nazis?" I remembered when Günter was explaining the Lebensborn project to me, he had mentioned it was created by a man by the name of Heinrich Himmler. I had recently learned he was also the mastermind behind the extermination camps. "What will happen to Herr Himmler?"

"He tried to hide, but the Brits found him and took him into custody. He will pay for his crimes."

"Good," I whispered. Though I didn't believe any punishment would be sufficient for his evil deeds.

"What about you, Jack? What will happen to you?"

"Me?"

I nodded as tears pricked like tiny needles behind my eyes. This man who I had initially wanted nothing to do with had won my heart—his gentleness and compassion, his goodness, and his strength…all of him.

He tugged my chin upward until our faces were parallel. He grinned only slightly as he leaned down and pressed his lips against mine. They were soft and warm. He maneuvered his mouth to open mine and guided me with loving emotion and passion. Slipping his hands beneath me, he lifted my body onto his lap without breaking the kiss, then wound his hands along my back and up through my hair. I responded with equal fervor, my chest rising and falling to the desire that grew within—a longing unequal to anything I could possibly define.

I had never been kissed before, and now, never wanted to be kissed by anyone but him.

CHAPTER FORTY-TWO

12 July 1945

"ALEKSANDRA, we have some prisoners of war being brought in. They were detained just north of the city." Dr. Kimball announced when I arrived at work.

"Prisoners on which side?"

It was a logical question. Two months ago, the prisoners were British and American, now I wasn't sure who the enemies really were.

"They are German."

I sighed. *Can't we just agree the war is over and each can go back to their own sides, move on, and live life as they did before?*

"Will any need surgery? Should I prep the room?"

"I'm unaware of the extent of their injuries but make the preparations in any case."

I nodded and did as I was asked and, within the hour, nine German soldiers were transported into the ward with varying injuries and a handful of guards who wore a band with the initials MP on them.

One of the soldiers looked to the staff. "These men are to receive adequate treatment and be released to our care. No one is allowed to visit them, and they are not allowed to leave. Do you have any questions?"

Simultaneously, we all said no. This was not the first time we had treated a patient who was under guard. I grabbed the appropriate clipboards and corresponding papers. "Who will be able to give me their names?" I looked to the soldier who spoke first.

"We don't know their names. They aren't talking."

"Did you try in German?" I asked.

"Our interpreter was called away for another purpose."

"I can do it. I speak both languages."

"Very well, you may try but I doubt they'll talk, they've been trained not to. If they don't, just assign them a number."

I briefly addressed the men, but it was true, they wouldn't speak…not even to me, and the three who were unconscious most likely would have joined their comrades in their silence. When Dr. Kimball arrived to make his initial assessments of their health, I dutifully followed behind him and took notes.

"This one needs surgery immediately," he said, pointing to prisoner number four. "He has a bullet wound in the thigh. They have put a tourniquet on to stop the bleeding, but the wound appears infected."

I wrote everything down. It was probably best he was unconscious.

"This one also needs surgery." He pointed to the next unconscious man. "If he awakes, we might need to amputate his arm."

I cringed. We had always made every effort to heal before resorting to amputation.

The last of the three unconscious men had a severe head wound. The imprint of a blunt object was found on the back of his head. The doctor checked his pulse—it was barely perceptible.

"He certainly won't survive surgery—I doubt he'll even make it through the night. Please just make him comfortable, Nurse Vogel."

I nodded. Even though this had become an everyday scenario, it still tore at my heart. *He belonged to somebody.*

He moved on to those he determined to have lesser injuries. "This prisoner has burns on his legs and feet, they will need to be treated and rebandaged.

"Yes, sir."

"Prisoner eight has sepsis." The man with flushed, clammy cheeks, shivered violently. "We need to find out where his infection is."

I placed a blanket over him and called an assistant over to help him immediately.

"This one." He stopped at the next man. His hair was unusually long and ragged and a full beard covered most of his face. He did not look like a soldier, though he wore the remnants of a uniform.

The doctor seemed to have trouble finding anything wrong with him. Yet when he examined his arms and legs, he stopped short. "He has cuts and bruises."

My brows furrowed. They *all* have cuts and bruises, but he never mentioned that before. "Anything else?"

He lowered his voice so only I could hear. "He has severe lacerations around his wrists and ankles." He took a breath. "As if he wore shackles for an extended period of time."

I stopped myself from gasping. *How sad.* To go from one prison, now to another. I glanced at the nearby guard and wondered if he or his men were responsible for the wounds. Then I peered down at the prisoner. His eyes were closed—it seemed unlikely that he would be unconscious, but he could be suffering from something more serious internally without the typical indicators.

"Do you want me to treat them?"

"Yes, ointment and bandages."

Dr. Kimball moved to the next man. "This prisoner has a gash on his side that needs to be cleaned and sutured. At least a dozen stitches, I would estimate." He stepped closer and examined his face. "Sir, can you see me?" he asked the man.

I quickly repeated the question in German. "Kannst du sehen?"

The man made no attempt to answer.

"I believe he is blind."

I marked his chart. Two more to go.

Thankfully, the final two only exhibited minor injuries and nothing that would require surgery or extensive medical care.

Once the doctor was finished, I stopped him before I went to gather the supplies. "Do you prefer me to assist in surgery or treat the ones here?"

"Stay here, your language skills will be more useful here."

"Yes, Dr. Kimball."

I began with the prisoner with the most soiled bandages. Prisoner number seven, the one with the burns. Although he should have been writhing in extensive pain, he somehow kept his discomfort contained. I gently unwrapped the horrid coverings and, while I had grown used to many foul smells, the putrid scent of burnt flesh has always been the worst. Ever so carefully, I cleaned his wounds, applied ointment, then rewrapped them with fresh, clean linens. And every time I encountered someone who suffered from burns, I thought of Werner Genau, then Liam.

"Thank you, Fraulein."

I looked up, surprised to hear him speak. "You're welcome." Then I quickly followed up with, "What is your name?"

He shook his head as if he intended to keep that the extent of our conversation. I smiled and moved on to the next one.

One by one, I washed, cleaned, and bound their wounds. Most were superficial but, on occasion, I had to stitch an open cut and each time I moved to the next patient, the last person ended with, "Thank you, Fraulein."

Until I reached prisoner number five.

When I folded back his sleeves to reveal the marks on his wrists, I cringed. Examining the depth of the cuts and proximity to the radial artery, I was stunned the man hadn't bled to death. I doused the cotton balls in alcohol and gently dabbed them on the man's injuries which had scabbed over in most places. He shuddered but did not open his eyes or speak.

"I'm sorry if this hurts," I said. "I am trying to be gentle."

Once they were cleaned and a medicated ointment was applied, I bandaged them and repeated the process with his ankles. When I gathered up the supplies, the man's eyes opened. I smiled and waited for the *thank you, Fraulein* but instead heard…

"Thank you, Aleksandra."

I gasped, then stared. Leaning forward, I searched for recognition when the man's striking green eyes pierced me with shocking precision.

"Günter?"

He didn't smile or nod. He remained silent.

"Is it really you?" I whispered, edging myself a bit closer. Reaching for a clean washcloth, I dipped it into my water basin and squeezed out the excess liquid. With gentle strokes, I cleared the dirt and grime from his face wherever the hair did not consume. Tears filled my eyes as he came into clearer view. He was older…but so was I.

"What happened?" I kept my voice low so as to not be overheard, even by the prisoner in the next bed. My eyes flitted to the wounds on his wrists that I had just cared for. "I thought you were heading to France or Spain?"

He glanced down briefly then back up. "I didn't make it."

I nodded as I dipped my washcloth into the water again and continued to clean his ears, neck, and upper chest. "I'm so sorry."

When he stared at me again, his eyes softened. "You were supposed to be in Dresden."

I smiled partway. "Luckily, I am not."

He nodded. There couldn't have been a person in Germany who didn't hear of what happened there.

"I'm glad you are safe," he said. He might've even been smiling, but it was hard to tell through all that hair.

"You know that I am safe because of you."

He shook his head. "You are safe because you're brave."

I put the washcloth down and squeezed his hand gently. "Are you hungry? Can I get you something to eat?"

"No, thank you."

"Nurse?" A voice called for me from the opposite end of the room.

I turned to find the lead soldier approaching. "Did you get anyone to speak to you?"

My face flushed as I glanced away. I had never been a good liar, but I would not risk Günter's life. "No sir, they are just mumbling incoherently. Nothing substantial."

"Very well. Let the doctor know I'm leaving two of my men at the door overnight and I'll return in the morning for an update."

"Yes, sir."

After the soldier left, I turned to Günter. "Rest for now. I will be back, I promise."

That night, I stayed late, way past my regular hours. Although I had plans to meet Jack, I sent word with a messenger that I needed to cancel, then waited for the ward to grow dark and most of the men to fall asleep. When the clock chimed midnight, I placed a chair next to Günter's bed. He was wide awake.

"What happened?"

He shook his head. "I made too many foolish mistakes."

I shrugged my shoulders. "You're not the only one."

He reached out and took my hand in his. "Tell me."

I relayed the details of the night of the Dresden bombing and what Liam forced me to do. Though Frida was speaking to me again, it wasn't like before, and I wondered if it ever would be.

"You did the right thing, Aleksandra." Günter insisted. "You all might've perished if you hadn't left when he told you to. You also couldn't have forced him to get back into that car."

"But why would he do that? Why would he leave his wife, his family?"

"I don't know the man, but I know the honor embedded into thousands of German men. We are duty-bound."

"But you pursued a way to break free from that burden. Couldn't he have done so as well?"

"His calling was to be a doctor. Do you think he would've been fine living here in Leipzig, knowing he could have saved a life in Dresden? He would have felt guilty living, even amongst his family. I say this, though I realize it's all relative, only twenty-five thousand residents died that night, it could have been hundreds of thousands."

"Twenty-five?" My eyes widened. "No, Günter, it *was hundreds*, hundreds of thousands…over two hundred and fifty thousand."

He shook his head. "It was misinformation, Aleksandra. A comrade of mine, another convict, used to report directly to Joseph Goebbels, the Reich Minister of Propaganda before my friend fled. Herr Goebbels inflated the numbers by adding a zero to the number of casualties. He wanted to draw sympathy from the world on Germany's behalf."

"It was a lie?" I held my hand over my open mouth. *What else have they told us that isn't true?*

"Yes. Though twenty-five thousand is still tragic, it was not the entire population as they portrayed. Liam could very well have helped people before he died. If he died."

"What do you mean *if*? It's been five months."

"Unless his body was found, there's always an if."

I thought about what he said. We checked the lists. He never showed up on the list of the dead. Never. I glanced back over at him.

"What happened after you left us?"

He closed his eyes. "I made the mistake of going home."

"Moselle Valley?"

The corners of his mouth lifted into a faint smile. "You remembered."

I grinned in return. There wasn't much about our interaction I had forgotten.

"The year before I left my military unit, I got word from my sister that my father was ill. I wanted to see him one last time before I departed the country."

"Did you? Did you see him?"

He smiled. It was a warm, genuine, memory smile. "Yes. He was bedridden, practically at death's door, but he recognized me. Mama and my sisters run the bakery now. I promised him I would return and take my place. He understood why I needed to leave though. He knew—he saw things, terrible things, even in Hatzenport."

"I'm sorry, Günter. I'm sorry for your loss."

Our fingers were still interlaced. "Thank you."

Peering around the room, I noticed it had remained mostly quiet. Several of the men snored so it gave us the right amount of background noise to not alert others to our conversation and, of course, the two men who were assigned to stand watch remained outside the doors of the ward and neither one entered the entire time we spoke.

"Günter, can you tell me what they tried to force you to do? Back at the camp near Dresden."

"I can't say, Aleksandra, and I promise you, you don't want to know."

"Why the shackles?"

"I was apprehended before I reached the border. Most deserters are shot right on the spot. I've seen it myself. I believe the only thing that saved me was the fact that there was no one around to witness it—no one to see me become an example. They took me to a prison outside of Berlin and condemned me for *defeatism*."

"How did you get out?"

"The prison was overrun with deserters, so they thinned the ranks. They sent the most able-bodied men to work in a *Strafbatallion*."

"A penal battalion?"

"Yes. A unit designed for dangerous missions…clearing minefields, defending front-line positions against attacking forces, repairing defenses. If we were shot or killed, it was of no loss to the regime."

"A suicide mission."

"Precisely."

"Where did you fight?"

"Mostly between Berlin and here. Our role was to cripple any advancements on the city by the Allied forces."

I tried to wrap my head around this information. "But the Germans surrendered on the 8th of May, nearly two months ago."

"Our commanding officer told us to keep fighting or he would shoot us himself."

"The German pride to the end." I frowned. "Even with the all-powerful Hitler…who hid in a bunker, then committed suicide."

"He was not the only one." Günter sighed. "Besides Eva Braun, many of our so-called leaders took the cowardly route…even a woman and her five children."

"In the same bunker?"

"Yes, Magda Goebbels. Her husband, Joseph, was the man who propagandized the Dresden attack. I overheard the officers talking about it. Though my commanders pretended the news of the suicides did not deter their mission, the spineless act affected them."

"How did you come to be detained by the Americans?"

"They sniped the officers three days ago, but not until after most of the men in the unit were already dead."

"Did you tell them you fled the Germans? That you tried to get away?"

"They don't care, Aleksandra. We still appeared to be defending the Nazis."

I bit my lip and fought the emotion building in my chest. "What do you think will happen now?"

He shrugged. "I've heard rumors…prison, labor camps, it depends on whether the Americans turn me over to the Soviets or not."

I fought my tears. *He cannot be a prisoner.*

"The Americans can't imprison *all* the German soldiers, that would be nearly every German man."

"No, but we were the ones who didn't surrender."

My heart sank. My own father was given an impossible choice too. *Do this or die.* "Oh, Günter." I leaned down and kissed his hand. "I'm so sorry."

He brushed my hair off my face with his free hand and moved it to my cheek where it rested in his palm. The warmth of his skin comforted me.

"Though I wish you weren't here under these circumstances," I said. "I'm happy to see you."

He smiled. "It's good to see you too, Aleksandra."

CHAPTER FORTY-THREE

T HAT NIGHT, I didn't even go home. Once Günter had fallen asleep, I settled into an empty exam room and curled up on the table with a blanket for the three hours of night that remained.

When the sun cracked through the small window, I immediately rose so as to not draw any undue attention. Washing my face in the sink, I then put on a clean white ward dress, which helped me feel physically refreshed, but I couldn't shake the heavy feelings I carried from my conversation with Günter.

It tortured me to think that such a good man—a man who risked his life to save me and my friends—would face a horrible future because of circumstances out of his control.

When the lead MP arrived for an update, I exaggerated several of the men's injuries just a tad, including Günter's, believing if I could stretch out their stay another day or two it would buy me time to figure out a plan.

"Have you been informed that two of the men died?" I asked as we met.

"No, I wasn't aware of that."

"Yes, the soldier with the severe head trauma and the one with the sepsis infection. The one with the bullet wound in the leg was operated on. His condition is quite critical."

"Six still alive." He said this more as a statement to himself than a question to me. "Have any of the men given you their names, ranks, any information?"

"No, sir. They haven't." I bit the inside of my cheek to hide my lie.

"Very well, I will be back tomorrow at the same time for another update."

I nodded my understanding.

After I saw to each of the men's bandages, I retrieved shaving tools from the supply closet and with a bowl of warm water, soap, and a razor, I took my seat next to Günter's bed.

We knew better than to speak in the daytime, but his curious eyes seemed to have relayed a full conversation by the time I reached over and angled his jaw for a better look.

"Well, soldier." I chuckled. "It seems like you're due for a trim." The last time I had seen him, his hair was longer than the normal cut of a typical soldier, but not this disheveled, and his facial hair was now wildly unkempt.

One of his eyebrows raised.

"Trust me, I used to shave my papa all the time." I dipped the soap in the water and lathered it on both hands before I spread it over his very thick beard. Wiping my hands on a towel, I then reached for the razor and carefully scraped the blade along his skin. It took nearly an hour, but the finished product was well worth the time. His smooth skin revealed the Günter I remembered, *and* he didn't fight me over it. Next, I took the scissors and clipped the frayed ends of his hair. It wasn't perfect, but he looked like a whole new man.

Before I left, I leaned down and whispered, "Now, it's *really* good to see you." He smiled in a way that only I would have recognized.

That evening, two additional MPs were assigned to the ward. I wasn't entirely sure why they doubled their guard. Maybe the lead MP thought I was lying about the dead soldiers and suspected something nefarious happened overnight. Although the thought seemed ridiculous, it wasn't entirely wrong. If I knew I could sneak Günter out unseen, I would.

Their presence meant I could not stay and visit with Günter tonight as I had the night before and this discouraged me. Especially when all I could do was say goodbye with my eyes before I departed for the night.

As I stepped off the trolley, a man stood in my way. I'd been looking down at my shoes, not watching where I was going and bumped directly into him.

"Oh, I'm so sorry," I said without looking up.

Two hands reached for my arms and a deep chuckled emerged. "You must've been deep in thought to not see me, beautiful…"

I peered up to see Jack watching me with that heart-stopping smile of his.

"Or are you avoiding me?" His smile waned just a bit.

My grin was less than enthusiastic but not because I wasn't happy to see him for, I was…but I had so little sleep and what space remained in my head was filled with thoughts of Günter. I worried about my friend non-stop. "No, I'm not avoiding you, I promise."

Pulling me into a warm hug, he kissed the top of my head. "I've missed you Aleksandra, I haven't seen you these last two days. Has something happened at the hospital?"

"No…well, yes."

He drew me back so he could see my face. Tears had already formed and bubbled on my lashes. He reached for my hand and led me to our park. The sun had already set, but the summer warmth kept the night temperate. Once on our bench he pulled me to his lap and held me.

"Tell me what's happened."

I sighed. That was the one thing I could always count on from Jack—he was an engaged listener. "A German soldier I met a few years back is in the hospital now. He has been held as a prisoner of war…" I wiped my eyes. "But he has been wrongfully detained."

"How do you know he's a good man, Aleksandra?" The muscles clenched in his jaw. Something bothered him.

"I know," I whispered.

"I've heard the confessions of many German soldiers. Their roles in the war and the harm they caused without even blinking an eye. They are not good men."

"This one is…he saved me."

"Saved you? How? When?"

I started at the beginning—the day I was taken from my school. It took nearly an hour for me to tell Jack the entire story. One that seemed more like ages ago and not just four years past.

"Please say something," I pleaded when silence hung thick in the air.

Jack didn't speak but wrapped his arms around me and drew me in. When his lips met mine, he communicated his emotion thoroughly, leaving me breathless. When he finally released, his deep voice sounded barely above a whisper. "I can't even begin to understand the heartache you've been through, leaving Poland…the forest, then Dresden, and the bombing that brought you here…" He rested his forehead against mine. "Forgive me, Aleksandra."

"For what?"

"For judging you…your history, your strength. You are the most incredible woman I have ever met."

"You already apologized." A simple grin slipped through.

"I know, but it doesn't change the fact that my words were thoughtless and cruel."

"No, please, Jack." I held his face in my hands. "You are a loving, caring man."

He tucked a loose strand of hair behind my ear, then caressed my jaw. "So, this Günter…he is in your hospital now being guarded by MPs?"

"Yes, but I don't know for how much longer."

"What are his injuries?"

"When he was arrested by the SS for being a deserter, they shackled him. He has deep lacerations on his wrists and ankles…other than that, he's okay."

"Hmmm." He rubbed his chin. "He must be a decent man if he chose to leave them willingly."

"Yes."

Jack slid one hand to my neck and leaned in. "But he also saved you and that makes him a *great* man." He tenderly kissed my forehead, my eyes, nose, and jaw, and when he reached my lips once more, I melted into him.

Taking a breath, he soothed. "Trust me, Aleksandra. I promise to help your friend."

CHAPTER FORTY-FOUR

Of all the mornings this would happen...it had to be today.

"Aleksandra!" Karina nudged my shoulder.

"What?" I answered reluctantly and turned away from her.

"Aleksandra." She prodded again. "I woke you up two hours ago. Why are you still in bed?"

I shot straight up. Karina stood next to me with both hands on her hips. Wrinkles multiplied on her forehead. "What's going on? You're never late for work."

When I scrambled to get out of bed, the quilt that was wrapped around my legs nearly threw me to the floor. "What time is it?" I cried.

"10:17 a.m."

"Oh, no, no, no!" I panicked and rushed to the wardrobe, grabbing the first work dress I could find. They were all generally the same, but some were longer than others.

"What can I help you with?" Karina called as I fled to the front door.

I blew her a quick kiss. "Nothing. I will see you later."

Taking the steps two at a time, I could not get my feet to move any faster. I was even determined to run the whole way to the hospital if the trolley hadn't been coming down the street at that precise moment.

By the time I reached the front doors of the hospital, the air in my lungs had evaporated, but I still didn't stop and ran straight for the men's ward. Coming to a sudden stop, I stared at four empty beds.

"No!" My hand flew to my mouth. All the prisoners were gone except for the man whose arm was amputated and the one who had a bullet wound in his leg. "No, please no," I cried as I reached out and touched the blankets to confirm that no bodies hid underneath. Sure enough, Günter's bed was vacant. Tears sprang from my eyes as Dr. Kimball approached.

"What's wrong Aleksandra? You seem upset."

"I—I, uh." *I couldn't tell him why.* "I, uh had a terrible night...a nightmare, actually. I'm sorry I'm late this morning."

"Don't concern yourself. No new patients have arrived since last night."

I nodded and wiped my eyes as subtly as possible.

"Wh—what happened to the other four prisoners?"

"They're gone."

"Gone, as in, um, the guards took them?"

"Yes. I cleared them myself an hour ago."

I bit my lip, trying not to cry in front of him. "Thank you, doctor." I rushed to the water closet where I could sob in private. *I cannot believe I wasn't here. I didn't even get to say goodbye.*

I clenched my fists over my eyes and sank to the floor. *If only I had told Jack the night before and not stayed up with Günter, he would have had more time to help.*

Angry at myself, I didn't have the strength or motivation to be at the hospital today. When I stepped into Dr. Kimball's office he seemed to understand and quickly approved my release for the afternoon. The tear-stained cheeks and swollen eyes may have helped.

Once home, I gave both Henry and Luisa, a volley of kisses and headed straight back to bed, avoiding the family's probing questions, at least for the next several hours.

"Aleksandra?"

Karina's voice slipped into my dream like it had just this morning. I couldn't get my eyes to open. Was it daytime? Nighttime?

Her gentle touch caressed my cheek. "Aleksandra? A message came for you. Do you want me to read it for you?"

I finally opened my eyes. Concern covered her face. "I'm worried about you," she said.

I reached for her hand and kissed it. "Thank you, sweet Karina. I promise I'm okay. It's only exhaustion."

"Oh," she exhaled. "I'm glad you're not ill."

"Thank you."

"For what?"

"For being my sister, my friend, my family. I love you so much." I never wanted to make the mistake again of not saying how I felt about someone only to find out I might never get that chance again.

She smiled and snuggled her head against my chest, then wrapped her arms around me as best she could while I was lying down. "Oh, Aleksandra, I love you."

When we released, I sat up and she handed me the folded paper. "This came about an hour ago, but you looked so peaceful I hesitated to wake you. Are you certain everything is alright?"

"Yes, of course." Even if it weren't, seeing her always made me feel better.

She smiled and winked. "I will leave you to your love note then," she announced and walked out.

I turned on the lamp light and unfolded the paper.

Aleksandra,

I went to the hospital to walk you home and was informed you left early. I hope you are well. You know I would come to you if I could. If you are able, meet me at the park tonight.

JD

I reached for my watch on the desk. 7:08 p.m. *He might still be there.*

I rushed to change out of my work uniform and hustled out of the house once more.

Approaching the park, a tall, dark figure leaned comfortably against the lamppost closest to our bench. No doubt, the strapping silhouette belonged to Jack. Tears bubbled again. I had never been so emotional. *Why is this happening?* In all the times I had faced difficulties, I seemed to cry more often since arriving in Leipzig.

"Oh, Jack." I ran into his outstretched arms and buried my face in his muscular chest. Weeping, I could barely get a word out. "I missed him," I whimpered. "Somehow, I slept in this morning and was late to work. By the time I arrived, Günter was gone."

Jack kissed my forehead. "I know."

I sniffled. "I should have let you know sooner...I should have told you and given you more time to figure something out. Now he's going to prison."

He held me out just a tad and tilted his head down. His eyes warmed over me. "Didn't I ask you to trust me?"

My mouth parted.

When he leaned in and brushed his lips past my cheek and reached my ear, the vibration of his voice tickled. "Günter is on his way home."

"What?" I cried and gripped his arms to steady my shaking body. Jack's hands went to my waist, and he easily lifted me up and twirled me about. When my feet reached solid ground again, I peppered him with questions. "Really? How? Are you certain?"

He smiled at my impatience. "Let's just say someone who has more authority than me owed me a favor."

"A favor for what?"

Jack cleared his throat. "Saving his life."

Curiosity strangled me. "How?"

"That's a long story for another day."

I wrapped my arms around his neck, enjoying the closeness of his body. "Please tell me what happened with Günter."

He tilted his head and captured my eyes. "I can't, I'm sorry, but I promise you, he's safe."

I pictured Günter's sweet reunion with his mother and sisters in his hometown village of Hatzenport, safe now that the war was over, and taking his place as the man of the house and baking his bread. The very images brought a smile to my face and a balm to my heart.

"Thank you, Jack." I nuzzled into his neck. "Thank you so much."

He laughed and held me tight. "I hope you know, Aleksandra, I would do *anything* you asked me to."

CHAPTER FORTY-FIVE

2 August 1945

"Nurse Vogel." Jack appeared at the door of the ward. A look of concern crossed his face and his body appeared rigid and stiff. He also rarely called me by my official title.

I glanced at my wristwatch, fearing I had stayed past the time we had agreed to meet tonight, but it was only half past four. I waved him over. "My shift isn't finished yet, can you wait?"

He shook his head. "I need to talk to you now. Please see if it's okay. I'll wait outside."

Now he had me worried.

He had never asked this of me before. I placed my papers aside and rushed into the lead nurse's office and within seconds flew out the hospital doors and right into his arms.

"What's wrong? What's happened? Did something happen to Mr. Ochoa?" I knew that they had been in contact since his cousin returned home.

"No, no that's not it. Scott's fine." He pulled me back and cradled my face in his hands. "Oh, Aleksandra, I don't even know how to begin."

I braced for terrible news. "What? What is it? You're scaring me."

His breath warmed my lips as he spoke. "You know I care for you, don't you?"

Tears built in the corner of my eyes, but I didn't know why. "Yes."

He released his hold and paced away from me. When he suddenly turned around, frustration emerged. "I don't know what to do. I've spent the last two hours trying to figure out a way for me to stay here."

"You're leaving?"

"Our platoon is being reassigned to Berlin."

I choked. "Berlin?"

"We've received orders to go and assist in the peace process."

"Why Berlin?"

"Many troops are being sent there. It's total chaos. The streets are still filled with Nazis, and they don't seem to know their country has surrendered."

"I'll go with you."

He took two long strides and fervently reached for me. The kiss tingled my toes and sent unidentifiable emotions throughout my limbs. Though the intensity of his touch excited me, it was when he slowed his lips that made me weak in the knees. The kiss communicated more than just desire…it tasted of desperation.

When he leaned back, I could see tears welling in his eyes. "It's too dangerous."

"I've faced worse," I whispered.

"I know." He kissed my nose. "You have more courage than I do."

I didn't believe that. "Please don't go," I cried. "Can't you tell them you need to stay?"

He shook his head. "If I refuse, I could be court-martialed."

"What does that mean?"

"I'd face a military court; they could sentence me…even imprison me for such a refusal."

My hands wound around his waist, and I clung to him as if he might vanish before me. "When? When do you leave?"

"In two days."

I buried my face in his chest. The smell of apples made me cry.

"Aleksandra?" He lifted my chin. "I'm asking for a special leave before I go. It will only be for one night. Will you come with me?"

"Where?"

"Anywhere we can be alone."

CHAPTER FORTY-SIX

17 August 1945

IN THE WEEKS following Jack's goodbye I faced a cavalcade of emotions. The only thing that kept me standing upright was the memory of our one night together in a small village outside of Leipzig, I don't even recall its name. We stayed in a family-run inn under the guise of being a newly wedded couple and over the next sixteen hours, spent every moment together. I never believed love could be that perfect.

By the next morning, I had entered a different realm…a place where only mature women could claim to have gone. The recollection of Jack's gentleness and the way he tenderly loved me kept my smile from being devoured by the sorrow of his absence…that and his promise to return. He assured me with absolute conviction that he would marry me. He would even take me back to Poland if I wanted, so we could raise our family in Łódź.

My sentimentalities were not the only reason my emotions were frenzied.

Though Germany had surrendered in May, the Japanese continued their fight in the South Pacific all summer and in some rather daring, dramatic moves to stop them, the Americans dropped a colossal bomb on the Japanese…*an atomic bomb.*

One bomb that had the ability to obliterate an entire city…the first on the 6th of August on Hiroshima, Japan and the second three days later on Nagasaki, Japan. In all, it was estimated that one hundred and twenty thousand people were killed…five times the number of casualties over Dresden.

Once again, all the feelings of that night in Dresden and the subsequent months were dredged up to the surface. The deaths of so many people who happened to be in the wrong place at the wrong time, all to change the face of the war.

It succeeded.

This "new and cruel bomb" as it was described by Japan's Emperor Hirohito, had led to Japan's unconditional surrender two days ago on the

15th of August 1945. Sadly, this might've been avoided had the emperor heeded the undeviating cautions from the United States, Great Britain, and China. Details of the July 26th ultimatum from Potsdam were published by the news press worldwide prior to the bombings. Sadly, the Japanese leadership promptly rejected any terms of surrender and ultimately brought the destruction upon their own people. Another example of poignant arrogance.

Finally…World War II was officially over.

I spent the afternoon on Wednesday in solemn contemplation outside the hospital as the celebrating commenced inside. Regardless of what side you fought for, the losses were insurmountable and the pain of losing loved ones was incomparable.

My thoughts went to Jack. Despite the news being favorable for America, I knew his work was not over. I clutched his first letter in my hands and reread it for the tenth time today. At the time he wrote it, the surrender had not yet taken place.

August 10, 1945

Dear Aleksandra,

I cannot begin to explain the pandemonium that has occurred in Berlin. Four different countries with four different agendas have descended not only on the country but on a broken and divided city. Though the Americans, French, and British are working together, the Soviets are not as accommodating, and this has stirred up old disputes and infantile opposition placing the frightened people of Berlin into various predicaments depending on their geographical boundaries.

My platoon has been assigned the task of hunting down the men responsible for the reign of terror—the Nazis—and bringing them to justice. Though many discarded their uniforms at the time of the surrender and are harder to identify in civilian clothing, I'm certain their cowardice will come to light. Unfortunately, there are still a fair number of German residents who are defending them, even hiding them. It is astonishing that in the midst of their country's losses, some still believe they will rise from the ashes and regain dominance. These are the ones who are the most dangerous.

But enough of war talk. I MISS YOU, Aleksandra! You cannot imagine how often I think of you, your smile, the way you wrinkle your nose when you get mad, the way you fit perfectly in my arms, and the way you loved me that last night we spent together.

When this war is finally behind us, I promise to return, to marry you, and take you wherever you want to go. Trust me...I'm yours and yours alone.

JD

Though the edges of the letter had already begun to fray, I read it another two times before folding it neatly at the creases. Lifting the parcel to my nose, I hoped to catch even the slightest hint of apple, but to no avail. Oh, how I missed that man.

Just yesterday, Dr. Kimball announced his departure. He stated that due to the decrease of active fighting and wounded soldiers around Leipzig, he too was being ordered to Berlin. I wanted to hide in his luggage at the very least, and at the very most, I was tempted to ask for the opportunity to come along. Truthfully, though, the unknown frightened me. What if I traveled to Berlin and couldn't find Jack? Or what if he returned to find me gone?

Overall, Leipzig was rebuilding. Though the city itself sustained little damage structurally, the greater obstacles came when the fighting had concluded. Forgiveness had become quite an insurmountable hurdle for some. In the end, it was apparent that most of the people of Germany wanted to move on—coming together in their efforts to put the ugliness of the war behind them and begin healing. This, I hoped, was happening all over Germany...*and Poland.*

When Nata had shared the news about my parents in her building, I immediately wrote to them, but if they had written back, the correspondence would have gone to our Dresden flat, months ago. I tried again upon our arrival to Leipzig, no longer fearing the discrimination of being a Pole.

When an envelope with my mother's handwriting arrived at Uncle's house this afternoon, you would have thought it was Christmas day as excited as I was. Though I hadn't read Polish in years, I understood every word.

Dearest Aleksandra,

I cannot tell you how many times I lit a candle at the Basilica of St. Stanislaus Kostka for you and Ivan. I feared you both were lost to us and could not bear the thought that I would never see you again. Your grandmother's cross never leaves my neck, and I am often found on my knees, praying for your safety. To receive your letter was like a gift from God.

I am unfamiliar with the cities in Germany, but Pani Dabrowski, my neighbor, has a foldout of a European map. She showed me where Leipzig is and I kissed it, then kissed her. You are not as far away as I believed, and you are alive. That is all I can ask for my sweet girl.

I am sad to say, your father is quite weak. After the occupation and loss of his legs, he did what was necessary to keep his family alive. When you disappeared, he lost his will to live. We had no knowledge of your whereabouts or survival...only speculation. I prayed to God you would not be harmed and from your letter, I see my prayers have been answered.

I worry Szymon may not live much longer. Most days he spends in bed, sleeping. On good days, he will eat a potato and sometimes a cracker, on others, nothing. Wilk stands watch and rarely leaves his side; he makes a good nursemaid. I have taken on sewing work to pay dues. Ration shortages are so extreme we are lucky to get anything. Through the goodness of others, we have enough for a modest supper nearly every night.

Before we were evicted from our home, we received a letter from Ivan. He was sent to France with the Wehrmacht but said little else and now it has been over two years since we have received word. When I read about all the fighting that occurred in France these last years, I wept. I have no love for the German troops only for my son and your brother. His fate is now in God's hands.

With the European conflict over, can you not join us? I beg of you, dear Aleksandra, can you not return to your family and your home?

I look forward to hearing from you soon.

Mama

For a brief moment, I considered her pleas, but for the same reason I didn't follow Dr. Kimball to Berlin, I needed to remain here in Leipzig. Though I ached to see her again and wished to see Papa, my heart and soul were tied to Jack's promise. He said he would come for me. For if all were truly coming to an end, it was here and here alone, where he would find me.

CHAPTER FORTY-SEVEN

5 September 1945

"ALEKSANDRA, what's the matter?" Karina knocked on the bathroom door. "Are you ill?"

I wasn't sure if I had picked up some sort of bug from the hospital, but it had upset my stomach for several weeks now.

"Please open the door. Let me help you."

Her words were cut short as I dove for the toilet seat once more and discharged the rest of my breakfast. I couldn't recall any contagious illness that had spread through the patients recently and caused such ongoing nausea, nor aware of any type of food poisoning that lingered for weeks.

After washing my face, I stepped out of the bathroom to not only see Karina standing there but a very concerned Frida by her side.

"I'm alright." I moved to step past them when Frida blocked my way. Our relationship was strengthening slowly, but it still had a long way to go.

"Aleksandra," she said in the gentle voice she used to reprimand her children.

I stared.

"When was your last bleed?"

My cheeks heated. What was she suggesting? *Could. I. Be...?* Gasping, I rushed past her and back to my room, but she followed me. Then a very surprised Karina followed her.

"Could you be pregnant?" she asked as she sat down next to me on the bed. Reaching for my hand, she held it lovingly. I knew that intimacy led to babies, but it was only *one* night. Could I really be with child? My mind spun. The very idea should've been my first deduction...for heaven's sake... I'm a nurse, but how could Frida know? *I never told anyone.*

"Have you been intimate with a man?" she persisted.

My lips trembled. I couldn't speak, I only nodded. She wrapped her arms around me and held me against her. This was the first time since our arrival from Dresden that I had felt her touch. I wept into her shoulder.

She wiped my tears and lifted my chin. "I think…my sweet Aleksandra…" She smiled. "I think you are going to be a mother."

How? How can I be a mother with no husband? A thousand thoughts whirled wildly in my head—the most poignant being that Jack was not here. What if he didn't want to be a father?

"When did you…um," Frida's words were laced with caution. "Karina, would you mind leaving the room for a moment?"

Karina stomped her foot like a toddler and folded her arms across her chest. "No, Aleksandra is my sister. I should like to know what's going on. I am eighteen after all."

Frida smiled. "And when Aleksandra is ready, I'm certain you will be the first to know, but right now I need to speak with her alone."

Karina rolled her eyes and walked out. She was both an adult *and* a child in so many ways.

Frida reached for my handkerchief lying on the desk and handed it to me. "Tell me about your love."

My eyes widened. I could not tell her he was an American soldier.

"I won't judge you, Aleksandra. You forget I was in love once too."

I never forget.

She held my hand again and rubbed my fingers. "When did you spend time together…alone?"

I thought of the night I cherished in every waking moment. "The 4th of August."

She nodded.

"What's his name?"

I pursed my lips.

She patted my arms. "Do you remember how scared I was when I found out I was pregnant with Henry?"

I nodded. She was petrified. Henry was her second child, but her first with a man she loved. The first child she gave birth to, a daughter, was turned over to the Reich's Lebensborn program, but she had only spoken of her once.

"I wish I had my mother by my side." She squeezed my hand. "I am not your mother, and I also haven't been very…considerate of you since we left Dresden." Her eyes glistened as they met mine. "But if you'll allow me, I would like to be there for you."

She had barely finished her sentence when I lunged for her. I nearly smothered her from gratitude. I missed her more than I could explain. She had been such a strength for me for so long that I didn't quite feel whole without her.

"Thank you, Frida, thank you," I said. Not only for her offer but for her intent to move past the anger she harbored. If it was true...if I am carrying Jack's baby, there was no doubt I needed her.

I would need a mother now more than ever.

CHAPTER FORTY-EIGHT
22 April 1946

"IT HURTS!" I cried out to both Nurse Ilse on one side and Frida on the other. Dr. Hahn, the man who took Dr. Kimball's place was at my feet.

"You're doing well, Aleksandra." He spoke calmly despite my sharp tongue. "One more push and your little one will be here."

I recalled the babies' births I had been present for and not one in my recollection was pain-free. Even Frida in her sweet, charming ways had a nasty thing to say a time or two while in labor.

A second later, I felt as though a gush of water slipped out, though I knew it had to be more substantial…and substantial it was. Several little smacks against a bare bottom and a tiny cry rang out.

"You have a daughter," Dr. Hahn announced.

Ilse swiftly cleaned the infant, then wrapped her in a blanket and laid her on my chest as the doctor finished up with me. Her tiny mouth trembled as each weak little cry came forth. The sound both precious and heartbreaking to hear.

I placed one finger next to her tiny palm and she immediately gripped it. *Strong…very strong*, I admired, then justified…she will need her strength as we proceed alone.

It had been eight months since I'd heard from Jack. His last letter was posted on the 20th of September of last year. He didn't even know I was pregnant.

I leaned in and smelled her new baby skin, a scent I remembered from my time in the women's ward and helping Ruta. In the brief moment she opened her eyes, I smiled at the sight. Adela has her father's eyes, chocolate brown.

Adela, the name of Karina's little wooden doll that went through all the same challenges we did, up until Dresden. Sadly, that was where she, and all our other belongings, turned to ash overnight. When Karina learned

I would be naming her Adela if I had a girl, she was beside herself with emotion.

Frida had been true to her word and stood by my side through the pregnancy…even through the continuous nausea and back pain. She spoke little of her own concerns, though I knew she had gone back to Dresden twice after the bombing. Once in March of last year, and the second time, three months later.

Her dear sister Helene and her husband perished, and only a few months ago we learned Olga and Inga, who lived with Helene, were now listed amongst the deceased.

My dearest friends, who had survived the cruelty of our strenuous journey to Dresden, fought for survival to the end only to lose the duel with the devil. Though I had mourned them in February… seeing their names in print paralyzed me all over again.

Then there was our beautiful flat with Frida's lovely paintings. Karina told me that our building had collapsed, and though Frida tried to pick through the rubble, attempting to find anything that belonged to her beloved Liam, the process produced nothing.

Three months before Adela's arrival, Frida shared with me the details of her visit to the hospital in Dresden. Through heartbreaking sobs, she described the condition in which she found it. The battered ruins exhibited the same signs as other torched buildings did…only in this case, one solitary wall remained standing with little or no damage. It was as if the hospital taunted back…you can wound me, but not destroy me. *A statement I understood all too well.*

Though I recognized the significance of being taken into Frida's confidence, all I could picture was the street where Liam had gotten out of the automobile, then commanded me to drive. The memory—no matter how hard I tried to forget it—was etched into my soul forever.

The next bit of news she shared surprised me. Frida had tracked down a former nurse who worked with Liam. A woman by the name of Uta Lata Huber…the woman I knew as Nurse Huber. Through Frida's diligence, she discovered her at one of the evacuee camps located near the clinic. Like many others, Nurse Huber had felt compelled to remain close by and assist as needed even as the first anniversary of the bombing approached.

Nurse Huber told Frida about Dr. Meier's final days.

She said he appeared at the hospital that night during the bombings and toiled nonstop, regardless of the continued assault. Somehow, through it all, the hospital received little damage. "Until the 15th," Nurse Huber said. "That Thursday, the third day of the bombings, we had such a shortage of supplies that I told Dr. Meier I would go in search of anything we might be able to use. The never-ending burns were only part of the challenges we faced. I rummaged madly through the neighborhood for linens…I even took clothing off the dead if it was salvageable."

Frida told me that Nurse Huber struggled terribly to share the rest of the story. "In my absence, the hospital was hit. The sight…more devastating than you could imagine." Frida herself struggled to say the next words. "The whole building ablaze and no one…" She repeated Nurse Huber's declaration. "*No one* could have gotten out in time."

The one thing that brought an element of peace to Frida was hearing how Liam had helped many, many people. Nurse Huber said he barely rested in the two days he worked and once he patched people up as best he could, he arranged to get them transportation out of the city. He was responsible for saving the lives of hundreds of people.

"Look, Aleksandra." Karina cuddled little Adela and brought my thoughts back to the present. "She's smiling at me."

I glanced over to the infant in her arms. Her eyes were closed, and she did seem to have a curve to her lips, but to say the three-week-old was smiling was a stretch. "Her father must've been quite handsome." Karina caressed the child's cheeks.

"Are you saying her good looks could not have come from me?" I teased.

"I'm not saying that, but she has this lovely brown color to her skin. Will you not tell us who he is?"

"You don't know him," I mumbled.

"When will we meet him and why hasn't he come to see his baby girl?"

"Because he is probably not here," Frida said as she walked toward us from the kitchen. She glanced at me and sat across from us. "He's a colored man, isn't he?"

I stared. I could not read her emotion.

"And an American, I presume. For I don't know a single German man with black skin."

"Oh…" Karina must not have heard the subtle strain in Frida's voice. "That's why she has such a beautiful complexion, she is half-white and half-black. That's wonderful!"

I looked to Frida again and fidgeted under her gaze. Taking a deep breath,

I lifted my chin. "His name is Jackson Driggs. He's a sergeant in the United States Army and he is a very good man."

Frida's jaw tightened. "No American can be good, Aleksandra. You can try telling yourself that, but we know…" Her voice cracked. "We know what they did to us and now the Japanese people know, too."

"And now we also know the horrifying things Germans did to the millions of Jewish people in those camps. War is a deadly game."

"So, you are justifying what happened in Dresden?"

"No, Frida, but Jack didn't do it; in fact, he was part of a unit that liberated one of those camps. He's a decent man and he will return to us."

When she scoffed, it nearly broke my heart. The joyful guise we had enveloped ourselves in since my pregnancy came to light had finally cracked. It was apparent the wounds I had caused her with my actions the night of the Dresden bombing might *never* heal. She took very good care of me while I was pregnant and through the birth, but at this very moment, I knew it would never be what it once was. This child would always be a physical reminder of her loss.

Taking Adela back into my arms, I marveled at her tiny perfection. She had given me something to remember Jack by, but in dark contrast, she gave Frida something to grieve.

Though I will never forget the goodness and love Frida offered me at a desperate, painful time in my life…that time had come to an end.

I must now face my future alone.

CHAPTER FORTY-NINE
14 July 1946

I HELD THE BASKET's handle tightly between my fingers. The strain on my limbs was nearly more than I could bear. Though the summer rains had ceased for the day, the chill lingered as I trudged down the street in near blackness. The sun had yet to rise, but that's precisely why I chose this hour—to remain unseen.

The silence of the journey was deafening with the streets of Berlin so eerily quiet—mostly due to mandatory curfews, but I was certain the people of Germany also slept soundly for the first time in years.

I had arrived by bus in Berlin seven weeks ago, having taken all of my saved Reichsmarks with me—yet within hours discovered they held little value. The Allied forces were printing money to be exchanged. Money that didn't include Hitler's image or the associated swastikas. But the disbursements proceeded slowly.

Through the goodness of a stranger I met on the bus, her mother offered to take me and little Adela in. If it weren't for her, we might have ended up in a migrant camp.

Before I left Leipzig, I said my emotional goodbyes. Karina would not let go. Her tears stained my cheeks, and her cries filled my ears, but I had more to worry about now and I knew she would always be in good hands with Frida.

Frida. Though our farewell came with tears, she did not persuade me to stay. We both knew my departure was imminent. Adela would have been a daily reminder of her pain and the blame she placed on men like Jack would always be present…for I had done the same.

I could not bear the thought of any animosity towards this innocent child or her father.

Every day since my arrival, I went in search of answers. Though I had Jackson's rank and unit number, there were too many troops from the various countries and so much city to cover. Even when I approached men in official capacities, my inquiries were ignored...the priorities in the city had little to do with locating a lover. I got nowhere.

Deeply discouraged, day after day I returned to my temporary quarters unsuccessful. With my last correspondence from Jack, now dating ten months ago, it was very possible he was no longer in Berlin or even in Germany, for that matter. I refused to believe the worst may have occurred, but the stories of random violence aimed at any foreign soldiers had come to light.

Helga, the kind mother who took us in, had been more than obliging, though she herself had little to share. She let me know that she would be leaving Berlin to live with a sister in Steinbach and that Adela and I would need to move on as well. In her kindhearted and truthful manner, she helped me recognize my options, though none of them were very good.

Holding Adela in my arms yesterday, after yet another day of disappointments, I realized how little I had to offer her. With no husband, no work, and the last of our money gone, our outlook appeared bleak. And now, within the week we would be homeless. Adela's tiny fingers curled around mine as I watched her sleep, imprinting every line of her face into my memory. My next move, by far, would be the most difficult thing I would ever do.

Reaching the correct street, I paused. I had been over this scenario a thousand times wishing painstakingly for a different outcome. The bundle before me stirred, then settled once more. Tears filled my eyes. She would have a chance at life, at stability, and a future...with me, everything was unknown...*everything*.

I had located the correct building the day before. A kind man who owned a shoe repair shop across the street confirmed to me the existence of such a place, but each step I took that drew me closer, ripped my heart open a little more.

I paced slowly. My eyes blurred with tears. Will she ever know how *much I love her?*

I set the heavy basket down and peeled back the top layer of fabric. Scanning the baby's beautiful olive skin and perfection, I whispered. "You will be taken care of, my darling girl." I sniffled out the rest of my words. "I hope you understand why I must leave you."

Reaching into my coat pocket, I retrieved the note I had written before we left...

Please care for my sweet Adela and tell her I love her.

Placing both the note and the single photograph of me taken last year at the May Day Festival, I tucked them both against her chest, then tugged the blanket up to her little brown nose. Her eyes remained closed and the precious rise and fall of her chest beneath the blankets nearly took my breath away.

I quickly lifted the knocker and slammed it down three times. There had to be no doubt someone would come to the door. I bent over, kissed her forehead, and scrambled down the steps.

Rushing across the street, I leaped toward the darkness of an alleyway, allowing only a second to catch my breath, then peered around the corner.

A light appeared through the crack of an open door. A short heavy-set woman stepped out, looked around, and then glanced downward. Placing her hands on her broad hips, she openly sighed, then scanned the street once more. I pulled back farther into the darkness. When I gathered the courage to look again, she and Adela were gone.

Slipping to the ground with my back against the wall, I sobbed. Of all the sadness I had faced since the war began, this was the worst—the most painful of them all. Even as images of my parents, Ivan, my friends, Günter, Frida, Liam, and Jack flashed through my mind.

Adela was a part of me—my very blood flowed through her. She had been created through love, pure and perfect love.

Wrapping my arms around my middle, I fought the desire to go back to the building, knock on the door and ask for my daughter back. Anger surfaced at my circumstances. I wished with all my heart I could care for her on my own…reality proved otherwise.

One day, I hoped she would understand my decision and forgive me… though I could hardly forgive myself.

Stepping out from the shadows, the golden rays of the sun's emergence peeked between two buildings. Its sudden brightness brought little comfort to my shattered heart, but somewhere, inside, a voice told me my daughter would be okay.

I faced the quiet orphanage once more and blew a simple kiss, "I love you, my little princess. Goodbye, sweet Adela."

…And left my heavy heart in Berlin.

Epilogue
May 1947

I STEPPED OFF THE BUS and instantly a cool breeze wafted over me and filled my nose with the airy scent of fish. The rolling sounds of a nearby river instantly relaxed my tense shoulders.

The day-long journey had brought me dangerously close to scenes from my past life— the train from Łódź, the bus passing the ruins of Dresden, and a sorrowful ride along the roads I had driven the night of the bombing. Had the bus stopped anywhere near Leipzig, I might've gotten off and never gotten back on.

After leaving Adela in Berlin, I traveled back to Łódź to find a fragmented, hollow shell of a city. With the SS in hiding from the Allied forces, they deserted quickly, leaving the people free but without structure, sanitation, food, or resources. Nothing of value could be found within its boundaries and there was nobody to rescue them. Much of the focus had gone to both Warsaw and the largest, most deadly extermination camp two hundred kilometers away from Łódź—Auschwitz-Birkenau. Not only a horror-filled torture chamber but the last resting place for millions of Jews.

Upon arrival in my hometown, I followed the directions to find the flat my parents occupied. While I had come to expect my father to be gone, I didn't want to believe my mother, too, had lost her will to live. According to their neighbor, Pani Dabrowski, Mama died just short of one month before I arrived.

Starvation and disease had hit the city terribly hard, and she was not strong enough to fight it all. She, like Papa, was cremated. The kind woman who had been so good to them directed me to the warehouse that housed their ashes and, though it was against the law to remove them, I did so, and within days, they were spread across the fields surrounding Papa's childhood farm.

Now, there really was nothing left for me in Poland—no past and no future.

Only one place came to mind.

Turning away from the river, the first white structure appeared, preceding a cluster of colorful brick buildings that made up the rest of this quaint town. As I walked forward, the peace that surfaced from the sight had me wondering if the war ever reached this part of the world. It was a very different scene from the ones I'd grown accustomed to in Germany and Poland and one I never truly believed existed.

Especially now, with the onset of the newest war... *The Cold War as they called it.*

Last year, tensions mounted between the Soviets and the Americans, progressing to a psychological standoff, each with their own allies, but without the characteristics of hand-to-hand combat. This war, though no casualties might arise from battle, would be no less damaging to the innocent inhabitants.

With one hand gripping my valise that held my only possessions—a few dresses, an extra pair of shoes, a hat, and a small pair of Adela's first booties—I walked down the street toward the edge of town. Its appearance was almost exactly how it was described to me two years ago and that image had never really left my mind—the cobblestone roads, the skillfully crafted structures, the lamplights glowing with fire, and the black spire with a white cross atop the village church rising above it all.

Before I entered the village, a short distance away on a grassy field, a large white cross centered two rows of smaller wooden crosses...ten on each side. A flower wreath hung from each...likely the fallen soldiers of this little town.

I set my belongings down and clasped both of my hands in a silent prayer for these men who lost their lives in the war. Though it was doubtful I had ever met any of them, someone, somewhere mourned their absence and I prayed that if my brother met that same fate, someone honored him in death as well.

Taking a deep breath, I picked up my bag, turned, and took the first few steps into town. Instantly met with timid smiles from the townspeople, I shuffled up the walk while they closed their shops for the night. Many showed far less fear of a stranger than my fellow countrymen in Łódź. *This was a good sign.*

Stepping past each door and window with caution, I glanced slowly at each of the handcrafted signs—the cobbler, the bookstore...a millinery shop...the pub...*and the bakery.*

I stopped before the tall, wooden door frame and took another deep breath. *This is it.* Placing my hand on the iron handle, I turned until it opened. The door creaked loudly at my efforts and a small bell above my head tinkled. My arrival would be more than noted.

I first took in the sights of this charming room with its lovely pastries on display, but it was the scent of yeast and freshly baked bread that kept me frozen in place. In that one instance, a simple odor made me feel warm, safe, and at ease. *Astonishing.*

"I will be with you in a moment." The broad back shoulders of a man faced me as he lifted a large, weighty bag off the ground and placed it on the counter. Red marks—most assuredly scars—could be seen on his wrists when the sleeves of his shirt cinched upward with the exertion. His tall frame made his presence seem so out of the ordinary for such a tiny shop, but oddly comfortable, too.

When he turned around and faced me with his flour-covered apron, clean chin, and handsome face, his smile broadened with recognition and his green eyes sparkled with delight.

I easily matched his smile. "Hello, Günter."

"Welcome home, Aleksandra."

ReadMore Press

DISCOVERING THE NEXT BESTSELLER

Would you like a FREE WWII historical fiction audiobook?

This audiobook is valued at 14.99$ on Amazon and is exclusively free for Readmore Press' readers!

To get your free audiobook, and to sign up for our newsletter where we send you more exclusive bonus content every month,

Scan the QR code

Readmore Press is a publisher that focuses on high-end, quality historical fiction. We love giving the world moving stories, emotional accounts, and tear-filled happy endings.

We hope to see you again in our next book!

Never stop reading, Readmore Press

Language Glossary

- Vorwärts! Kinn hoch! Arme nach oben! – Step forward. Chin out. Arms up.
- Gute Länge – Good length
- Mach Notizen (sg) Macht Notizen (pl) – Take notes
- Generalne Gubernatorstwo – General Government (Polish)
- Dreh dich um (sg) Dreht euch um (pl) – Turn around
- Siebzehn – Seventeen
- Auskunftsabteilung – Intelligence department
- Blitzkrieg – Flash war
- Litzmannstadt-Formerly known as Łódź, Poland
- Judenräte – Jewish Council
- Weitergehen – Move on
- In Flammen – Alight
- Pan/Pani – Mr. and Mrs. (Polish)
- Zieh deine Sachen aus (sg) Zieht eure Sachen aus (pl) – Take off your clothes
- Ja – Yes
- Sie ist stark und gesund – She is strong and healthy
- Lebensborn – Fount of Youth
- Urodziny – Birthday (Polish)
- Alle raus – Everybody out
- Spricht jemand Deutsch – Does anyone speak German?
- Das tue ich – I do
- Beweg dich jetzt (sg) Bewegt euch jetzt (pl) -Move now
- Geh schnell (sg) Geht schnell (pl) – Go fast
- Müll – Trash
- Hündinnen – Bitches
- Scheiße – Shit
- Glückliche Männer – Happy men
- Komm her (sg) Kommt her (pl) – Come here
- Die beschissenen Briten haben die Hauptstraße gesprengt – The f-ing British blew up the main street
- Geh hinein (sg) Geht hinein (pl) – Go inside

- Zatrzymać – Stop (Polish)
- Motył-Butterfly (Polish)
- Reichsmark – German currency
- Stille – Silence
- Sprich nicht (sg) Sprecht nicht (pl) – Do not speak
- Bitte – Please
- Wo ist er hin – Where did he go?
- Er wird bezahlen – He will pay
- Halt – Stop
- Herrenrasse – Master race
- Hauptbahnhof – Central Station
- Staatliche Kunstsammlungen – State Arts Collection
- Fettbemme – Rye bread topped with pork and gherkins
- Holunderbeerensuppe – Elderberry Soup
- Quarkkeulchen – Curd dessert
- Jestem tutaj, aby pomóc – I'm here to help (Polish)
- Proszę, uspokój się – Please calm down (Polish)
- Landesbank – State Bank
- Helfer (male) Helferin (female) – Helper
- Sächsische Zeitung – Saxon Newspaper
- Luftwaffe – German Air Force
- Frauenkirche – Historical Dresden Church
- Wasser – Water
- Mit Kohlensäure – Carbonated (with bubbles)
- Lekarz musi sprawdzić twoje obrażenia – A doctor needs to check your injuries (Polish)
- Nationalsozialistische Volkswohlfahrt – National Socialist People's Welfare
- Ta Dorotka – This Dorothy – A traditional Polish lullaby (Polish)
- Polesie – In the forest (Polish)
- Fastnacht – Carnival
- Glühwein – Mulled wine
- DRK/ Deutsches Rotes Kreuz – German Red Cross
- In Gefahr – In Danger
- Kannst du sehen (sg) Könnt ihr sehen (pl) – Can you see
- Strafbatallion – Penal battalion

Acknowledgements

This statement has been expressed time and time again in my books but holds true today as much as the very first publication. I would not be where I am without my insightful, honest, and talented critique team. They each bring something different to the table, and I am forever grateful to Maria Carrasco, Nicole Gardner, Wendy Hargrave, Melisa Harker, Stacy Johnson, Josette Mari, Greg Moyes, Kim Moyes, Diane Norris, Susan Provost, Rachel Schnepf, Lani and Lina Taunima.

Thank you, Dawne for your skill and talent with the pen, I appreciate your ability to see things differently and are not afraid to tell me.

To my family and their loving support of my work and especially to my husband, Greg, for always being the first to read my manuscripts and the first to shout it from the rooftops... *You're my #1 customer!*

About the Author

Leah Moyes is a wife and a mother, a former teacher, and a coach with a background in Anthropology. Her best-selling historical fiction novels have won multiple awards and come from unique stories she has stumbled upon around the world. She loves popcorn and seafood (though not together) and is slowly checking off her very long bucket list.

Printed in Great Britain
by Amazon

52504664R00148